CONNEC

The Legacy o *...d Dors*

By Niema Ash

In collaboration with Jason Dors-Lake

Purple Inc Press

purpleinc@fastmail.fm

Connecting Dors

The Legacy of Diana Dors

In Collaboration with Jason Dors-Lake

By

Niema Ash

ISBN: 978-0-9550301-2-3

COVER DESIGN and ART WORK by DENIS SMITH
Email: denissmith@me.com

Photographic Compilation by Marcella Trowell

Published by Purple Inc Press
in conjunction with Writersworld Ltd.

Purple Inc Press,
5 Eagle House, The Parade,
Broadstairs, Kent, CT10 1LZ, UK

Email: purpleinc@fastmail.fm

To buy this book directly from the author with
autograph and dedication, visit

www.niemaash.com

Printed and bound by www.printondemand-worldwide.com

WRITERSWORLD
2 Bear Close, Woodstock, Oxfordshire, OX20 1JX, England

www.writersworld.co.uk

The text pages of this book are produced via an independent certification process that ensures the trees from which the paper is produced come from well managed sources that exclude the risk of using illegally logged timber while leaving options to use post-consumer recycled paper as well.

Acknowledgements

Heartfelt thanks to Jason for his no holds barred, moving and often disturbing story.

Special thanks to my lovely daughter, Ronit Corry, to cousin Marny Shuster, to my very dear friends, Maggie Mahomed and Andrea Chappell for their support through the difficulties of writing this book.

Also special thanks to Mark Hoser both for his support and for rescuing me from my computer.

Extra special thanks to the acclaimed author and very dear friend, Jamila Gavin, not only for her personal support and invaluable editorial help, but for her encouragement, which kept me going.

Thanks to Linda Sears, Marcella Trowell, Denis Smith and dear, dear, William Carter (Billy Snapper) for their input and advice.

Thanks to all Diana's and Jason's friends who so generously shared with me their experiences with Diana and Jason, especially to Jozy Pollock, Maya Sendall, Fi Fi Denison and above all to the incorrigible David Malin.

Very special thanks to Andy Barrett of La Trappiste for providing nourishment for the soul and just for being Andy.

And thanks to Graham Cook of Writersworld for his devoted and expert assistance in bringing this book to fruition.

For

Jason

Contents

Part One

Part Two

DIANA

"WHATEVER YOU CAN DO OR DREAM YOU CAN, BEGIN IT.
BOLDNESS HAS GENIUS, POWER AND MAGIC IN IT."

GOETHE

Chapter 1
Stars in her Eyes

An eight year old girl looked at herself in the mirror, her glasses were askew, there was a black patch over one lens to correct a 'lazy eye' and her mousey brown hair was dishevelled. She stared hard at the image.

Then, she said out loud, as though the sound of her voice would help make things come true, 'When I grow up I am going to be a film star and have a big house, a swimming pool and a cream telephone.'

She repeated each phrase slowly, watching her lips form the syllables until she could imagine the sounds turning into pictures. She waited a few moments for her words to enter the universe, then, holding them tight in her head, like a prayer, she made her way into the garden. Sitting cross-legged on a special patch of grass, she squeezed her eyes shut until the cream telephone appeared in the dark behind her eyelids. Perhaps if she thought hard enough about it, when she opened her eyes it would be there, sitting on the grass, right beside her. She knew she couldn't expect the swimming pool or the house, they were too big and would take a lot more wishing. But she was ready for that.

Jason loved the story from the first time his mother told it to him, when he was just old enough to be mesmerised by its magic. He made her tell it to him over and over, again and again, listening intently with his child's fairy-tale imagination, until it became embedded in his consciousness, like an inheritance. And, as he listened, a secret plan gradually took shape in his thoughts. He knew he would have to wait until he was eight years old to carry it out, because he didn't want to jeopardise the magic by changing any of the story's details. But when he was eight, and that was only two years away, he too would sit cross-legged in the garden, on a special patch of grass, scrunching up his eyes and wishing hard for what he wanted.

All his mother's wishes had come true, even those wishes bigger than her dreams. She was certainly an important film star. Even as a small boy he knew that, from seeing her on their giant television screen, and because people were always wanting to take her picture, talking to her like she was a queen, and because she looked so beautiful, especially in her sparkly dress with the white fur softer than their angora kitten, and because she smelled so good, even better than the flowers she brought for them to smell together.

Orchard Manor, their home, was certainly a big house, really a mansion, he even had his own separate house just to play in, with a pool table, for when he was older, fruit machines with flashing lights that jingled and jangled and played tunes, and all the toys and pets he wanted, many more than any of his friends had. And he especially loved the swimming pool with its underwater lights changing the colour of the water and the two giant black panther statues his nanny let him sit on, running his hands over the silky-smooth stone, feeling all high and mighty; and there was a cream telephone in most of the rooms, including his.

He did not doubt, not even for one minute, that when the time came, if he wished long enough and hard enough as his mother had done, and followed exactly all the things she had told him about, whatever he wished for would come true. For hadn't she discovered the magic formula on her very own and wasn't it right for her to pass it on to him, her only really true son – the others were like visitors, they lived far away, not like him, he lived in the big house with the swimming pool and the cream telephone with his mother, and, of course, his father too, who was not their father and who didn't read stories to them in all different voices like he read to him. Meanwhile he would think about what he wanted most, because right now he could go to the circus as many times as he liked and he was allowed to talk to the animals, because his mother knew Billy Smart, the man who owned the circus.

* * * * * * *

It was not hard to understand why the young Jason supposed some special formula had been evoked in the miracle that had transformed a seemingly unexceptional eight year old girl, living in an unexceptional English town, with unexceptional parents, into becoming Diana Dors, the UK's most famous film star, and, indeed, a living legend. What he could not know was what the components were that went into the miracle which had made Diana, at age 14, the youngest student ever at London's Academy of Music and Dramatic

Art (LAMDA); at age 20, the youngest registered owner of a Rolls
Royce; at age 24, Britain's highest paid film star adored by the British
public and a sex symbol so popular, so much in demand, she was
considered Britain's answer to Marilyn Monroe.

The young Diana, too, sitting on the grass consumed by
fantasies of stardom, could not know what price she would pay for
the miracle to unfold. She saw only the brightness of a cream
telephone glowing in her film star dream. She was unaware of the
crushing disappointments, the heartbreaks, the scandals, that would
line her path to that stardom, unaware of the failures, dotting the
successes, the tragedies both personal and national which would be
endured. For the year was 1939 and Britain had just entered World
War Two.

The young Jason, too, could not know how the miracle came
into being and knew only the wonder of its reality. He saw only the
brightness of wishing, like candles on a birthday cake burning in a
darkened room making wishes come true, as his mother's wishes had
come true. He knew nothing of the bitterness of the journey between
those wishes and their fulfilment, just as, when the time came, he
would be unaware of the dark shadows falling between his wishes
and their fulfilment.

* * * * * * *

A 14 year old girl hurried along a deserted London street. It was so
early that it was still dark and it was so cold that wearing the heavy
winter coat her mother had obtained from a friend, and walking as
fast as she could did not stop her from shivering. Turning into a main
street, at that hour without traffic, she made sure to keep to the middle
of the road in case some robber, or worse, some murderer would leap
out of an alleyway and stab her. She knew it was silly, but from the
time she was little she had a fear of the dark, imagining monsters
reaching out of the darkness to grab her and maybe kill her or bury
her alive. Being alone in a strange city brought back all her old fears
and even made them worse. And living in the YMCA didn't help.
Sometimes it reminded her of a prison with its screaming alarms and
chilly corridors. It's not as though she would ever like living there,
having to get up early in the morning in the dark and cold and she
hated all the rules especially having to be in by 10 at night because
she was only 14, while the other girls didn't have to be in until 11

because they were older. But it was all necessary to make her dream come true, and she was determined to do everything that was necessary to make that happen, no matter how hard.

However, despite her fears and dislikes, there were some moments when she experienced an indescribable joy. She had finally escaped her birthplace, the dark, grey, uneventful Swindon which she hated; she had escaped from a dreary school run by two boring spinsters, who were always criticising her – they weren't even happy when she won a prize in a beauty contest. 'Better to attend your studies instead of wasting your time with trivialities,' was all they could say. In fact they disliked her so much they had dismissed her from the school – good riddance to bad rubbish. And she had escaped from the endless arguments with a strict, disapproving Victorian father who didn't like her either and who was opposed to all her dreams.

It's true, there had been some good times, like when she went with her mother to dances at the camps where the American soldiers were stationed, because of the war, with her hair curled, wearing makeup, which was forbidden by her father, and her precious nylons, which were hard to get because of the war, and high heels and dresses that showed off her curves, pretending to be seventeen instead of thirteen and dancing with the most handsome GIs. The soldiers were always inviting her to their camp parties and even some of the teachers were jealous of her. She needed little urging, delighted to go, thrilled to be with real Americans. They made her feel closer to Hollywood; they spoke like film stars and were so romantic, whispering compliments in her ears and bringing her gifts. They made her feel grown up, and above all, she wanted to be grown up. Her mother was proud of her being so popular, helping her to make friends with the camp cooks and bring home things that were hard to get, because of the war, like sugar and butter. But all that didn't make up for most of the boring times, and anyway she always knew she would have to leave Swindon to make her dream come true, because nothing magical could ever happen in Swindon.

Her one small regret, if she had any regrets at all, was leaving her mother, who was always on her side, defending her against her father who wanted to control everything she did and didn't want her to have any fun. Like her auntie Kit, her mother not only shared her dream of her becoming a glamorous Hollywood film star, but encouraged it, even initiated it by taking her to see lots of films, often three or four times a week, from the time she was three years old, and then sneaking her off to the cinema when she was supposed to be in school and keeping it a secret from her father – although that wasn't too hard as he was always busy with his Masonic club. She wanted so much to be like the glamorous film stars and wear beautiful clothes and live in a beautiful house and go to exciting night clubs and have romances. Not like the people in Swindon who were dowdy and small-minded and spoke about nothing except working for the railway. But she hardly thought of all that now, because with the help of her mother, they had convinced her father to send her to theatre school in London to become an actress, although they pretended to him that she was studying to become an elocution teacher. That was another of their secrets.

And, here in London, even though it was winter and cold and even though she had to share a room with three girls, she was on the way to becoming a famous film star. Even if the beginning was scary and hard and everything was dowdy, without one flicker of glamour, she knew magic was often disguised as something else. But she had taken the first step and her aunty Kit said, it takes just one step to begin a journey. London, the YWCA and LAMDA were that first step in her journey. She would willingly make sacrifices, like in the films, for in her heart she believed this was the start of the magic, because, like Judy Garland, in The Wizard of Oz, she had left her boring old life behind and was on her way on the yellow brick road to the magical land of Oz, with all its beauty and adventures.

Chapter 2
The First Miracle

The first miracle was one that Diana was unaware of at the time, for it was the miracle of her own birth.

Mary, Diana's mother, longed for a baby but her body conspired against her, or perhaps it was her husband Bert's body conspiring against them both, for childbirth eluded them. It was at the post office in Swindon, a railway town in south west England, where Mary Payne met Albert Fluck, better known as Bert. Mary had come from Wales to Swindon to find employment. The move proved auspicious for not long afterwards she became one of England's first female postmen, a prestigious position which assured her attention and acclaim and of which she was rightfully proud. So the encounter was not that of a routine post office occurrence.

Perhaps in ordinary times the meeting would have been a casual one, with no special significance, but the times were not ordinary. World War One was raging in Europe and the soldiers on leave from military duty did not know if this would be their last visit home. Bert was a military man, an army officer, home on leave. Mary was already a war widow, her first husband having been killed in action. But she was still young, in her twenties, and very pretty with her long flowing hair reaching below her waist, which Bert so admired. Bert was tall and handsome with the posture and bearing that displayed a confidence Mary so admired – a dashing army captain who cut a striking figure on the dance floor. And how she, too, loved to dance. Dancing had cemented their brief courtship.

Mary wasn't the only one who had found Bert attractive. He was popular with the ladies and enjoyed escorting them, sometimes with one on each arm, to the dances and parties sponsored by the town folk of Swindon for the soldiers stationed in the area. Entertaining everyone with his impressive piano playing made him the life and soul of the party and all the more desirable. Wartime has a way of creating urgency. Home-grown men, especially talented, handsome men, are at a premium. Bert had no shortage of admirers. But with hardly the opportunity for courtship, and before the war ended, it was the lovely, vivacious, Mary whom he married in March of 1918. Wartime also has a way of disrupting the expected patterns of living. It makes no concessions to married life. The groom returned to service. The bride remained behind.

After the war ended Bert returned to Mary but not quite in the same condition in which he had left her. He had contracted malaria while serving in India, which resulted in a heart condition, and a mustard gas attack left him with damaged lungs. Mary, concerned about Bert's health persuaded him to see a doctor. The doctor was equally concerned and advised Bert that he must change his lifestyle, must stop the drinking, the smoking and the late nights. However, Bert chose to ignore both his condition and the doctor's advice. Even the threat that he would be dead in ten years if he did not heed the warnings did not deter him. If his football playing suffered some minor adjustment, the parties and dances continued uninterrupted. Rather than changing his lifestyle, Bert preferred changing his doctor.

Bert felt no compunction to delay starting a family, something both he and Mary wanted. Wasn't that expected of every happily married couple? And they certainly appeared a happily married couple. All their friends could attest to that. Even people who hardly knew them would comment on what an attractive couple they were, especially on the dance floor. They looked made for each other.

However, for whatever reason, the baby refused to make an appearance. Mary was heartbroken for she dearly wanted to be a mother. Bert, too, was disappointed, albeit more for Mary's sake than his own. But after the initial disappointment they chose not to dwell on the misfortune but rather on the advantages being childless afforded. Not having the responsibility of a family had its own rewards especially for two sociable, fun-loving people. Without the expense of children they were able to buy not only a lovely modern home on the coveted Marlborough Road, in Swindon's upscale neighbourhood, but also a car. This ultimate luxury allowed them to indulge in country frolics and seaside holidays. Not having children meant they were free to attend parties in London and to give their own, which were much celebrated. Mary had trained as a singer, and accompanied by Bert's piano playing they were a talented duo, much admired and in demand to entertain at various social events. They enjoyed not only performing together but the resulting popularity and acclaim. Being childless they had only themselves and each other to please.

If their freewheeling lifestyle was as sweet and multi-layered as their wedding cake, the icing topping that cake was one Gerry Lack. Gerry Lack was a great friend of both Mary and Bert. For a time, Gerry not only shared their pleasures, he enhanced them – the country jaunts, the London escapades, the seaside adventures. He was even part owner of the car. Together they formed an inseparable trio, dedicated to good times and to their unusual friendship. Whereas, in the past Bert had been known to appear at parties with two females in tow, Mary now enjoyed the attention of two males. And how well they complemented each other, both committed to catering to Mary's social and cultural well-being, sometimes together and sometimes in turn.

Although their socialising and excursions were usually conducted as a trio, there were occasions when an outing as a couple was preferable, and often the couple was composed of Mary and Gerry. There were times when Bert, who had become a committed Mason, preferred an evening at his Masonic lodge or at one of his clubs, to some more demanding and less appealing activity Mary had planned, like attending a concert or going to the theatre. Gerry was pleased to be Mary's escort and Bert was pleased that his devoted friend, Gerry, relieved him of that duty, allowing Bert the pleasure of a relaxing evening with his companions.

Swindon was a conservative town with limited access to titillation, where whispers inevitably mushroomed into rumours. However, it wasn't gossip that destroyed whatever the formula was that kept the threesome in happy harmony – it was something far more formidable.

* * * * * * *

After thirteen years of marriage, at the age of 42, long after giving up all hope, Mary became pregnant. She was ecstatic. Bert far less so. He did not welcome any disruption to his most satisfactory existence, although he could not have fully anticipated the extent of that disruption or the upheaval it would cause to his well-ordered life.

Bert was content with his lot in life. He adored his wife and enjoyed the privileges and attentions of being the centre of her life. He had a good job in the accounting department of the railway offices with excellent prospects for promotion; he held the title of 'Worshipful Master' at his Masonic lodge, a title denoting honour and esteem, allowing him the privilege of presiding over lodge meetings; he was popular with his friends and well-liked by his colleagues. He continued to enjoy an active social life despite the predictions that he would have to curtail it due to health problems. The Flucks were known for their parties some of which continued well into the night. Often after such a late night party their good friend Gerry Lack would stay the night. The house was certainly big enough to accommodate guests, and Gerry was more than a guest, 210 Marlborough Road had become his second home. Bert wanted for nothing. He considered himself a very lucky man indeed.

Parenthood, had long ago been eliminated from Bert's agenda. In fact he now saw it as an unnecessary interference. However, if he viewed the advent of fatherhood with trepidation, Mary rejoiced at the idea of motherhood. Nothing could please her more. Becoming pregnant was the miracle she had longed for. Her cup was overflowing

But all did not go well. Mary was in the nursing home for a week giving birth. Her labour was so difficult, so agonizing, that the staff feared for her life. They were so concerned and so focused on saving Mary's life, that the baby when it finally arrived, was almost irrelevant. In any case it was dismissed as stillborn and cast aside to be disposed of. But not only did Mary survive, the baby, who had almost suffocated was revived by a nurse. As it turned out, the miracle of the pregnancy was compounded by the miracle of the birth. The baby was named Diana, goddess of beauty.

Bert's detachment from all things involving the newborn Diana was evident even before she was born. He was not at Mary's bedside during her terrible labour. While she was in the throes of a life and death struggle in the nursing home, a short distance from Marlborough Road, he was at his Masonic Lodge giving a talk to his fellow Masons. Although at the time it was not customary for husbands to be involved in the details of childbirth, especially those involving labour; Bert was not involved in the nursery details either. He left everything in Mary's hands.

From the very beginning of that near fatal birth, Mary focussed all her attention on baby Diana. She had hoped Bert would do likewise but soon realised that Bert was anything but the doting father she had so wished him to be. Mary's sister, Kit, more than adequately stepped in to fill the vacuum. Kit had been all too happy to partake in the event of Diana's birth and eager to lavish attention on her. It was Kit who cared for Mary while she was recuperating from her ordeal. And it was Kit who cared for baby Diana from the day of her birth. Although Kit was childless herself, she had more knowledge about child care and was far more competent than the inexperienced Mary. Mary now spent considerably more time with her sister than with her husband. Bert became more and more irrelevant and more and more resentful. Baby Diana rather than bringing a new joy into his life, managed to obliterate the old one. She was like a wedge driving apart those aspects of his life he had found so rewarding.

Mary, who had been a hair's breadth from losing her baby, became the ultimate over-protective, doting mother. She refused to allow anyone but herself and Kit to look after Diana. This meant that she and Bert were no longer free to attend parties in London, nor could they host their own as there was now a baby in the house whose sleep must not be disturbed, although Bert felt that his own disturbed sleep did not merit the same consideration. The carefree days were over. Their social life dwindled to a pin head. In fact, Mary became a social bore, totally preoccupied with motherhood to the exclusion of all else and to the consternation not only of Bert but of Gerry as well.

Gerry, now affectionately called 'Uncle Gerry', did not survive the title for long. Although he had attended Diana's christening when she was less than two months old and although he was one of her godparents, he increasingly distanced himself from the new regimes in Marlborough Road. As a matter of fact, he probably considered his attendance at Diana's christening his final concession to mother and baby, for, to Mary's chagrin, he disappeared shortly afterwards – fleeing the scene, accompanied by a lady love, probably in panic of becoming embroiled in matters too domestic and baby-centred. Bert was not only losing his wife, but had now lost his best friend as well. He withdrew further and further into his preoccupation with his clubs and lodge, immersing himself in his Masonic involvement. All the things which had fulfilled his existence now suffered the irreversible trauma of Diana's birth

Chapter 3
Bells on her Toes

If, for Bert, baby Diana was a thorn embedding itself deeper and deeper, infecting the most tender parts of his being, consuming all Mary's attention, all her affection, like a greedy newborn animal; for Mary, Diana was a precious gift, a treasure to be cherished above all else. From the moment Mary discovered her baby was not dead but had miraculously survived the horrific birth, Diana became her infant miracle. The wonder of that miracle imbued her with unparalleled dedication. Diana was wrapped in a mantle of adoration. She became mummy's little princess, to be pampered, indulged, catered to, in her determination that Diana would have everything Mary never had, being one of many children growing up in a poor Welsh household. Her sister Kit applauded Mary's resolve. Diana would have the very best, she would have 'Rings on her fingers and bells on her toes.' She would have 'Music wherever she goes.' Together they constructed a wall of determination to assure Diana's specialness, to honour it, to guard it, to nourish it, a wall impervious to objections, to warnings, even to good sense.

And so it was. If Bert protested to the over-indulgences – the expensive clothes, far more fashionable than those worn by the neighbourhood children; the lavish treats; the catered birthday parties celebrated in costly venues; the private schooling; the elocution lessons, dance lessons; the catering to every one of Diana's whims, his protests fell on deaf ears. Knowing beforehand that Bert would disapprove, Mary didn't bother with advanced warnings, so that more often than not, when Bert discovered some objectionable deed, or some outrageous behaviour, it was after the fact, too late to voice effective disapproval, or even to have his opinion considered. Like the time Mary allowed Diana to have her hair permed because Diana wanted to emulate the Shirley Temple look, which was then in vogue. She wanted her straight hair, which she regarded as a cross to bear, re-incarnated into fashionable curls. Bert was most upset. He accused Mary of ruining Diana's hair as she had ruined her own luxurious hip-length hair, which Bert dearly loved, by having it cut short into the latest stylish bob. He had refused to speak to Mary for weeks.

If, on occasion, Bert's frustrations became too vocal, his complaints too vigorous, Mary pretended to address them, but would employ all manner of subterfuge to carry out her original intentions, keeping Bert in the dark, preventing him from discovering the deception. The wall of determination could not be breached. This secrecy and subterfuge, establishing Bert as an outsider, an adversary, an obstacle to good times, an obstacle to romance, imagination, inspiration, was instrumental in shaping Diana's attitude towards her father and in determining their relationship.

Mary loved going to the cinema, where she could escape into the glamour of another existence, and she began taking Diana to see films when Diana was just three years old. By the age of five, Diana was going to the cinema three or four times a week, although Mary had agreed to a once a week limit. When the time came for Diana to begin her education, attending school made little impact on the established ritual. Diana considered school an interference, an obstacle to what was of foremost importance to her – the magic world of films. For Diana, films became more than entertainment, distraction or escape. Films became an alternate life, far more exciting, far more rewarding than her reality. She lived in the Hollywood mansions, swam in their Olympic-sized swimming pools, spoke on the cream telephones. Hollywood and the stars who inhabited it became her beacon, her guiding light, her future.

Mary had no objection to Diana missing school to see a film. On the contrary, she conspired with Diana and Kit to make it possible. If Bert objected, outraged by Mary's irresponsible behaviour, the truancy was simply hidden from him. Diana, Auntie Kit and Mary plotted to deceive him, taking pleasure in concealing their secret. The cinema escapades continued uninterrupted. This attitude of undermining Bert's authority, of setting him up as an impediment to pleasure and fun, an impediment to dreams and ambition, was to have a profound influence on Diana's life and career. No doubt it also influenced her choice of men.

If, as it is said, many women are attracted to men with qualities like their father's, Diana shunned men like her father – dependable, law-abiding, down to earth, no surprises men; predictable, sensible men; men content with limited expectations. (It took her almost a life time to appreciate the fact that her father was only interested in her welfare and doing his best to shield her from terrible disappointments). Diana was drawn to the unpredictable, the impulsive, to men who lived on the wild side, who could supply the hit of adventure, drama, excitement; gambling-type men who took chances in life, who walked on the edge, who feasted on daring and exhilaration.

Diana also shunned Bert's family and their narrow-minded 'what will the neighbours think' mentality, their Salvation Army milieu. She rebelled against their Victorian morality, which Bert seemed to increasingly embrace, which he increasingly adopted as he put his carefree days behind him and accepted the responsibilities of parenthood. Diana took her cues, as well as her name, from the maternal side of her family, especially from her maternal grandmother, Georgina Dors, whom she adored. Georgina was so unconventional she had run off with her brother-in-law, hiding in the forest, pursued on horseback by her cuckolded husband. Without money or any form of security she took her four children to Wales, where she 'lived in sin', until abandoned by her lover.

From an early age, Diana became especially keen to defy her father, to flout his values, to block his voice. Almost as soon as she was aware of having a father she disliked him and the dislike eventually grew to hatred, which she openly admitted in future writings. For her, Bert's was the voice of dull reality and repressive 'good sense', a conservative voice, a voice which confined her to small-town restrictions and ambitions, to living within her station in life, a voice which limited her to the mundane, which slapped her hand when she reached for the stars, which made no allowance for magic, for fantasy, for grand aspirations.

And Diana, from a very early age, was consumed by fantasy and grand aspirations, with ambitions unlike those of her contemporaries. Whereas they responded to the question 'What would you like to be when you grow up?' with the usual nurse, teacher, fireman or policeman, Diana had responded with the astonishing statement, 'I am going to be a movie star'. She was not hampered by hesitation or doubt. It was as though somehow she knew it was her birthright to become a film star, to become rich and famous.

Perhaps this is not as strange as it may seem. There is nothing like praise and adoration to instil in an ordinary looking child – and Diana was certainly ordinary looking, with mousy brown hair, glasses, and a patch over one eye – the self-esteem and confidence of an acclaimed beauty. It was the combination of the promises of the Silver Screen coupled with this confidence and self-esteem, nourished by an adoring mother and aunt who turned everything Diana did into gold, that enabled Diana at age eight to make this seemingly preposterous declaration; to even consider the possibility of becoming a movie star, while living in a country an ocean away from the home of movie-making, in a dreary working man's town, worlds apart from the glamour of Hollywood.

Diana did not dream alone. Her mother and her aunt Kit added weight to her dreams, fleshed them out, believing with her. For Mary, the dreams were not pie-in-the-sky illusions, doomed to end in grief, as they were for Bert, but genuine possibilities, realistic, attainable. She believed her miracle child, her little princess, was fated to achieve greatness. She lived Diana's dreams with her. Diana became her path to stardom, to glamour. Mary too had once dreamed of a Hollywood-style life when she had trained as a singer. But her ambitions had been thwarted, her expectations dashed by the bitter limitations of her life. She would make certain Diana did not suffer those limitations. Mary would fulfil her own expectations through the possibilities she afforded Diana. Diana would be her currency to success. Mary, Kit, Diana, Hollywood, stardom, were all wrapped up together, part of the same whole and Diana was its focal point.

* * * * * * *

At an early age, Diana had heard about Gerry Lack, her mother's 'best friend'. Mary harboured a deep resentment toward Gerry for abandoning her, and, no doubt, she was further displeased because he had left accompanied by another woman. Kit fuelled that resentment and Diana absorbed it. Not really understanding the circumstances, or even having known her uncle Gerry, as a child she had always referred to him as 'bad uncle Gerry'. Then, when she was old enough to understand the significance, Auntie Kit filled her head with troubling whispers. She told Diana that Gerry had been more than a best friend, that Mary was besotted with him, insinuating they had been lovers. She told her that once she had found baby Diana left on her own, utterly incredulous as Mary would not even entrust Diana to a babysitter, while Mary was off pursuing Gerry, who was rendezvousing with a lady love. And even more disconcerting, when Kit reprimanded Mary, Mary was abrasive and guiltless.

Kit's revelations were deeply distressing for Diana. She was not only shocked but confused. Now she could never know for certain if Bert was really her father. She became obsessed by questions to which she could find no answers. Her mother, for once, did not bow to her demands and would give her no information, resolutely refusing to discuss the matter.

Eventually Diana found a way of turning the distressing confidences to her advantage. When she was furious with Bert for attempting to prevent her from carrying out some pet agenda, or for stamping on some cherished dream, or attempting to anchor her to earth when she wanted to fly, she used Kit's revelations as an excuse for disobeying him. To justify her disobedience, her impertinence, her brazen disrespect, she fantasised that Bert was not her real father and therefore he had no rights over her and she could defy him with complete impunity. She had found a way of rationalising her anger towards him, her resentment, and after Kit's revelations, her utter contempt.

What child when deprived of something they want by the authority of a parent and feeling thwarted and resentful has not fantasised that the parent isn't really theirs; that someone else is their true parent, someone mysterious, glamorous, far more exciting? But Diana had more reason to believe this than most.

Chapter 4
The Miracles Begin to Unfold

Diana's wishing rituals combined with Mary's support, practical assistance, and implicit belief, must have had a major influence on the forces shaping Diana's destiny, because things began to move in a most unpredictable but promising direction. Heaven-sent opportunities were dropped on the Flucks' doorstep which Mary eagerly scooped up, using each one as a building block to create new possibilities, new potential, as a key to opening the door to the next triumph. But miracles have a logic of their own. Some can have a cautious, guarded nature. Some need time to unfold and are slow to reveal the full extent of their magic, especially miracles of this magnitude. Some may even present a dark side at first to frighten off those who believe only lightly; to ascertain staying power.

Things didn't begin well. Against Bert's better judgment, Mary enrolled Diana in Selwood House, an exclusive and expensive private school, as the first step on the journey to success. It was where many of Swindon's choice families; successful, well-heeled pillars of the community and those aspiring to these credentials; sent their offspring to imbibe the best Swindon had to offer and to smooth out any offending edges. In line with her no-expense-spared policy, Mary considered this to be a worthwhile move in guiding Diana along the path to fame and fortune. As it turned out Selwood House was a near disaster, redeemed only by an auspicious, but unforeseen saving grace.

The school was run by Miss Ruth and Miss Daisy Cockey, two prim grey-haired spinster sisters. They were everything that Diana was not: unbearably proper, oppressively formal and completely devoid of humour and wit. Diana did not fit the well-behaved, genteel, proficient mould they attempted to squeeze her into, a mould which produced polite, refined ladies, who could pass as educated and cultured and would fit into a well ordered, predictable and edifying lifestyle, a mould which made no concession to spontaneity and originality, to unusual children with unusual dreams. They were not accustomed to dealing with a child who could fight her own corner, who had that special confidence from knowing she had the unqualified support of a devoted mother. They were not accustomed to dealing with a child who not only knew what she wanted but was determined to get it. Their method was to inculcate the children with what they were supposed to want and then teach them how to get it.

From the start Diana loathed them and their repressive little school. It belonged to her father's world, a world rife with rules and regulations, with work ethic, with knowing one's place, a solemn world devoid of fun. She hated the boring lessons, the endless repetitions, the monotony of copying, and so she developed ingenious methods of coping with the unrelenting tedium she was forced to endure. She especially disliked maths classes and would pretend to pore over her exercise book, but instead of solving a math equation, she would extend the lines forming the symbols and numerals to form instead the names of film stars which she then doodled in the margins; instead of memorising the rudiments of French grammar, she would gaze into space, dreaming her film star dreams, in a world far removed from droning voices and squealing chalk.

She resisted attempts to discipline her, to make her sit with folded hands, to stand in line with rigid back and arms held close to her sides, to walk at a measured pace and never to run, skip or hop. It wasn't long before she developed the reputation of a trouble-maker, decidedly a bad influence on the other children. With her habit of missing classes, ignoring homework assignments and being on the wrong page of any lesson, she was held up as an example of what not to do, how not to behave.

The dislike was entirely mutual. Miss Ruth and Miss Daisy disapproved of everything about Diana. Not only did they disapprove of her school work, her unwillingness to heel, her perceived arrogance, but they disapproved of her clothes, more appropriate for a fashion display than a classroom, and of her mother who allowed her to wear them. To Diana it seemed they disapproved of her very existence. It was their well-considered and firmly held opinion that Diana would never amount to much, an opinion they took pains to impress upon her; and in his heart of hearts Bert couldn't help but agree.

Once Diana overheard Bert angrily confronting Mary. He raged over Diana's poor grades, her lack of effort, her lack of achievement. He accused Mary of ruining Diana's future. Another time, after an especially dismal report card, Bert was not only outraged, but despairing. He was worried that with the kind of school record Diana had, she would be virtually unemployable. He feared for her prospects. He had hoped Diana would get a good office job when she left school. Diana's poor performance was putting an end to that hope. He held Mary answerable, saying that with her indulgent, permissive approach to Diana's education, Diana would be good for nothing when she left school, except, with luck, going into domestic service and that it was all Mary's doing. For once Mary, who always defended Diana, who was always ready with excuses and rationalisations, held her tongue. However, Bert's accusations, his anger, even his despair, did little to dent her designs. As had often occurred in the past, she pretended to consider his concerns but continued much as she had before, only careful to conceal more and more from Bert.

One day Bert, as a final act of desperation decided to have a fatherly talk with Diana. Even though she was still a child, he believed in preparation, in planning ahead. Instead of reprimand and castigation he tried a calm, composed approach. 'You know, my dear, when you leave school I would like to see you get a good job, possibly that of a secretary.' Then came a statement that sent chills down Diana's spine, that made her blood run cold and her heart drop to the floor. It was a statement that would remain to haunt her for the rest of her life, because for her it was a forecast, a terrifying premonition, her personal apocalyptic vision:

'Eventually I'd like to see you settle down and marry a decent sort of chap.'

Even at her tender age – she was not yet ten, she knew this was the voice of doom. This was the voice of the wicked stepmother preventing Cinderella from going to the ball, the voice of the witch, pushing Hansel and Gretel into the oven.

She didn't want to settle down, she didn't want to become a secretary, and most of all she didn't want to 'marry a decent sort of chap'. Settling down was tantamount to condemning her to the prison of Swindon. 'A decent sort of Chap' was the prison warden. Her crystal ball glowed with Hollywood dreams: her big house, her swimming pool, her cream telephone, fashionable clothes, parties, romances, all the things the decent sort of chap, a chap much like her father, knew nothing about. But even as she became aware of the stinging tears she was trying not to shed, and the dread she was trying not to feel, she was sure of one thing: she would never become a secretary, never marry the decent sort of chap, never live in Swindon. Just because she hated school and had bad report cards, it didn't mean she couldn't become a film star and live in Hollywood. But she was deeply shaken.

It was Mary, as usual, who came to her rescue, who restored her hope, her confidence, telling her that low grades were nothing to worry about. Miss Ruth and Miss Daisy were old maids with no dreams of their own, besides they were only temporary and unimportant in the greater scheme of things. What in the world could anyone do with algebra anyway, and besides no one in Hollywood speaks French.

That night, after her mother put her to bed with the solace of hugs and kisses, Diana made a promise to herself.; she would hold on to her dreams even tighter, she would wish even harder. For if Diana had no other virtues, she had staying power. She would in no way relinquish even the tiniest morsel of her dream, nor the certainty it would come true. She knew from the stories she had read that miracles didn't come easily, they set up challenges, stumbling blocks, hurdles, to test the worthiness of their recipients. She would be worthy, she would believe, like in the movies she would wish upon a star. The decent sort of chap would never be able to find her.

The saving grace made its appearance exactly when it should have. It came disguised as an elocution teacher. Mary managed to convince Bert that if he was concerned about Diana's future employment possibilities, the best remedy would be to give her after-school elocution lessons. She persuaded him that whatever the cost, this would be a worthwhile investment, as a well-spoken girl would have many advantages in the employment market, opportunities denied to less privileged girls. Since Bert was concerned that Diana lacked marketable skills, elocution lessons would address that concern, would give her an edge over her competitors. Employers put much store by accents. The right accent carried considerable weight, it was an indication of breeding, of intelligence, even of virtue.

In truth, Mary's real concern was that Diana's accent could be detrimental to her film career – Bert's secretarial objective was not even a consideration. She wasn't sure exactly what accent was required to become a film star but she was certain it wasn't the broad

Swindon accent Diana spoke with. That wasn't the way movie stars spoke. Diana's accent would mark her as a simple, unsophisticated, small-town, West Country girl, someone of little consequence. Since Bert was so concerned about Diana's future employment, what better ploy than to pretend she was likewise concerned and convince him that the lessons were necessary to give Diana a better chance in the world of commerce and industry.

To everyone's surprise, Diana not only enjoyed the lessons but excelled at them. She liked the idea of talking in a way that was different from most people, besides, it was fun. She could switch from being posh to being ordinary. The lessons involved not only a transformation of speech patterns and accents, but practice in reciting. They involved different stances, different gestures, different expressions. For her it was a kind of acting.

To relieve the boredom of living in Swindon, and, no doubt, to escape the pressures of her inglorious academic career, from an early age, Diana had not only frequented the cinema, but had immersed herself in books. Now she was keen to act out some of her favourite passages. She was especially good at the recitations bringing the texts to life with nuance and voice variations. But her favourite was poetry. She had an instinctive feel for words, for rhythms, for emphasis, that delighted and impressed her teacher. Suddenly, instead of reprimands, she was receiving praise, instead of rebukes, compliments; instead of being regarded as a failure, she was a success.

Her elocution teacher, Mrs Barraclough, came from Cheltenham, a nearby town, known for hosting writing festivals and sponsoring competitions. Early on, she recognised Diana's talent and began to enter her into poetry festivals and competitions. For Diana, the letter proclaiming her a winner of her first competition entry was the most cherished, the most unbelievable letter anyone could ever receive. She read it over and over, even keeping it under her pillow. For her it was like winning the Academy Award. And it was Mary who accepted it.

Encouraged by Diana's success, Mrs Barraclough entered her once again and again she won. Each time Diana was entered in a competition she won. It was remarkable, beyond belief. It didn't take long before she had a collection of shining medals. The medals were her pride and joy until they were outshone by an even more brilliant trophy. In a local newspaper there appeared the caption, 'Swindon

Child Prodigy Does It Again'. Under the caption was a photograph of Diana. Diana could hardly believe her good luck. From someone who would never amount to much, she had become a child prodigy. And the child prodigy was really herself as evidenced by the photograph. The glory of the newspaper report was compounded by the public recognition it engendered. Strangers stopped her in the street to congratulate her. Even her mother was complimented for having such a talented daughter. Mary and Aunt Kit were over the moon. The acorn they had planted was beginning to sprout. Even Bert had to sit up and take note.

It was only Miss Ruth and Miss Daisy who refused to be pleased. If they were secretly impressed by Diana's sudden acclaim, they were at pains not to show it. They had branded her 'a right little madam' who would not amount to much and were determined to allow nothing to challenge that assessment. In accordance with their policy of shrinking 'swell heads' of preventing any child from becoming 'too big for their boots', of curbing any vestige of pride resulting from a success they did not approve of, instead of congratulating Diana when she proudly showed them her awards, they dismissed her achievement as inconsequential. They reminded her they were far more impressed with good conduct and application to school work, than in show-off medals and flashy newspaper headlines. In fact, they resented her achievements considering them inappropriate, of doing Diana no good at all, of being detrimental to character building. Their critical attitude, their inability to so much as utter the words 'well done' made Diana all the more determined to adopt a 'one day I'll show you' attitude.

Diana was eventually dismissed from the school, much to her delight, and ironically it was Bert, who had been opposed to her going there in the first place, who appealed to have her reinstated. But although Miss Ruth and Miss Daisy had a high regard for the steady, respectable Bert, who was in tune with their methods and means, they had a more than equivalent disrespect for his daughter. Diana would never be an asset to the school, she could only lower its tone, bring it into disrepute. She was definitely not Selwood House material. They politely, but firmly, refused.

Miss Ruth and Miss Daisy never relented, never wavered from their staunchly held opinions and principles regarding Diana. Many years after Diana had been dismissed from Selwood House and had become a famous film star, one of the newspapers wanted to interview them, as the heads of the first school she had attended. Miss Ruth and Miss Daisy refused. They were keen to emphasise they wanted no fuss made over the school because the now famous Diana had once been a pupil there, shunning the honour and glory of having the school associated with a famous film star. They wanted the school to be valued for its own merits, not because Diana Dors had passed through its portals.

But, in truth, they were unable to admit they had committed a gross error of judgment, had been unable to appreciate Diana's talent, to realise her potential. They had been so wrapped up in their rules and regulations that they would have been incapable of recognizing a gem even when its sparkle was blinding. In all probability, they were too embarrassed to admit they had, in fact, rejected Diana as a waste of time, and had finally dismissed her from the school, refusing to reinstate her despite her father's appeal. They could claim no credit for Diana's success. It was probably embarrassment rather than any principle that caused them to decline the interview.

However, despite the resounding vote of no confidence from Miss Ruth and Miss Daisy, Mrs Barraclough was able to recognise her pupil's special gift. For both Diana and Mary, the elocution lessons and the rewards and attention they led to were a clear indication that the journey had begun, the first step had been taken, the first applause heard. For Diana, the miracle had revealed a tantalising glimpse into her future, she had received a special sign that her belief had been acknowledged, her wishes heard. The miracles were beginning to unfold. She would not have long to wait. And how right she was.

Chapter 5
Early Days

It is said that everyone is born with their own blessing. Diana's blessing, however, was of a volatile yet elusive nature and could, with imperceptible ease, be transformed from blessing into affliction. Her special gift was a unique power she exerted over men, an auspicious gift indeed, yet throughout her life she struggled to prevent that gift from becoming a poisoned chalice.

From early childhood she instinctively knew she possessed a mysterious power over the opposite sex. But because, like her grandmother Georgina, Diana adored men, she did not abuse the gift, did not use it in any strident feminist sense, to liberate herself from men, to decry, disparage or dominate them, but merely to attract those males she was drawn to and to make sure they were drawn to her. This is a great advantage for any female at any time, but was especially advantageous for a female at a time when it was the male prerogative to pick and choose and for the female to wait to be chosen. For a female to be considered 'forward', 'brazen' or 'easy' was to equate her with having loose morals, and to brand her with the label 'bad reputation' – a label which could prove disastrous for her relationships with men and abandon her to the fate of the undesirables when it came to choosing a marriage partner.

However, Diana's magnetism was so powerful, so compelling as to transcend censure. Even as a child, when little girls were supposed to be demure and adorable, she had a forthright boldness which, combined with a provocative femininity, even before that femininity became explosive, proved irresistible to men. Diana never had to wait for the phone to ring.

When she was just five years old her special gift was already evident. At a birthday party Diana was the belle of the ball, the centre of male attention and had the boys – even at kindergarten age – eager to do her bidding. By age seven her gift took on a new dimension. On her first day of school, instead of being intimidated and clingy, she broke away from her mother and rushed headlong into the new adventure. Deprived of male siblings, she was delighted to discover that her fellow pupils were boys as well as girls. Avoiding those children who appeared timid or who were in tears, she singled out one of the more confident looking boys and approached him in a direct, determined manner. All went well at first. He told her his name was Eric Barrett, he told her where he lived, he even showed her a pen that could write without ink. Then, suddenly, for no apparent reason, he pulled his cap over Diana's face and punched her in the eye. The injury was so severe that Diana had to be sent home with a black eye. It also may have been the cause of her subsequent eye problem which necessitated wearing the hated black patch.

The incident did not serve to make Diana wary of boys or anxious to avoid their bizarre behaviour. When she returned to school she simply turned her back on Eric Barrett and transferred her interest to David Colbourne, the only boy in her class. The relationship blossomed and it wasn't long before they declared they were sweethearts and soon afterwards announced their intention to marry.

These initial incidents marking Diana's passage into the world of gender mystery established a pattern which would be repeated throughout her life. No matter how many black eyes Diana received from men – metaphorically and actually, she never ceased to love them, never wanted to be without them, impetuously agreed to marry them. Diana loved life, she loved acting, but most of all she loved men.

* * * * * * *

Despite her early successes, or possibly because of them, Diana couldn't wait to grow up and have proper romances, glamorous ones like those she saw in films. However, the unremarkable town of Swindon wasn't exactly the glamour capital of England and she had to make do with what was available to her. By the time she was 13 she'd had several local boyfriends including the horrid Eric Barrett who by now was more interested in kissing girls than in giving them black eyes, and Desmond Morris, who was to become a world famous anthropologist and author of the influential book *The Naked Ape*. Desmond was an especially auspicious choice because being older – he was seventeen – he had his own car, most convenient for necking sessions. He was her first real boyfriend.

Fortunately for her, Diana's body had cooperated with her desire to grow up quickly. Even before she had entered her teens the angles of childhood had given way to the curves of womanhood. The transition had been accomplished without the usual pubescent awkwardness and angst. Diana slipped from girl to woman with the ease of a creature shedding an unwanted skin.

Not only did Diana's body oblige in her quest for male attention but history colluded by providing the appropriate males. Diana's main loves: the male sex, and America/Hollywood (the latter two inextricably linked in her mind), combined happily with the arrival of American soldiers in England. America officially entered World War Two in 1941 and joined the Allied forces fighting the Germans, sending troops and equipment to England. When the soldiers came to Swindon in the early 1940s, Diana was ready for them.

Although at this time World War Two was raging in Europe, Swindon experienced relatively little major disruption. There were occasional bombing raids, mainly in 1941, which resulted in some deaths and destruction, but by 1942 the last bomb had fallen in Swindon. Compared to cities like Portsmouth and Plymouth, and especially Coventry where German bombers destroyed most of the city, killing hundreds of men, women, and children, whose bodies were burnt beyond recognition, Swindon escaped with relatively few casualties. The Fluck family were especially fortunate. They lived in a roomy semi-detached house in one of the best suburbs of Swindon, there was no shortage of money, they went on regular holidays, and their daughter went to a private school. The war had little negative impact on their lives.

If anything, the war had decided advantages for the folk of Swindon and for Diana in particular. It added an element of excitement and sparkle to an otherwise lacklustre town. Although the inhabitants suffered the usual inconveniences of war: food and clothing rationing, blackouts, deafening sirens heralding air raids, there was a heightened sense of community, of pulling together. This was especially evident in war efforts like the *Dig For Victory* campaign which encouraged people to grow their own food, a project Bert enthusiastically embraced much to Diana's delight, as it diverted his attention from her. The residents of Swindon proudly turned flower gardens into cabbage patches and discussed vegetable recipes instead of flower arrangements. Women who had been housewives, whose lives centred around caring for husbands and children, became involved in the 'war effort', their horizons and interests expanding, their activities more engaging, more purposeful. For Diana the war was a thrilling addition to an existence short on thrills.

A major factor contributing to the excitement and sparkle, especially for Diana, was the encampment of the American soldiers close to Swindon. The townspeople took it upon themselves, as an act of patriotism, to welcome the soldiers – after all, they came all the way from America to fight for them. Parties were organised in their honour and a Saturday night dance became a regular event. This dance was to become an important occurrence in Diana's life.

In the few short years during which the American soldiers remained in Swindon Diana became a young lady with a hue of sophistication far beyond her years. Suddenly, from a little girl tap dancing to Bert's piano accompaniment and singing little girl songs like *The Good Ship Lollypop* to entertain the troops, she was sashaying down the street with a wiggle in her hips, a flirtatious glint in her eye, makeup glamorising her eyes and lips, clothes hugging her curves – an evocative miss strutting her stuff – tantalising those very same troops. It is little wonder that the soldiers greeted her with whistles, catcalls of approval, and invites. When a group of admiring soldiers invited her to her first dance she thought she had died and gone to heaven. These were real Americans from the land of Hollywood. For her they were almost movie stars. After all, they spoke just like the men in the films. She could hardly contain her excitement.

Diana was determined to attend the dance although she knew Bert would have strenuous objections, no doubt feeling that a girl of Diana's age would be better off in bed instead of carousing with American soldiers well into the night. However, it wasn't difficult to obtain Mary's cooperation in concealing the invitation from Bert. Finally the day of Diana's debut arrived. She was striking, beautifully made up – a skill perfected practising tips from Hollywood stars gleaned from magazines – and wearing a tight fitting dress emphasising all the right places. She let it be known that she was seventeen and no one doubted her. Diana was an instant success and soon became a regular at parties and dances, much to the chagrin of some of the older women who waited in vain for invitations. The soldiers adored her, whispering compliments, vying to take her on dates, giving her presents. She was in her element. Mary, who accompanied her to the parties and dances was delighted by her daughter's popularity, especially as it helped to obtain various items of food from the cooks which were hard to come by.

It was no wonder that at the age of thirteen, when Diana entered a beauty contest with Mary's contrivance, again giving her age as seventeen, she had no difficulty being accepted. The contest was sponsored by Soldier Magazine – a magazine dedicated to the troops – and the winners were to become pin-ups. Mary had managed to keep Bert in the dark about the contest as his inevitable objections could have had disastrous consequences.

Diana looked stunning. She filled every inch of her scarlet and white bathing suit and her matching red, high-heeled shoes emphasised her lovely long legs. Her hair was several shades lighter with chemical help, and she wore it long in the style of her favourite Hollywood film stars, tossing it over her shoulder with a practiced disdain when the occasion arose. She strode along the equivalent of a catwalk with such grace and poise, it was as though she had been born into it. The catwalk was her path to the stars and she embraced it with an instinct so powerful it was as though it was her God-given right.

She won third prize. Part of the prize was having her photograph in the local Swindon Advertiser, which meant Bert had to be told. Bert was predictably angry. He was angry about her participation in the contest, about the multiple deceptions and especially angry about his young daughter's provocative near-nakedness staring out from the newspaper for all the world to see. However, by now Bert's protests had become increasingly irrelevant, buried under the heaps of male approval and flattery. The teeth of his protests had lost their bite and even Bert was aware of this.

It may seem incredible that a girl, barely 13, had already developed the skills, the wherewithal, the whiles and above all, the confidence to compete in an adult world as an equal; to enter a beauty contest with the composure of a professional; to be dated by the most desirable American soldiers; to walk the line between the overtly seductive and the subtlety intriguing with perfect ease and to have grasped the knack of attracting the opposite sex with the surefootedness of an experienced femme fatale.

Diana's assurance was the result of a combination of factors. Foremost was an obliging body and the ability to display it to maximum advantage. Secondly, an even more obliging mother whose delight in her daughter's popularity and successes, whose help in deceiving a strict Victorian father, whose approval and encouragement, which could always be relied upon, were powerful elements in contributing to Diana's race towards womanhood. Most important of course was Diana's inherent abilities, especially her ability to imitate the style and antics of the Hollywood stars she saw in films and read about in magazines.

Diana had been fed on the Hollywood ethos from the age of three. She had not only breathed Hollywood, but devoured it and now its influence was shaping her life. In a town she found stifling, in a school she hated, Hollywood was the oxygen of her survival. Her indomitable resolve to become a movie star influenced every move she made and she measured her success by her progress in achieving that goal. An important notch on the yardstick of success was her involvement with the male sex; with love affairs, romances, conquests. By the age of thirteen she had an eighteen year old American G.I. boyfriend and had already fallen deeply in love. Hollywood, male attention, film stars, romances, were all bound together in a great whirl of excitement and she was at its centre.

Diana would not have made such spectacular progress into the world of womanhood if it wasn't for her mother. Mary was Diana's main ally in her desire to bypass the innocence of girlhood and rush headlong into adopting the affectations of a self-styled sophisticate. Instead of curbing Diana's increasing vanity, Mary encouraged it; instead of restricting her flirtations, her preening and primping, she encouraged them; instead of discouraging her obsession with all things Hollywood, she encouraged it. She was Diana's collaborator in deception, her coach, her mirror, her conspirator in doing whatever was necessary to fulfil Diana's film star dreams – for they were Mary's dreams as well.

When the war was at an end, history once again colluded with Diana in achieving her goals. The G.I. Bill of Rights was signed in June, 1944 by President Roosevelt. Its purpose was to provide greater opportunities for servicemen who had fought in World War Two. One of its main aims was to grant them wider educational opportunities especially in the fields of higher education. In accordance with this bill, the Shrivenham American University was opened in Swindon and the Americans stayed on. A staff of highly trained professionals was sent from America to organise and teach the courses. This initiated a chain of events which could not have been more auspicious for Diana.

Unlike the Miss Cockeys, who disapproved of Diana's outlandish ambitions and who did their best to thwart them, the college staff, typical of Americans, appreciated ambition and enterprise and did their best to further them. They valued individuality and boldness, regarding them as virtues instead of as character flaws which had to be eradicated.

One of the professors seeing Diana's photograph in the newspaper as a beauty contest winner, asked her to pose for his art class on a regular basis, for which she received a fee. Diana was delighted. Even better, responding to her intention of becoming an actress, which Diana did her best to publicise, she was given roles in dramatic productions at the school. She received rave reviews in the campus newspapers which led to more performances and more acting roles. Several professors, appreciating her talent and sympathising with her aspirations and her irrepressible spirit, encouraged her efforts by providing her with additional opportunities. She was given the chance to sing on the college radio station. One of the professors even arranged for Diana and Mary to attend a film studio session in London. They were thrilled. Unlike Shelbourne School, Shrivenham University took Diana under its wing and nurtured her potential, even though she was not one of their students. She was no longer treated as 'unsuitable', but as eminently suitable and worthy of encouragement and assistance, which must have been a great boost to her confidence.

To add to her glory days, after she was dismissed from Shelbourne School, Bert, who was at the end of his tether regarding her vocation and despairing of her future, was convinced, not only with Mary's help, but with the help of the Shrivenham staff, to allow Diana to attend private drama classes once a week at London's prestigious Academy of Music and Dance – LAMDA. It was Bert's understanding that Diana would study for a teaching diploma and become an elocution teacher when she returned to Swindon. Nothing was said or done to dispel this illusion. Diana was thrilled. Mary accompanied her each week to the class. The acting, the singing, the rave reviews, the drama lessons, all contributed to her belief that she was indeed on her way to Hollywood. Everything was falling into place. Her cup was running over.

The war ended in May, 1945. Inevitably the American soldiers went home and Shrivenham American University was closed. Diana was devastated. Her brief encounter with glamour, with success and acclaim, was over. The joy went out of her life. Swindon once again descended into relentless dullness, to a colourless place where dreams were crushed. Her desire to leave Swindon became overwhelming. She would soon be 15 and felt life was passing her by. One thing she knew for certain, she had to find some way of escaping from Swindon or she would die together with her dreams.

Chapter 6
Fluck Becomes Dors

Diana's movie star compulsion, coupled with the intense will driving that compulsion, did not allow her to waste time bemoaning her circumstances, instead she set herself with renewed tenacity to pursue her film star dream. With an uncanny knack of knowing which steps were necessary to further that dream, Diana became intent on attending LAMDA full time. LAMDA was probably the best choice Diana could have made. Founded in 1861, it was not only the oldest drama school in Britain but probably the most famous and prestigious school of its kind. Its high standards, excellent teaching methods and superb facilities produced first class actors in theatre, film and television, not only in Britain but throughout the world. If any place could do it for Diana, LAMDA was that place.

Diana had no problem convincing Mary that LAMDA was a matter of life or death. The problem was convincing Bert. He was understandably reluctant to allow his fourteen year old daughter to leave home and embark upon a career he considered not only inappropriate but morally questionable. As a responsible parent he was unwilling to entrust someone so young to the suspect world of film making with its wicked temptations and moral laxity, let alone subject her to the uncertainties, indeed the dangers, inherent in a vast metropolis like London. Before even considering such a hazardous step he needed to obtain some serious assurances.

First he consulted with the head of LAMDA, a Mr Wilfred Foulis, expressing his concerns. Mr Foulis allayed his fears, convincing him that Diana would be perfectly safe at the school, that there were many young people attending the courses, and most important, that he would take personal responsibility for her well-being. Bert also had to be satisfied that Diana would have a suitable place to live. He discovered there was a YMCA close to the school and received assurances from Mrs Whipp, who ran it, that Diana would be well cared for in her establishment. He also obtained a promise from Diana that she would visit her parents every weekend, and her renewed assurances that she would return to Swindon to teach once she received her diploma and abandon her acting aspirations – a promise that Diana had no intention of keeping. With these multiple assurances and with the help of Mary, Aunt Kit and the elocution teacher Mrs Barraclough, who was enthusiastic about the LAMDA plan, Bert reluctantly acquiesced.

On a cold day in January, 1946, Diana stood on the Swindon station platform flanked by Bert and Mary, her green suitcase by her side, her return ticket tucked safely away, waiting for the London train to arrive. Bert was giving Diana a final talking to, reading her the riot act, warning her that she must focus on her studies and work hard. He impressed upon her, yet again, that in agreeing to the LAMDA plan, he was allowing her this final opportunity to prove herself and failure to do so would be devastating. Diana listened but said nothing, unable to understand how anyone could consider becoming a glamorous film star hard work. Mary, too, was quiet but she must have been consumed by doubts, wondering if she had done the right thing. She had certainly received enough flak from enough people to cause her to question her eagerness in getting Diana to London. Critical tongues had been wagging profusely.

'What mother would allow a young girl to live in London on her own; and what a cheek to think Diana could become a film star. The utter absurdity of it all.'

There was not a smidgen of doubt that Diana would be running back to her mother soon enough with her 'tail between her legs'.

In fact Mary had been most generous in helping to make the move possible for Diana. It was an indication of her great love for Diana and her faith in her daughter's abilities. Since her birth Diana had been the centre of Mary's life and the two had grown increasingly close as Diana grew older. From childhood onwards Mary had lived through Diana, fighting her battles at school, conspiring with her to subvert Bert's moral imperatives, rightly or wrongly providing her with the approval and confidence of growing into womanhood when she was still a child. Mary aided and abetted Diana's plans to become a movie star, rejoicing over her successes, sharing her acclaim, accompanying her to London for her weekly LAMDA classes, to elocution lessons, to the film studio to witness filming first hand.

Mary featured in Diana's film star dream, Diana filled her days, provided her with excitement, with possibilities, with the promises of life itself. Diana was her world. Now Diana would be gone leaving a terrible vacuum in her life. Mary was losing not only a daughter but an entire ethos. She was losing a life. The change in her existence would be cataclysmic.

There were no tears as the train pulled out of Swindon. Bert had been more involved in administering advice and warnings than in thoughts of missing Diana or at the sadness of her departure. For Diana, leaving Swindon to become a film star, which was all she had ever wanted, was a celebration rather than a wake. Her heart beat with excitement. And if Mary felt tears welling up she managed to blink them away for Diana's sake.

* * * * * * *

As it turned out the green shoots of Diana's acting career were abundantly nourished in LAMDA. But they just as easily could have withered and died in the demanding institution that was LAMDA combined with the intimidating grimness that was London. Leaving a life short on discipline, in a comfortable home with a loving supportive mother, in a town which had lavished acclaim on her and finding herself alone in a cheerless, alien city in the cold of winter, unknown and unloved could easily have defeated a less gutsy candidate with less formidable dreams.

Aside from having to adjust to living in a dreary place with strict rules and regulations, even stricter for her as she was the youngest student – actually the youngest full-time student LAMDA ever had – she had to overcome the multiple fears of her childhood. After all she was only fourteen and despite her sophisticated exterior, more a child than an adult. She was still afraid of the dark and had to leap into bed from a distance, terrified of having her ankle caught by some malignant force hiding under the bed; she still feared walking alone in a dark street convinced that some thief or murderer would leap out of the darkness to accost her. She struggled to defeat her many personal demons, or at least to learn to live with them. However, she clung fiercely to her dream which gave her the strength and the discipline to brave the initial terrors and persevere with the hard work demanded of her. It was a tribute to Diana's incredible willpower and determination that she was able to endure the hardships furthering her aims necessitated. And it is a tribute to her talent and abilities that she excelled at what LAMDA had to offer. LAMDA became a major force shaping the miracle.

The eighteen short months Diana spent at LAMDA saw a fledgling drama student, who even the head of LAMDA didn't think would amount to much, blossom into a fully-fledged actress. She quickly adjusted to the fact that the path to glamour and fame was not strewn with roses. On the contrary it was pockmarked with much that was distasteful and tedious. To add to the distress of cold and damp, of fear and loneliness, her limited allowance meant she was always short of money. She dreaded asking Bert to increase her allowance for fear he would use the excuse of limited finances to curtail her time at LAMDA. When the opportunity arose to become a photographic model she jumped at the chance to earn some money, although she found the work tedious. She even posed nude to earn extra money although she found this not only tedious but unsavoury, and struggled to overcome her aversion to it.

But she loved her classes, the acting techniques, the voice lessons, improvisations, make-up classes, fencing instruction, the reading of plays and especially the enacting of pieces from Shakespeare. She always had a book under her arm, usually a volume of Shakespeare and she used her spare moments to read and to try her hand at various roles. Her hard work was complemented by her very obvious talent. She adapted to LAMDA so perfectly, it was as though she had been born into its world.

However, hard work and talent do not automatically equal success, they have to be supplemented by luck to complete the equation. Diana was doubly fortunate as her stroke of luck came early in the LAMDA experience. First, a contact in Swindon, unbeknown to her, had sent her details to a film agency and it didn't take long before she acquired an agent – a Mr Gordon Harbord. Harbord had been so convinced of her ability that he was prepared to keep her age a secret. But most important was an event which took place at the conclusion of each term as part of the LAMDA curriculum. The term concluded with an acting exam and with the presentation of medals for the highest achievers. Diana was awarded a bronze medal at the end of her first term and tried for a silver medal at the end of her summer term. The exam involved acting pieces of several well-known plays as well as a piece from Shakespeare's *As You Like It*.

The adjudicator, Eric L'Epine Smith. happened to be a casting director. He was so impressed with Diana's performance that he not only awarded her the silver medal but, taking her out of earshot, divulged something astounding. He was casting a film called *The Shop At Sly Corner* and told her she would be perfect for a small role. Diana could hardly breathe with excitement. From the first time she had visited a film studio, when back in Swindon, she was fascinated by the camera and longed for the opportunity to have it focused on her. However, there was the usual hurdle to overcome.

The role in question, the girlfriend of the villain, called for someone older than Diana. Smith knew that Diana was an unbelievable fourteen years old and was certain that if the producer became aware of her age he would think him insane. But so taken was he with Diana's ability he asked her to keep her age secret, to pretend she was seventeen, until after the screen test. Once the producer saw the results of the screen test, Diana's age would cease to be an issue. The words 'screen test' were twin stars in Diana's heaven. Pretending to be seventeen was no problem, indeed, it had become a way of life for her. Her dream was becoming a reality, she could almost touch it. Lights were beginning to ignite in the cinemas, bearing her name.

The screen test was a triumph, the role of tarty girlfriend made for her. The salary was an incredible £8 a day. The contract was drawn up by her agent, Gordon Harbord, who was delighted with his discovery – his belief in Diana had paid off big time. However he foresaw one problem – Diana's surname. The name 'Fluck' was an irresistible invitation to obscene modifications. And, as Diana herself was later to comment, what if, when her name was up in lights and due to some electrical malfunction the lights went out on the letter 'L'. It was too risky. 'Fluck' had to go. However, Bert had to sign the contract as Diana was too young and he objected most strenuously to a name change. He protested that the name 'Fluck' had served generations well, and he saw no reason why it should be changed. After much deliberation and persuasion, Bert finally agreed to the name 'Dors', which was Mary's suggestion, the name of Diana's maternal grandmother. Dors was a family name, so all was not lost. And so Diana Dors was born.

After only three days of filming, Diana returned to her LAMDA classes with her status greatly enhanced. She was now a professional actress. The staff and students were delighted. One of them had made good and that good was reflected on all of them. Mr Foulis was forced to revise his original assessment. But the person who reaped the greatest and most deserved satisfaction was Mary.

She was over the moon. The rewards were far in excess of anything she had anticipated so early on.

When Mary attended the opening of the film as an honoured guest, walking down the cinema aisle with Diana and Bert to their reserved seats, with Diana in a white satin gown, its silver sequins twinkling, and Bert in evening dress complete with a black bow-tie, it was more than she could have desired. Then when the cinema manager ushered Diana onto the stage to deliver the speech Bert had written for her, it was as though she was living everything she had ever wished for. And when the film began to play in cinemas Mary herself became a celebrity. For Bert it was all too bewildering. How could his fourteen year old daughter earn more in a few days than a grown man with a family to support earned in a month. It made no sense.

Coming to London fulfilled Diana's two great loves – her love of acting and her love of the opposite sex. The magic she exerted over men and the fascination they exerted over her found rich soil in the male-dominated film world. Aside from her acting success contributing to her popularity, Diana's cleavage was taking on a life of its own enhancing that popularity. Her intriguing physical attributes were complemented by a bright, fun-loving nature and winning openness which verged on the cheeky. It didn't take long before she had a boyfriend, then another and still another. Old and young were drawn to her, from the unfledged student to the seasoned professional. Age and status were immaterial. She even developed a relationship with a man almost three times her age. But now it wasn't just necking in a car, more was expected.

Diana, however, was not willing to give more. Although she was seriously tempted she guarded her virginity with the iron determination of a chastity belt – the same fierce determination with which she pursued her film career. Both Bert and Mary had a hand in shaping that determination. She had been raised on a diet which combined Bert's moral advice and Mary's practical concerns. Diana feared being 'disgraced' and with child, which would end her acting career, as her mother had warned, or 'easy meat' for men who would then abandon her, as her father had warned.

The parental warnings rang in her ears, determining her responses to amorous encounters. In her refusal to 'go the whole way' those encounters often ended up more a battle than a delight and she sometimes felt that holding on to her virginity was an affliction curtailing relationships she longed to maintain. However, although her relationships with men were subjected to the inevitable trials, disappointments and heartbreaks inherent in the search for love and romance – a quest that would plague Diana most of her life – her acting career suffered no such setbacks.

With a film to her credit, Harbord, her agent, was able to get her several small film roles. A short time after the release of *The Shop at Sly Corner* she was hired to do the film *Holiday Camps* at an astonishing £10 a day. And shortly after that she was offered, and accepted, a ten year contract with the prestigious J. Arthur Rank film organisation beginning at £10 a day with an escalating pay scale. She was still only fifteen. In signing the contract she became a J. Arthur Rank starlet and found herself with small parts in one film after the other, among them *Dancing With Crime* in 1947, which featured Richard Attenborough and David Lean's production of *Oliver Twist* in 1948.

Joining the J. Arthur Rank organisation wasn't exactly an easy ride towards glamour and fame. It was more a trial by fire. The film work was exceedingly difficult. She had to get up at 4:30am for the 7am shoots. The studio was often freezing cold and dark due to power cuts, and make-up would have to be applied by candlelight. It also meant acting in a series of B movies with small roles, which rarely gave Diana the opportunity to act as she would have liked to.

Diana was prepared for the difficulties that filming presented. But she resented the mandatory participation in the 'Charm School' demanded of all those under contract to Rank. The 'Charm School' was an off-shoot of the Rank setup. It aimed to create Hollywood-style stars to act in Hollywood-style films with glamorous leading ladies and handsome leading men. In effect, its goal was to develop a British Hollywood. Despite its glamorous name it was really a hyped up schoolroom which taught would-be stars the basic techniques of the acting profession – elocution, singing, dancing, deportment and so on. For Diana it was a waste of time, excruciatingly boring and even insulting. She felt like a graduate student forced to attend kindergarten.

However, despite the many negative aspects of Diana's experience with the Rank organisation and its Charm School affiliate, the positives far outweighed them. She was now securely ensconced in the film world and had met some of its present and future leading lights, like Christopher Lee, Richard Attenborough, David Lean and Alec Guinness. She no longer approached a film studio with timidity and trepidation but with the confidence of familiarity. She came to know the individuals that people the film world: the actors, directors, producers, cameramen, designers, extras, as well as the structures that support it – the backstage components like sets, costumes, make-up. And she received an invaluable education in the behind-the-scenes complexities involved in making a film. The film world had surrendered its mysteries and if the magic was somewhat dulled by familiarity, it was now her world.

In effect, the Rank experience subjected Diana to the extreme rigours of the acting profession. If she could endure those rigours anything else would seem a blessing. And in those moments when she counted her blessings, she knew she had to be a starlet before she could become a star. From the age of eight, when she had dreamed her dream of stardom, she vowed she would do whatever was required to become a famous film star, no matter how hard the work and how many sacrifices she would have to make; and then the miracle would happen. The Rank Organisation was a vital part in bringing about that miracle.

Chapter 7
The Casting Couch

Although career-wise things were developing beautifully for Diana, romance-wise they were far less rewarding. The male sex was letting her down big time. She was surrounded by a pride of males, attractive, interesting, desirable but was unable to connect with any of them in the way she wanted to. Her early successes were unfulfilling and in any case they seemed to dwindle. This was partly because of her insistence on preserving her virginity, partly because of something she only became aware of much later on and partly because of a brief but significant all-consuming, at least for Diana, love affair, which proved a terrible disappointment. Even when romance was within her grasp, the relationship she yearned for eluded her.

Her sixteenth birthday signified her coming of age and marked an important stage in the development of her love life. She greeted the day with all the excitement and expectation such a major event deserved. That evening she was all dressed up and ready to celebrate, waiting by the phone for the man she was in love with to call and whisk her off on some enchanting adventure. But the call never came.

The man in question was the 37 year old film star, Guy Rolfe. Diana was madly in love with Guy. It all began when she was intrigued by the sound of a beautiful voice emanating from somewhere in one of the studios and was compelled to meet its owner. She was not disappointed. Guy was as beautiful and as striking as his voice, not only tall, dark and handsome but elegant and with an air of confidence and experience lacking in the LAMDA fledglings.

For Diana it was love at first sight, reinforced by the second sight of manliness and sophistication. Guy, somewhat world-weary and verging on the cynical must have found Diana's energy, her youth, her optimism and determination refreshing, to say nothing of her winning cleavage. An instant connection developed between them. For Diana that connection had a deep emotional impact. She had never met anyone like Guy; someone who knew all the answers, all the right people, the right wines, the right postures, the right possessions. For Diana, Guy was not only a sweetheart but an education. He swept her off her feet in a whirlwind of discovery. He took her to the fashionable restaurants, to the 'in' pubs, to the theatre, on country drives, and on visits to his actor friends. He had a car, a luxurious apartment, access to fine dining when rationing was still in effect. And most amazingly he respected her virginity, keeping well within her sexual boundaries. Diana was flattered by the attention and good times he lavished upon her. For the fifteen year old Diana, Guy represented the world she longed to be part of, and when she was with him she became part of that world, some of his suaveness and glamour spilling over onto her. Inevitably she grew increasingly dependent on him, on his approval, his judgments, always longing to please him, always on hand.

In her eyes he was perfect. She suspected he was married to an actress but was willing to forgive that minor imperfection. He gave her no cause for jealousy or concern. There was no evidence of a wife to cause her discomfort or distress. Although he had to juggle their frequent dates to fit in with his wife's acting schedule, he managed quite nicely. Diana had to be back at the YMCA by ten o'clock which gave him ample time to collect his wife after her show. But the night of Diana's birthday something must have gone wrong. Guy's call never came. The broken-hearted Diana waited in vain, sobbing uncontrollably, unable to contain her disappointment and hurt. Her world had suddenly collapsed.

Although Guy phoned the next day to apologise, the incident proved to be an omen marking their future. The dates became more and more infrequent. The adoration became muddied by neglect. Diana hung on, waiting, hoping, until the final realisation drew blood. Diana walked into a restaurant and found Guy dining with his wife. He did not so much as glance in her direction or offer even a crumb of recognition. It was as though she did not exist. The relationship was over. In its own way the incident was a continuation of the punch-in-the-eye syndrome initiated by Eric Barrett on her first day of school. But this time Diana was devastated.

Even before the Guy affair it seemed Diana suddenly did not exist for the males who dominated the studios, who had been so obviously attracted to her and with whom she had happily flirted. It took her some time to discover the reason. Unknown to her, a memo had been circulated stating that Diana was under sixteen and therefore jail bait. The warning must have sent shivers down the spines of the most ardent old lechers and young studs alike. On the whole it seemed to cool the hottest of lusts, except for the occasional lapse like when a senior, high-powered Rank producer, equipped with the confidence of status, devised an inventive ruse to circumvent the warning. After all, lust will be lust.

One day Diana was summoned to the office of this top-ranking producer. It was well known that a novice being summoned to his office was tantamount to being offered a leading role in a film and a new contract. She was thrilled. Her big break had come. She got all dressed up for the occasion and practiced her responses to the inevitable offer: her words of acceptance, her facial expressions, her thanks. How was she to know that the old pro had conjured up a sly seduction scenario?

Pretending to be concerned by rumours that Diana had gained weight which he considered detrimental to her career, he asked her to undress so he could assess the matter for himself. With these instructions he left the room saying he would return shortly. Diana was overcome by a mixture of disappointment and despair. Aside from hating the idea of standing naked before this aging man, she dreaded what would happen once she was undressed and standing before him like the 'easy meat' of her father's warning. And what was he up to in the other room? In equal proportions she feared obliging him and refusing him. He had the power of life and death over her. Miserably, she began to undress, taking off her jacket and loosening her skirt. Suddenly there was a knock on the door and a surprise entrance by the secretary, who, no doubt, was keeping tabs on the situation. The unexpected intrusion broke the spell. The plot was foiled. She was dismissed with a warning about puppy fat.

Sex-wise this was a bewildering time for Diana. She was beleaguered by dichotomies. She had the beautiful sexy body of a woman but was unable to use it as a woman would, beset by adolescent ineptitude and parental warnings, let alone male insistence which seemed to regard having sex as the focus of any relationship. It was true that she didn't exactly discourage men. On the contrary, she was well-versed in the art of seductive flirting. She wanted male attention, admiration, even the thrills of soft-core sex, of touching, kissing and cuddling. She used her body to provoke interest and desire but was at a loss to know what to do once that desire was provoked. But all that was about to change.

Diana was miserable about her break-up with Guy. In a short space of time she had gone from love-struck to grief-stricken. Whereas the former had lifted her to heights of excitement with moments of the ecstatic, the latter had dropped her into a pit with moments of despair. However, once again a combination of her own vitality and good fortune came to her rescue.

In the months before her sixteenth birthday Guy had more than filled her days and she had been content with the minor film roles she was offered. They demanded little from her and allowed her to focus on the adventure of being in love. However, now that she had been abandoned, bereft of the excitement and preoccupation that Guy had provided, the minor roles offered no distraction from her distress, and no satisfaction for her career. She felt disheartened, unanchored. But luck favoured her. At precisely the right moment she was offered some substantial acting roles, satisfying, challenging, which restored not only the promises of stardom but of romance.

The first role was in a film called *Here Come the Huggetts*. The film was based on the adventures of a family of that name, filmed as a pilot for a potential series. Diana played a capricious niece who causes havoc when she visits the family. It was a role she could sink her teeth into, and if the Guy adventure had caused her to slip from her career path, she regained her foothold and was soon back on track.

But the major breakthrough came with the filming of *A Boy, a Girl and a Bike*, filmed in 1949, the same year as the Huggetts film. This film not only firmly secured the path she was on career-wise, but added a new dimension to her life, reviving her other main interest: men.

The film was shot in the beautiful Yorkshire Dales, which Diana immediately fell in love with. The sensuality of the hills, the flowers, the proximity of the sky, the moon, the stars, had a profound effect on Diana. She felt inspired, released from the confines of London. The inspiration was compounded by the thrill of having, for the first time, not only her own room but her own suite in a fabulous hotel, instead of sharing a dormitory in an institution. The timing was perfect. Diana made a momentous decision. She would no longer be a virgin.

Before making that decision she had had a heart-to-heart with Jimmy, one of the older actors in the cast, who took a fatherly interest in her. That talk, no doubt, helped lay the groundwork for that decision. She had confided to Jimmy her torment about sex, the warnings, the fears, the frustrations. With patience and understanding Jimmy pointed out that attitudes had changed from those held by her parents. He told her Mary's opinion that sex for a woman was something to be endured was a relic of the past. Sex was to be enjoyed by males and females alike. Bert's 'easy meat' concept was no longer relevant, especially among the people in her world. He laughed at the nonsensical idea fed to Diana's generation that a girl could become pregnant by sitting on a toilet seat vacated by a man. Jimmy's influence together with the influence of the sky, the moon and the stars combined to create the perfect opportunity for Diana's momentous undertaking and she grasped it with both hands.

Diana already had her eye on one of the cameramen, a nineteen year-old, good-looking Norwegian with a beautiful muscular body, called Egil, Gil for short. In her own inimitable, direct, no-frills manner, Diana decided to go for it. Gil didn't take long to get the message, his eye too had been fixed on Diana and he was only too happy to oblige. And so it came to pass that Diana lost her virginity. However, instead of being transported to the heights of ecstasy, Diana was left wondering what all the fuss was about. But it didn't take her long to find out.

Gil was the perfect antidote to Guy, continually professing his love, being Romeo to Diana's Juliet. The setting was perfect for the romance Diana craved. Outdoors, the countryside was ideal for strolling hand in hand in meadows of wild flowers or climbing the purple hills to be entirely alone in the sweet smelling grass, or for lying together beside the clear running streams listening to bird song. Indoors, Diana had her own suite with the privacy she longed for, perfect for erotic activity without the fear of sanction or interruption. The parental haunts had been banished. Diana was finally freed from the bondage of her virginity.

The setting, the romance, the lover were all so perfect, so enchanting, that for a brief moment they eclipsed Diana's dream of stardom, and she fantasised about a rose covered cottage with a white picket fence in the beautiful countryside where she and Gil would live happily ever after. But the fantasy was short-lived.

When the announcement came that the Yorkshire filming was complete and everyone would be returning to the London studios to film the interior scenes, the lovely calm fulfilment Diana experienced turned to alarm. Gil and Diana had been spending all their free time with each other, virtually living together. What would they do now? Where would they go? Diana had to return to the YMCA, an environment which defied the most ardent of passions. Something had to be done, and with Diana's resourcefulness it didn't take her long to do it. She found a small flat in Chelsea. Money was not a problem. Her Rank contract was earning her £20 a week and she was well-satisfied with that. In any case money was not important to her, it did not excite her. What did excite her was her new-found love, her new-found freedom and independence.

Bert and even Mary were appalled by the idea of Diana living on her own with no supervision or care, but there was nothing they could do. Diana had flown the coop. She gave little thought to their concerns. Her main concern was preserving the relationship with Gil. She found the perfect place where their love could flourish and she couldn't wait to share it with Gil.

However she hadn't taken into account the effect of the city on that relationship, that love. The difference between the idyllic countryside with its sensuous allure and the harsh city reality, with its noise, pollution, traffic, crowds, its distances between A and B, with hardly a glimpse of the sky and the stars had a profound effect on their love. The strolling together hand in hand became rushing alone to catch the bus. The lying together under the stars became late night sessions at the pub. The setting was no longer able to sustain the romance. There was no stardust to sprinkle on their love. The relationship faltered. Instead of being keen to continue it, to Diana's dismay, Gil wanted to, as he confessed, 'cool it', a euphemism for ending it. Once again the punch-in-the eye syndrome had reared its head. Diana was left with carefully contrived props but with no player.

Chapter 8
A Taste for Anything

Diana had tasted the delights of a live-in lover, a taste she wished to savour. A replacement for Gil was an urgent requirement. She didn't have long to wait. At precisely the right time Anthony Newley, with whom she had acted in both *Oliver Twist* and *A Boy a Girl and a Bike* surprised her by confessing his love; a love she had been unaware of, having been so involved with Gil, a love that was now especially welcome

Diana and Tony had much in common. They were both the same age – sixteen, they were both actors under contract to Rank, they both earned enough money to amuse themselves in style. Tony had the right qualifications and it was easy for Diana to convince herself she was in love with him. Although still a virgin, Tony had no objections to being seduced by Diana and Diana wasted no time in seducing him. He slipped into the space vacated by Gil with the ease of a chameleon shedding an unwanted skin. Although he didn't actually move in with Diana, he spent so much time at her flat that it was almost as good as.

After completing *A Boy a Girl and a Bike*, their last film, there were few acting roles for either of them and what there was required minimal effort and even less time. With time, money and personality in abundance the pair became a good-times magnet for the Chelsea set and a major addition to its party culture. The borough of Chelsea had become a party centre, with clubs, pubs, after-hours venues with loud music and all night parties. It was a refuge for the fringes of humanity, harbouring high-bred aristocrats, mostly disowned and penniless; low-bred crooks, some recently out of jail; it was a haunt for radicals, actors, artists, poets, ladies of the night and their managers, hangers-on, ravers of every description.

Diana was fascinated by the variety of characters who peopled the Chelsea scene. She loved engaging with them, carousing with them, listening to their stories. If their backgrounds and class were widely divergent, they converged on one major fundamental – they were all members of the drinking class. Alcohol fuelled the fun, the poetry, the bohemian non-conformity, the wild times. Although she didn't drink with the same dedication as most of the others she not only 'developed a taste for anything,' as she later admitted, but for anybody, the more outrageous the better – a taste she cultivated throughout her life – some of her closest friends were criminals, low-lifes, people on the edge, as far a cry as possible from Bert's 'decent sort of chaps'.

In the long stretches between studio calls, with time and money on their hands, Diana and Tony frequented their favourite pubs, went to parties, gave parties, stayed up all night drinking, dancing, flirting, and having fun. 'Fun' became the operative word, dominating all else. Work became an intrusion, interfering with fun and fun was winning out. Diana began to resent even the occasional having to get up at the crack of dawn for studio work. None of the others seemed to be working, they were too busy enjoying life, too busy having fun. Why should she be missing out? Why shouldn't she be living the Chelsea fantasy? Once again the pursuit of her career took a back seat for Diana, but this time not for the love of a man, but for the love of good times.

It is not surprising that Diana devoured the Chelsea scene like a prisoner starved of experience. Her life had been devoted to seeking stardom, an all-consuming pursuit which didn't put much store on frivolity and gave no priority to having fun; a pursuit which demanded serious commitment, total devotion, hard work; a pursuit with an exacting task master – herself. In Chelsea Diana suddenly experienced heady liberation, she had been sprung from the confines of discipline, of regimentation, of concern with achieving. After all she was still a teen-ager and a teen-ager with ideal conditions to live the teen-age dream. She had her own flat with no restrictions, no parental supervision, no one to account to; she had money; she had a lover; she was at the centre of a fun universe. Who could blame her for submitting to it? And submit she did.

Just as things were getting out of control and Diana was surrendering to the pleasures of excess, her stardom dream obscured by the Chelsea good times, her good luck angel came to her rescue. She was offered a starring role in the film *Diamond City* , her first leading role. The offer was an instant sobering up.

The film, an attempt at a British-style western, was set in a mining boom town in the wilds of South Africa – the diamond rush replacing the gold rush of the American western. Diana played Dora

Bracken, a crusty, hard-edged bar hostess who ran a tight show in the saloon where the miners came to drink and indulge in the inevitable punch-ups. The role was a challenging one, especially for a seventeen year old. It not only required Diana to sing, dance the Can-Can and play the piano but to be convincing as a seasoned 30 year old, experienced with men, accustomed to wise-cracking with the miners and maintaining control when the drink took over.

Once again Diana found herself totally involved in acting, excited by the role, by the potential the film offered her career. She plunged into the discipline of acting as easily as a duck into water. She was back home, back to where she felt most comfortable, most fulfilled. She had returned to what really mattered to her. Her dream of stardom had been revitalised and her success was stunning. The role marked a turning point in her career. She was no longer a starlet. After pretending to be seventeen for all those years, she no longer had to pretend. She was seventeen, and with a major film role to her credit. Stardom was beckoning.

* * * * * * *

Tony was always going to be a stop-gap in Diana's life; someone to be with while she waited for someone else to arrive. And arrive he did. His name was Michael Caborn-Waterfield, Kim as his friends called him, or less kindly, 'Dandy Kim'. Diana first saw him on New Year's Eve, 1949, at the Cross Keys, the Chelsea club she frequented. The attraction was instant; that special twang on the strings of her heart, deliciously familiar. He had that promise-of-excitement look she was so drawn to, a look she had already learned to recognise and which she would succumb to all her life.

She watched him from a distance, intrigued by his looks, his stance, his style and especially by his charisma. She knew she had to meet him. Gradually inching closer until she appeared to be part of his group, she waited for the right moment to make her move. But things didn't go well. Although she managed to engage him in conversation she didn't manage to impress him. He refused to be smitten. He seemed cool, indifferent, even dismissive. Diana wasn't used to that kind of reaction from men. It was usually she who did the dismissing. Feeling somewhat deflated she slipped away as gracefully as she could. Although she didn't pursue further contact with him for fear of outright rejection, his behaviour left her decidedly intrigued.

She didn't bump into him again but several times she saw him and another male careering down Kings Road, the main Chelsea road, in impressive automobiles, a different one each time, motor revved to capacity. The effect was tantalising. Then one night they met. Again it was at the Cross Keys. But this time things were radically different. Instead of indifference, Kim displayed such intense interest in Diana that he insisted on whisking her off with promises of fun and adventure – magic words for Diana. He was charming, enchanting, intent not only on impressing her and showing her a good time but sweeping her off her feet.

They ended up in the West End, the main theatre and nightclub area of London. Kim was with Patrick, the same friend Diana had seen him with in Chelsea, tearing up the road. The trio did the rounds, ducking and diving from one club to another, drinking, laughing, high on alcohol and each other. Diana loved it. She was not only impressed by the clubs, far trendier than those in Chelsea, but by the fact that Kim and Patrick were greeted warmly by their owners and offered drinks by the many people they met. They seemed to know everyone. Kim introduced her to one person after another. To Diana they all seemed incredibly sophisticated, incredibly worldly. Some were aristocrats, some in government – a universe away from the Chelsea crowd. Diana was thrilled. They ended up going back to Kim and Patrick's spacious flat in Saint John's Wood, one of the most expensive and elegant parts of London. Kim had kept his promise, Diana had had a night to remember.

* * * * * * *

Many years later, by one of those fortuitous happenings, Kim turned up in my living room. By now he was in his early eighties. He was with his friend Lynne Brooke who had managed Diana's estate in the last years of her life. Sitting in my living room, Kim in a rocking chair, we drank wine and talked about their times with Diana – mainly Kim's. We had been drinking white wine and when that was finished I asked Kim if he drank red wine as it was all I had.

With a mischievous grin that said it all, he declared, 'I drink alcohol'. And so it was on to the red.

Kim was the essence of charming, an elegant gentleman with silver-white hair, twinkling blue eyes, and a trim, youthful body. Most intriguing was a blend of aristocratic polish etched with a roguish, defiant, naughtiness that inched towards the lewd but was saved by wit, humour and a boyish impishness. I could certainly see why Diana was so attracted to him.

There had been something puzzling me about Kim's initial meetings with Diana and risking a cheeky interjection, I said, 'How come you were so rude to Diana, so dismissive the first time you met her and then falling all over her, besotted with her, the second time?'

Kim seemed to relish the question.

'Of course I knew who she was,' he said. 'Everyone knew who she was. But I didn't want to be everyone so I pretended indifference to peak her attention. You see, I set out to intrigue her.'

'It really worked,' I said, 'And you reinforced the intrigue with those killer rides down Kings Road.'

'Exactly.'

'So it was all a ploy.'

'Exactly,' Kim repeated, with that blue-eyed twinkle. 'But,' he hastened to add, 'I loved Diana and I never stopped loving her. She was always precious to me and we remained dear friends throughout her life.'

After missing several trains to London, Kim finally roused himself to leave. His goodbye embrace was warm and affectionate like that of someone dear to me whom I had known a long time. And as he held me close in his arms I felt a connection with Diana, intimate, loving, inexplicable but real.

* * * * * * *

Diana's instinct about Kim had been right. Aside from being drop dead gorgeous, elegant, intelligent, witty; best of all, he was exciting. There was a wildness, an unpredictability, a devil-may-care attitude which immediately endeared him to her. His credentials were superb. He came from an aristocratic background and was as comfortable with the high and mighty as with the down and out. Although he was an actor with some highly paid acting roles to his credit, he was not committed to an acting career or to any career. He lived in the 'now'; the future held no interest for him. Kim was a perfect match for Diana and it wasn't long before she was in love with him and Tony knew it was over between him and Diana. (Coincidentally, almost twenty years later, Kim's daughter Campbell was the first girl Diana's son

Jason kissed, and with whom he played 'I'll show you mine…' Both were barely out of nappies.)

At the time Kim and Diana met he was earning £75 a week and with her assured £20 a week they were able to indulge in the good times, in rounds of clubs and parties that went on from morning to night. Sleep was for the dead. Even when Diana began rehearsing for *Diamond City*, a very demanding role, the extravagances did not stop. Night after night she would get to bed at 4.30, to be called for at 6.30 by the studio limo, in deference to her star status. At least there was no more walking in the dark or waiting for buses or trains. Each day when filming was over, Kim and his younger, less unruly, brother, John, would appear at the studio and Diana and her understudy Oona would speed away in two cars to begin their all-night cycle of carousing, drinking, dancing, pub crawling, club crawling, without a thought of tomorrow's heavy work schedule.

Once again having fun and enjoying each moment became Diana's primary concern, reinforced by the 'carpe diem' attitude of her beloved Kim. But unlike the Chelsea days when fun conflicted with career and it was an either-or situation, now it was not a question of fun replacing career. Diana wanted both. And for a time she had both. But over the months of filming her burn-out lifestyle took its toll and the dark circles under her eyes had to be hidden by make-up. Then the inevitable happened. As *Diamond City* filming was drawing to a close Diana collapsed in the studio and was in such a bad state that she was sent home to her parents to get well and recuperate.

Diana had been neglecting her parents and they had become increasingly concerned about her since she had moved into her own flat. When she arrived on their doorstep deathly pale and so ill she needed help getting into the house, they knew they had good cause to be worried. It took two weeks of Mary's patient nursing before Diana was well enough to return to London. During those two weeks Bert and Mary developed an intense dislike for Kim who kept phoning, urging Diana to return to London. Kim was the epitome of the 'indecent' chap Bert despised – a scoundrel who didn't have a decent job or earn a decent living. Bert lived in the slow, sure, steady lane and was unable to comprehend, or perhaps comprehended all too well Kim's fast, careless, hedonistic lifestyle and abhorred its influence on Diana.

Diana's return to London was not the anticipated happy occasion. She was greeted by the news that the lease on her Chelsea flat was not being renewed, hardly surprising considering the parties, loud music, boisterous behaviour and heavy traffic that went on there night and day. Kim and Patrick's flat was in trouble as well. Due to some difficulty with Patrick's inheritance they were no longer able to afford the rent. To make matters worse, Kim and Patrick were going to Dorset on a business venture and Diana would have to be on her own. And to further compound her difficulties, Bert and Mary's antipathy to Kim had reached boiling point and when Diana announced she was going to marry him, they were appalled. The arguments grew fierce and bitter. Diana, unable to defend the undefendable, was driven to tears of exasperation.

Diana had to vacate her flat in a hurry and the one she found reflected the dreary mood she was in. It was depressingly small, dark, with no natural light and close to noisy Piccadilly Circus. Fortunately Diana was able to escape the noise and heat of summer, for a two week theatre engagement. Mary joined her and they had a lovely two weeks rekindling their lapsed intimacy. Their enjoyment of being together even survived Mary's fuming anger which flared up each time Kim phoned.

Diana returned to London to more bad news. Kim's business venture had floundered as her father had predicted, and both he and Patrick had lost all their money. At least this meant he was returning to London. Diana had missed him terribly and was delighted to have him back. Although he found her flat claustrophobic and gloomy he had no choice but to move in with her. Being together was a gigantic plus for both of them even though they now had only Diana's £20 a week salary to live on.

Despite the lack of finances Diana and Kim managed to enjoy the rest of the summer in style. Their routine included a long afternoon session at the nearby S & F grill where they met fellow actors and actresses, all in between jobs. Toward evening they would move to a club across the way for drinks and then to some friend's house where they had great fun drinking, telling stories and jokes and playing pranks on people, all the while becoming increasingly outrageous as various stimulants were consumed.

One of their favourite pranks concerned a brand of tobacco called Prince Albert. Someone would phone a tobacconist and ask,

'Do you have Prince Albert in a tin?' 'Yes,' would come the reply. 'Then let him the hell out!' They would howl with laughter. The more absurd the prank, the more fun, the more hilarious the reactions. Diana loved it. She hated being bored and one of the best things about her relationship with Kim was that she never had to face that possibility. There were also jaunts to the country and to friends' swimming pools. Life was good, and it became even better when Honor Blackman, the actress whom Diana had worked with in *Diamond City* left her blissfully idyllic flat, and Diana and Kim moved in, although it was far beyond their means.

Of course the Rank Organisation wasn't exactly thrilled to be supporting Diana's playgirl lifestyle and when an offer came for her to tour with *Lisette*, a musical comedy, in the hope of an eventual London engagement, they made sure she accepted it. But just as rehearsals were commencing, a bombshell landed on Diana's doorstep. A fear that had haunted her for years, that had been etched in blood on her psyche, suddenly materialised. She was pregnant. Not only was she pregnant but she was desperately ill. Her attempts to quit the play were futile. The producer had discovered her secret and threatened to expose it both to her parents and to Rank if she pulled out.

Through sheer willpower and desperation she struggled through rehearsals and performances in three different cities. Fortunately *Lisette* had no further engagements. On her eighteenth birthday Diana returned to London and to Kim, to face the horrific ordeal of ending the pregnancy. Abortion was illegal and had become the illicit domain of back street abortionists who operated without anaesthetic in crude unhygienic conditions. Diana was given the name of someone who would get rid of the baby for £10. The money had to be borrowed. She was frightened, ill, emotionally fragile, and morally confused, as part of her wanted the baby. Fearing for her life, she underwent an agonising operation, which took several hours and was performed on a kitchen table.

Diana spent several months recovering from the trauma. It was a terrible time for her both physically and mentally. The only joy came with the release of *Diamond City* that winter of 1950. Nothing could match the excitement she felt seeing her name up in lights in Piccadilly Circus in the heart of London. She was thrilled. Her Hollywood dream glowed through the anguish of her distress.

At this point, Oona, Diana's understudy, was living with the penniless Patrick. It was ironic that when Diana had introduced Oona to Patrick, both Patrick and Kim had it all – a lovely flat, no shortage of money and cars. Now both Oona and Diana were supporting their flamboyant lovers on meagre incomes. However, while Diana and Kim were managing on Diana's weekly £20, Oona and Patrick had a stroke of good luck. Patrick's inheritance finally materialised, all £18,000. Of course this called for major celebrations: parties, treats, automobile excursions. Kim was delighted. He foresaw the pleasures of his own inheritance; an even greater sum than Patrick's, due the following year when he would be 21.

That spring Diana had a major role in a play, *Man of the World*, produced by Kenneth Tynan, a new arrival on the theatre scene, who was to become a foremost theatre critic. After some touring, the play moved to a prestigious theatre in London. Diana received great reviews and was named actress of the year by *Theatre World* magazine. It was through this play that she met fellow cast member Lionel Jeffries, a young actor who remained a very dear friend throughout her life.

After the play closed, Diana had little work and the summer once again reverted to fun times. With the money she earned from *Man Of The World*, Kim and Diana managed to buy an old car for jaunts to the country and afternoons at friends' swimming pools. They even went on a holiday to Cornwall staying in a lovely village by the sea. Although the money quickly evaporated, life was full of promise. Their friends were witty, amusing, exciting, the parties were continuous, the purpose of each day was to bring enjoyment, 'to experience everything regardless of cost.' And Kim's inheritance was just around the corner. Meanwhile Diana had the dependable Rank financial cushion to sustain them. The good times were rolling. They were both young. She was only 19, Kim almost 21. They were in love. The good times would be endless. But how wrong she was.

Suddenly, without warning, she was called to the Rank head office. Then the axe fell. Because of severe financial difficulties the contract actors were now redundant. Just like that. It was unbelievable. Diana was in shock. For the first time in her life she was cast out into the world to fend for herself. The results were not pretty. Despite evasion, promises, post-dated cheques, the debts piled up. The only hope was Kim's inheritance. But alas, on New Year's

Day, 1951, all hope vanished. Instead of receiving untold wealth, the check was for £50. The accompanying note explained that his father's business had been in difficulty and there was no more money. To add to the distress they were forced to move at once due to unpaid rent.

On a dismal rainy day they packed what little they had. As Diana stood by the window watching the rain, wondering where they would go and what they would do, Kim's brother John arrived in a big, power-blue Ford. The driver waited in the car while John made a fleeting visit. He too had no money and had come to borrow their radio in order to pawn it. However, the radio had already been pawned and John left in a huff. Diana, curious about both the car and its driver, asked who the car belonged to.

'Dennis Hamilton,' came the reply.

How could she know what a powerful effect this man was to have on her life?

Chapter 9
Enter Dennis Hamilton

The punch-in-the-eye syndrome begun by Eric Barrett reached new heights with the advent of Dennis Hamilton. At the time Diana met Dennis things were becoming increasingly rocky in her relationship with Kim. After being evicted from their flat, they were forced to stay with one friend after another sleeping on floors or at best on sofas before finally scraping the money together to rent a bed-sitting room. It was difficult to sustain passion in a crowded room and with an empty pocket. Kim and Diana began drifting apart, Kim becoming more and more embroiled in failing business schemes; Diana seeking distraction wherever she could find it. She was at a low ebb. She had no money. Her career was going nowhere. Her relationship with Kim no longer offered the excitement, the intensity, the fun, it once did. Life was stale, bland, miserable, without sparkle or even amusement.

Diana's misery was compounded by an offer to perform in a Broadway play. For a brief moment she was ecstatic. Her dream of stardom was closely bound up with going to America and both were suddenly about to happen. But when the offer fell through she was plunged further into despair. Then, true to the unpredictable nature of show business, with its emotional see-sawing from high to low and low to high again, she was cast in a leading role in the film *Lady Godiva Rides Again*, a satire on the glamour industry, for which she received the miraculous sum of £800. The film came to both her financial and career rescue. Despair turned to hope. (Coincidentally, Ruth Ellis, the last woman to be hanged in Britain, played a beauty queen contestant in the film. Five years later Diana's favourite acting role in the film *Yield To The Night* was based on Ruth Ellis.)

However, the joy at receiving both the work and the money was short-lived. The money quickly evaporated, mostly into paying debts – bounced cheques, promissory notes, unpaid rent. Diana's relationship with Kim was seriously deteriorating as he became both increasingly jealous as she looked elsewhere for cheering up and increasingly preoccupied with an upcoming court case concerning a dubious business deal. Her parents' disapproval of Kim was becoming a vendetta, sapping her endurance. The juices of living had run dry.

Enter Dennis Hamilton. Diana had met Dennis at her old haunt, the S & F café. She had seen him around and about since the first time she laid eyes on him in the powder-blue Ford parked outside her flat. She had even inquired about him, attracted by his good looks, but they had never made direct contact. This time she was with several friends and Dennis, on some pretence, managed to join them. Dennis's reputation was less than sterling and Diana had already been warned against him, but the warnings did not put her off, if anything, they piqued her interest. Tall, good-looking, with an air of confidence and virility, he exuded a magnetism Diana was drawn towards. She sensed in him an element of danger, of drama, which she found compelling and he sensed her fascination with him, which was an open door beckoning him to enter.

A master of the grand gesture, Dennis paid the bill for the entire group and then, in an even grander gesture, despite Diana's protests, he whisked her off to a prestigious Danny Kaye concert, for which he had obtained sought-after tickets, followed by a night of clubbing. Diana had a predilection for being swept off her feet. Kim had done it with an all-night round of fun and adventure and with his impressive first-name familiarity with the high and mighty members of society – although Diana was in no way a snob she was nevertheless in awe of the elite. Now she was being deliciously overwhelmed and much impressed by the Dennis adventure, to which she oh so willingly succumbed. The timing was perfect.

Although Dennis had dabbled in various projects, including acting in small film roles, at the time he met Diana he was selling sub-standard water softeners, not surprisingly, with great difficulty. He needed a new project and Diana became that project. Aware he had made significant inroads into her estimation, he reinforced his initial success with intensive wooing, swamping her with bouquets of flowers, cards inscribed with words of endearment, even poetry, and impressing her with his grand-gesture, flamboyant personality. Dennis managed to rekindle in Diana the dying embers of excitement with the promises of life.

Diana had only known Dennis five short weeks when Kim was convicted of a shady business deal and sentenced to two weeks in prison. Dennis took advantage of Kim's incarceration to make the grandest, boldest, most impetuous gesture of all – he asked Diana to marry him. Diana was so astounded, so taken by the drama, by the exhilaration of that gesture, so caught up in its romantic overtones that she said 'yes'.

She never did quite understand where that 'yes' came from. True, Dennis was strikingly handsome, with 'incredible ice blue eyes' and a 'dazzling smile', he was interesting, exciting, with a charm that could curl hair, and most important, he made her laugh, but she was not in love with him. She hadn't even experienced that special twang on the strings of her heart as she had with Kim.

In a later attempt to rationalise that 'yes', she listed the difficulties with Kim, his jealousy, his preoccupation with business schemes that required most of his attention. Added to the list were the continuous arguments with her parents who detested Kim – still refusing to have anything to do with him, or even speak to him. The intensity of their arguments led to bitterness, acrimony, even hostility which she was sick to death of. Then too, film work had become more or less repetitive with no significant possibilities in the offing. The horizon looked bleak without the faintest glimmer of Hollywood lights. The vision of stardom had become obscured, beset by dark clouds of reality. Then again there may have been a simpler, more mundane reason for that 'yes' which Diana didn't list. She discovered Kim had been sleeping with someone else while she was busy working, earning money to pay the bills. Marrying Dennis would even the score.

But most important, Diana was starved for adventure, hungry for excitement, for change, she needed a new interest, a new challenge and marriage seemed to fit the bill. It was a quick fix, providing the spice she longed for. Although she regretted the 'yes' almost as soon as it was uttered, she was carried along by the excitement, by the cheers and the toasting, by the waves of congratulations and well wishing, by the celebrations in pubs and cafés and by her parents' enthusiastic blessings.

Unconcerned with the reasons, Bert and Mary were delighted with Diana's decision. They approved of Dennis. He fulfilled one of their major criteria – he had a 'proper job'. They considered him mature – he was six years older than Diana. Besides, anyone was better than Kim. They heartily endorsed the marriage. The wedding was set for July 3, 1951.

The day of the ceremony was fraught with enough drama to satisfy the most voracious of drama kings. Since Diana was 19 and the legal marrying age was 21, it was necessary for her parents to give their official consent. However, Bert and Mary were away and unable to sign the marriage application. No problem. Their signatures of approval were simply forged by Denis.

Meanwhile, Kim had been informed of the coming wedding. He was both outraged and grief-stricken. He had to stop it. Impotent in his prison cell, he had a friend phone the court saying the consenting signatures on the marriage application had been forged. The registrar, a small officious man, was outraged by anyone bringing discredit to the solemn institution of marriage.

In a voice oozing with righteous indignation, he proclaimed, 'My office does not broker deception. I will not conduct the ceremony until this matter which is of the utmost seriousness has been investigated.'

Dennis was beside himself with fury. Taking matters in hand, he slammed the registrar against the wall and sneered, 'You'll marry us alright or I'll knock all your fucking teeth down your throat.' The ceremony was conducted as scheduled.

Diana was shocked but also somehow impressed. In her Chelsea days she had experienced the mix of excitement tinged with criminality, a taste she was to savour throughout her life. Criminals exuded a certain quality of glamour Diana was prone to – criminality being the dark side of celebrity. In effect, Diana had hardly the time to clarify her reactions. Exiting from the registrar's office Dennis was all grace and charm. With the ease of a chameleon shedding an unwanted skin, he had slipped from snarling killer to smiling groom.

As if this wasn't enough drama to enrich one marriage ceremony, Diana discovered, on the day of the wedding, that a woman with whom Dennis had an affair let it be known she would shoot herself right outside the registry office if the ceremony went through. The press was present with photographers ready to capture the impact of that revelation. Friends and fans were present to witness the spectacle. It was a full house.

The marriage ceremony, complete with sensational theatre, publicity, reporters, photographers and enthralled audience was a mere taste of the high profile, orchestrated events to follow – Dennis's gift to their relationship and to Diana's career.

There was no honeymoon, neither Dennis nor Diana could afford one, only a celebratory meal in an Italian restaurant. After the wedding, the newlyweds moved into a rather grand house in the exclusive Knightsbridge area. It was an extravagance they could ill afford. Diana paid the rent out of the £450 she earned filming a thriller she was working on, called *The Last Page*.

Diana dreaded the day Kim would be released from prison. If she couldn't justify her marriage to herself, how could she possibly justify it to Kim? She loved Kim. They had been together almost three years. They had come of age together. Their relationship had weathered formidable trials – the traumatic abortion, the thunderbolt discovery that Kim's eagerly awaited inheritance did not exist, Diana's sudden dismissal from the Rank Organisation. They had always stood by each other. Kim was not only her lover but her dear friend. Now she was formally separated from him, married to a stranger, and Kim had become the 'other man'.

When they finally met, the reunion was a tender, tearful one, but there was no going back. Everything had changed. This was made painfully evident by a threatening call from Dennis, whose spies had informed him of the meeting, demanding that Diana leave Kim immediately, reminding her, in no uncertain terms, she was now married to him and she was never to forget that.

Diana managed to stay in touch with Kim, despite Dennis's surveillance, secretly contacting him from the film studio, concerned about his deteriorating welfare, guilty that she had been a major contributing force. Finally Kim, surrendering to the inevitable, decided to leave England for France where he hoped to make a new start. Ironically, he went to France together with Tony Newley, the previous competitors now united by Diana's rejections. Diana gave Kim the fare for the journey, again from her £450. Somehow Dennis discovered this. Diana had already seen glimpses of Dennis's sudden rages, a prime example of which had been his attack on the registrar on their wedding day, but she was in no way prepared for the vicious, terrifying explosion of fury which he turned on her. Accompanied by nasty insults, he hit her so hard that she was thrown across the room. The initial explosion of violence instead of triggering contrition, inspired more violence. He kept punching her, yelling 'Faithless whore' in a rage, unable to stop.

If Diana had difficulty understanding why she had married Dennis, how much more difficult was it to solve the mystery of why she stayed with him after the assault? Yet stay she did. And that assault, that fury, was like a tea party compared with what was to follow.

Chapter 10
The Epiphany

Dennis was the ultimate con man, endowed with those quintessential characteristics that made him a master of that specialisation: good looks, charm, an illusion of sincerity, an ability to swindle without the merest tell-tale flinch, and a total disregard for morality. He was a five-star, off-stage actor, with a spectacular ability to innovate, invent, improvise, to bamboozle with winning dialogue – a skill that would put any method actor to shame. He not only wrote the scripts, he was producer, director and actor. His style was so convincing and his banter so captivating, that he was able to make people think white when their eyes saw black.

Diana was fascinated by these multiple talents, after all she had seen people spend years at LAMDA attempting to acquire those very skills and emerge far less accomplished than Dennis. Although, initially she balked at the lies, the deceptions, the blatant cheating, she was fascinated by the theatre, the superb performances and by the results they achieved. But most of all she was fascinated by the power Dennis wielded over people, including herself, and by his ability to bend others to his will, especially herself. It didn't take long before she was drawn into the adventure, the midnight flits to avoid paying rent, the window escapes to avoid paying hotel bills, the ducking and diving to avoid paying creditors, the pretence, the facades the implausible scenarios enacted before her eyes. It was akin to watching magic happen in one's own living room. No matter what else occurred between them, the terrifying moments when Dennis flew into demented rages; the indignity of being spied upon; the financial disasters; the unsavoury behaviour she found herself condoning; she was never bored with Dennis and that, for her, was a major prerequisite for any relationship.

Their rendezvous with exclusive Knightsbridge was short-lived. Neither Dennis nor Diana was earning any money. The see-saw of showbiz had hit the ground with a thud. From having her name in lights in the heart of London one moment, she was ignored and penniless the next. They were months behind with the rent, they were unable to pay their bills, no one would accept their cheques, and their creditors had progressed from persistent to downright threatening. Occasionally Dennis managed a mini triumph which bought them some precious time. Once he was able to fob off a group of debt collectors when they appeared at the doorstep, men in black suits and bowler hats, by adjusting his usual strategy. Instead of pretending he was not at home, he cordially invited them in. His charm, coupled with jokes, amusing anecdotes and large doses of alcohol, saw them off roaring with laughter and with much back-slapping but without the cash they had come for. Diana, hiding upstairs, applauded Dennis's Oscar winning performance. But the creditors were relentless. The blue car was repossessed and matters became so serious that even Dennis was concerned, unusual for him. Once again, as with Kim, the man-about-town who had overwhelmed Diana with his rich playboy style suddenly went broke when they began living together.

To add to Diana's distress at having no work and no money, Dennis managed to sabotage a fabulous opportunity that had unexpectedly come her way. Robert Lippert, an American producer who had worked with Diana on *The Last Page* offered her a film contract which would take her to Hollywood. She was over the moon. Hollywood at last. It was all she had ever wanted and coming at this low point in her life, it was the miracle of miracles. Suddenly she was being reborn, rising out of the ashes. However, there was one small snag. She would have to divorce Dennis. A married woman didn't fit the sexy blonde heartthrob image Lippert had in mind. He had no objection to Diana remarrying Dennis once the image had taken hold but she would have to be unattached until then. When Diana finally built up the courage to tell Dennis about the offer and its small print stipulation, he predictably flew into one of his rages. Fortunately, the object of his fury was not Diana but the 'fucking American' who had the arrogance, the damn gall to think he could interfere in Dennis's married life.

With the debt-collectors becoming virulent it was no longer possible for Diana and Dennis to remain in London. The only solution was to skip town and move to a cheaper house, somewhere the creditors would be unable to find them. Dennis found the ideal location in the countryside. Not only would they escape the creditors but he could con the local shopkeepers into allowing them to live on credit. The move was deeply depressing for Diana. She was a city girl. She loved London, the clubs, the restaurants the friends, the possibility of escaping Dennis's vigil. She had cut her teeth on the London buzz, it had become part of her life force. She hated the isolation of the country, removed from everything that was dear to her, with no money, no work and living on credit.

Dennis, on the other hand, loved their new circumstances. He liked living in the country, liked the challenge of convincing the locals how fortunate they were in having such a famous celebrity living amongst them and how divinely privileged to be given the opportunity of extending unlimited credit to such a superior being and her charming husband. But most of all he liked having Diana to himself. In London he had been forced to watch over her like a hawk, interrogating her when she was out of sight, always suspicious, always fearing she was fancying some other man. Now he could relax his guard. In this isolated neck of the woods, there was no other man to fancy. She was all his.

When Diana received the news that Lippert's Hollywood contract was no longer a possibility, she wept bitter tears. All her dreams had come to naught. She felt hopeless, burnt out, finished, buried in some remote nowhere place. Dennis, for once, rose to the occasion. He reprimanded her for declaring defeat even before engaging in battle. He, on the other hand was a fighter. The word 'defeat' was not in his vocabulary. If she would not fight her corner, he would fight it for her, he would take on her cause. He would win her battle. And, caught up in his oratory, carried away by his rhetoric he made an almighty proclamation.

Pulling Diana to her feet and lifting her head from its slump, he looked her in the eye with a steady gaze and said, 'Diana, I promise I will make you famous. I am going to build you up to be the greatest star this country has ever known'.

Diana, tearful, sceptical, distrustful, listened without hearing. How was she to know that Dennis was to keep that promise?

For Dennis, uttering those words, making that proclamation, that promise, evoked in him an epiphany. Suddenly he was beset by a vision and the vision was accompanied by the means to manifest it. He would make Diana into a star such as England had never seen. He would make her not only visible but so visible the light she emitted would blur everything and everyone else. As he excitedly verbalised his vision, ideas, plans, projects, flooded his imagination. He became inspired. And at that moment, through some mysterious form of osmosis, without any terms or conditions, without a written or spoken word of consent or agreement Dennis became Diana's agent, manager, and PR all rolled into one.

Dennis plunged into his self-created role with the zeal of a missionary eager to bring his message to the masses. He got right to work. While Diana listened with incredulity, Dennis telephoned one national newspaper after another with a steaming news item: 'Diana Dors, the successful, sought-after, highly acclaimed actress had just refused a lucrative Hollywood contract. England was her beloved country, her home and that's where she wanted to make her films, in England, not in Hollywood.' Diana was horrified. How would anyone believe that outrageous deceit when, in fact, she was desperate for work and couldn't get anything in England, let alone Hollywood? But to Diana's amazement, the press loved the story. The ruse, however thinly fabricated, had worked. Dennis was not only vindicated, but had demonstrated his ability to excel at his new endeavour. Diana was overwhelmed with publicity and Dennis had found his purpose in life.

Dennis's impressive success in motivating the media, and converting a negative into a triumph, wasn't beginners luck. It was as though he had been born for just that role, a role which relied on the ability to whet the media's appetite. His accomplishments in the art of con were ideal qualifications, as was his brazen confidence and his intimate relationship with the dark arts of exaggeration, distortion and hype. Above all, Dennis had an intuitive understanding of the psychology of fame, of how fame was the first step in the creation of celebrity and an essential component of the final goal of stardom. And most importantly, he understood the power of publicity. He was well ahead of his time in knowing how to initiate publicity, how to manipulate the image machine, how to fashion a celebrity. He believed in the ethos of 'say anything you want about me but be sure to spell my name right'.

Dennis was a superb salesman. His eventual failure in selling water-softeners was due to working with a product so flawed even the blind could see through the web of deceit he spun. But now he had ideal material to work with: an exceptional woman who was not only beautiful but talented, intelligent, ambitious and who was imbued with a bit of the devil. With his direction and skill the name Diana Dors would be on everyone's lips. She would be talked about, written about, quoted. She would be on the cover of glossy magazines. Journalists would be vying for interviews, photographers for photographs. Under his guidance Diana Dors would become a brand, a brand that everyone wanted.

It took some persuading for Diana to buy Dennis's vision. Her main interest was in serious acting, and she balked at the idea of being the glamorous, sexy, lightweight actress flaunting tits and bum, always courting sensation, always in the headlines – the image Dennis had drafted. But as Dennis fleshed out his vision, Diana was swept along by his enthusiasm, and was finally convinced that once she was a raging success as the blond bombshell no man could resist and every woman wanted to emulate, no matter what she had to do to sustain that image, to keep it alive in the popular imagination, she would be in a position to get the roles she wanted. Dennis would make her famous and once she was famous she could call the tune. And, until that time came, she could act that role as well as any other, it was the role she had been weaned on. And so it was to be.

Chapter 11
Mr Dors

The publicity generated by Dennis's sensational but bogus news item, claiming that Diana Dors had turned down a Hollywood contract, preferring to work in England, took a while to filter down to the movers and shakers in the entertainment world. But before the spin-offs from the media scoop metamorphosed into Dennis's grand design there were a few serious hurdles to jump.

Dennis and Diana had become so financially hard up they were unable to afford a Christmas tree and were reduced to stealing one. When the local shopkeepers and tradespeople discovered the 'famous' movie star and her 'charming' husband were penniless and unable to pay their bills, all credit came to an abrupt halt. Dennis solved the problem by resorting to the old dependable moonlight flit and relocating to virgin territory where their credit rating was unknown and they could embark upon a new round of deception. To add to the turmoil, Diana discovered she was pregnant. She longed to keep the baby. Dennis, however, was adamant. A baby was out of the question. The winning blonde bombshell image he had so carefully devised would be unable to survive the advent of motherhood.

After all, what glamour was there in a swollen belly and leaking breasts especially at a time when women, even if married, were trying to conceal their pregnancies under maternity garments? Being pregnant was not something to advertise, unlike today when females proudly display their bellies for all the world to admire, even drawing attention to them with navel jewellery in case anyone should overlook the remarkable projection.

And what glamour was there in a 'hausfrau' with a squealing brat clinging to her skirt? Dennis's idea in fashioning the Diana Dors image, aside from the obvious erotic titillation for the males, was to create a fantasy, an illusion of glamour to lift women out of the mundane, not to sink them further into it. The image of Diana Dors was meant to evoke dreams, to add a splash of colour, a dash of style, an antidote to the drab grey war years and the early Fifties' lingering aftermath of shortages and rationing; an antidote to the severe cut of women's clothing designed to save on materials rationed in the war years. With her ample bosom and curvaceous hips Diana epitomised femininity and her clothes were meant to further the image. The public wanted to fantasise about ball gowns, not aprons, about glamorous pin-ups, not overworked housewives, about penthouses, not basement flats, they yearned for the lavish, not the deprived. And Diana Dors would champion the fantasies of both males and females.

An abortion was an absolute necessity. This time the doctor was a discreet professional and the experience was not nearly as traumatic as the previous back street horror. Mercifully, Diana was able to pay the £50 fee from the one job she had managed to get: modelling furniture. Once again her desire to have a baby was thwarted. Her career took precedence over all else. Diana was more than Dennis's key to success, she was his path to glory, which he was not about to relinquish because of an unfortunate accident.

Then suddenly when finances, work and well-being were at their lowest ebb and desperation was the pervading reality, something wonderful happened, something so profound as to change Diana's life forever. It began with a call from a producer who invited Diana to London to discuss a possible role in a theatrical revue he planned to stage. Diana had difficulty disguising her excitement.

Driving in their rather rundown vehicle, Dennis spotted a black Rolls Royce bearing a 'For Sale' sign in a garage forecourt. To Diana's dismay he stopped the car, announcing he was going to buy it. He headed for the garage before Diana had time to voice her objections. She was appalled. How could he possibly buy the car when they had absolutely no money? She consoled herself with the assumption that nothing would come of it. But to her disbelief, Dennis re-appeared minutes later with the declaration that they were now proud owners of a Rolls Royce and with the documents to prove it. Once again, his fast talking, his exaggeration, distortion and hype had triumphed. Diana's protests concerning their ability to meet the hire purchase payments were swept away by Dennis's superb confidence.

'The Rolls is our first step to fame and fortune,' he declared, with unassailable certainty.

And again Dennis's intuitive grasp of the formula required to create a celebrity, of the ingredients needed to produce stardom, was spot on. The mantra that success breeds success just as money breeds money was his gospel. True to his assurances, the Rolls worked its magic. When Diana was chauffeured into London ensconced in the leather embrace of a Rolls Royce, Dennis making sure the producer was aware of the extravagance, she not only got the job but was offered more money as befitted someone who owned such a prestigious vehicle. Dennis was well and truly vindicated.

As he had predicted, the Rolls Royce was the talisman that changed Diana's luck and indeed, her life. He was to make the most of its high profile acquisition, astounding the press with the story that at age 20, Diana Dors was the youngest person in England to own a Rolls Royce, a formidable image enhancer, and one small step in promoting his premise that fame is an essential prerequisite for celebrity status no matter how it is achieved. Giant steps were to follow.

The revue Diana was cast in was called *Rendezvous*, and it opened in the coastal town of Brighton, before moving on to London. Diana took the critics by storm. Although they considered the play dull, they unanimously agreed her performance was not only brilliant but a 'show stopper'. Even the seasoned ultra-discerning critics were lavish in their praise. Kenneth Tynan, the acclaimed theatre critic wrote '….her personality is a blessing to our theatre and could easily develop into a legend.' Another wrote 'The blonde is the success of the evening.' To their amazement they discovered Diana Dors was not just a dumb blonde with a figure to die for, but a blonde who could sing and dance, a talented mime, comedienne and accomplished actress, with a figure to die for.

Opening night was a triumph. The audience loved her and would not stop clapping until she took multiple bows. Laurence Olivier was among the many celebrities in the entertainment world who came backstage to offer personal congratulations. Diana was a hit. As she herself quipped, 'London is truly at my feet.' As a result of her performance in *Rendezvous* she was inundated with offers: theatre, films, revues, everyone wanted her. Olivier wanted her for a part in *Beggars Opera*, a film he and Peter Brook were working on. She was offered a lucrative role for a summer season in a play at the resort town of Blackpool. Rejection was now her prerogative. From not being wanted for anything she had become the flavour of the entertainment month, the toast of the town.

Diana and Dennis decided on the lucrative Blackpool summer season, with Diana acting in *Life with the Lyons*. She and Dennis headed for Blackpool with all their belongings, including their animals. Blackpool; a popular holiday destination with its Pleasure

Beach, funfair attractions and amusement centres, catering to thrill-seeking, working class holidaymakers; was not to Diana's taste, and the heavy work schedule was exhausting, but the money made it all worthwhile.

While Diana was busy working, Dennis was learning the tricks of the show-business trade, the better to manage Diana's career, and, indeed her life. And, as she discovered some time later, while she was earning the money he was spending it, indulging in his favourite pastime: wooing the ladies. Blackpool proved to be fertile grounds for this preoccupation. With an abundance of women holidaying in Blackpool, many of whom were not averse to a holiday adventure, he was spoilt for choice. His charm, good looks, money and status, endeared him to the ladies, especially when he posed as a film director, spicing his seduction with promises of a film role. Diana was none the wiser. His clandestine pursuits had always been kept well hidden from her, their friends and acquaintances conspiring to keep his infidelities a secret, no doubt to protect her from painful revelations.

After the Blackpool season Diana and Dennis returned to London and rented a small house. Almost immediately Diana began work on another film, *The Great Game*, followed by a West End play. The money and the work flowed. Dennis took control of everything: negotiating contracts (often better than those her agent was able to negotiate), arranging money matters, publicity, which included planting stories in the press, perfecting Diana's image. He was now Diana's spokesman, publicist, dresser, stylist, banker, freeing her from the tedium of responsibility. The press began to refer to him as Mr Dors. Instead of taking the title as the put-down that was intended, Dennis loved it. As long as the name 'Dors' appeared in the press he was indifferent as to how it got there, even if it was at his expense.

Diana's professional success and the money it generated did little to improve her relationship with Dennis. She still feared his irrational outbursts, his terrible mood swings, which instead of improving had grown progressively worse. She was well aware it was he who had masterminded and maintained her success, it was he who set the pace, made the decisions and took care of all details. But it was this very reliance on Dennis, this control he had over her that she resented, that made her feel increasingly irrelevant, as though she had become merely an extension of him. At times she felt like a monkey on a wind-up organ, grinding out glamour to Dennis's tune. True, her life was luxurious, when she had time to live it, but her parameters were growing smaller, more confined.

Dennis watched her every move, was present at every event, always fearing she would be enticed by some other man, determined to prevent even the most minor flirtation. And, as in many cases, although it was he who was womanising, indulging in sexual escapades, he feared that she would do the very thing that he was actually doing. But although she resented being tethered to him, he also freed her from many of life's irritations. She was pampered, overprotected, and catered to. Life was served to her on a beautifully arranged platter and it didn't take long for her not only to grow accustomed to the service but to become dependent on it. Like an addiction, she needed Dennis, while, at the same time, yearning to be free of him, yearning to fall in love before it was too late – after all she was already 20 years old.

Her 21st birthday was a troubling occasion. It began well. Dennis had arranged a special party to celebrate Diana's official entry into adulthood, insisting on doing all the preparations himself. The results were outstanding. The decorations, something Dennis excelled in, were impressive, all original, and the buffet a sumptuous feast. Diana was delighted. The house was filled with adoring guests all having a wonderful time. With the party still in full swing, a reluctant Diana tore herself away and headed for bed. She had an early morning rehearsal, not conducive to hangovers. She was deep in sleep when she woke with a start to what sounded like the invasion of an alien force. Furniture was crashing, bodies seemed to be hurling into walls, voices were screaming abuse. Listening from the floor above she heard Dennis and a friend, both very drunk, cursing, threatening and beating up on each other. Although she was accustomed to Dennis's uncontrolled fits of temper, which friends dignified as 'brainstorms', she realised this was a particularly vicious fight.

Suddenly the friend shouted, 'I'll tell Dors the truth about you! I'll spoil your meal ticket.' Although the fighting raged on she was deaf to all else.

Diana didn't dare challenge Dennis, fearing a violent outburst. She preferred burying her suspicions. In all likelihood she didn't want them confirmed. But those words remained seared in her consciousness.

Money-wise, matters were flourishing. Dennis encouraged Diana to tour in variety shows because, 'That's where the real money is.' He considered theatre work 'acting rubbish' and actors 'boring and pompous, out of touch with the real world.' Although Diana hated touring variety when she had her heart set on serious acting, she did Dennis's bidding and, as he predicted, the money poured in. Dennis accumulated enough of Diana's earnings to buy a house which he set about decorating and furnishing with antique furnishings, something he was good at. Diana was excited about the acquisition of their own house – at least her hard work had produced something she took pleasure in.

Their bank account grew even fatter when a booklet of photographs of Diana was released, photographed in 3D, a process popular at the time. The photographs pictured Diana in saucy poses, almost naked except for strategically placed wisps of fluff. They were set against the background of their showcase home with its cocktail bar, goldfish pond and antique furnishing. The booklet was a raging success.

In addition to the financial success there was the publicity success which in turn further padded the financial success. Again, Dennis, relying on his mantra about success breeding success and money breeding money, circulated rumours that Diana was incredibly wealthy, that she had her own plane and flew it herself being the youngest pilot in England. He whispered choice tidbits into the right ears: 'Diana lived an extravagant Hollywood -style life.' 'She slept in a 'palatial bed covered in gold satin.' 'Her floors were strewn with tiger skins, her glassware was Waterford crystal.' The exaggerations embarrassed Diana, she thought no one would believe them they were so over-the-top. But newspapers and magazines couldn't get enough of Diana Dors, and the British public bought every word. Tired of the austerity of the war years, they longed to read about glamour, success, and affluence. Diana became a frequent news item and a sought-after magazine feature.

Diana and Dennis were riding high. Aside from the money there was also the prestige they both enjoyed, with Dennis becoming a popular figure in his own right. Diana was considered the English Marilyn Monroe, although in fact her success pre-dated Monroe's. A British film magazine had written as early as 1950: 'How much like our own Diana Dors this new Monroe girl is' – ironic in retrospect. Dennis was so successful in promoting Diana's affluent lifestyle that the matter of her wealth became an issue raised in Parliament sending the tax man to her door to investigate.

Dennis was now a renowned host and some of his parties were infamous, rivalling those of the later-day notorious madam, Cynthia Payne. The parties were carefully orchestrated by Dennis. The guests, mostly male, were ushered into a dimly lit room. Alcohol, erotic stimulants, willing starlets and exotic dancers contributed to a sexually charged atmosphere. The music throbbed, the dancing bordered on foreplay and inhibitions were suspended. As intimacy developed into arousal, each couple was led to a special room and allocated fifteen minutes, unaware that the room was fitted with two-way mirrors and their performance was a source of entertainment for select guests. Diana didn't exactly approve but she didn't exactly disapprove either and went along with Dennis's machinations considering them a harmless prank and indeed, lots of fun.

At one point, after one of Dennis's practical jokes seriously misfired, Dennis and Diana were arrested, and required to appear at court. During a visit to Blackpool to see friends, Dennis had decided to have a party at their hotel. Frank Rogers, one of the invitees lived nearby and they walked to his house to extend the invitation. Frank was not home so Dennis pried open one of the windows and they crawled in to await his return. After a long wait they decided to leave. Frank had the reputation of being a tight-wad and fearing he would not bring a bottle to the party Dennis decided to take several half-full bottles of spirits and serve Frank his own booze. When Frank returned home and found the drink missing, unaware who the culprits were, he reported a break-in to the police. Once the incident became a police matter, Frank was unable to retract the charge and they were booked for house-breaking.

Although the incident was a relatively minor one resulting in a fine for Dennis and a discharge for Diana, it was a feast for a media with an appetite for scandal. And a scandal it was. 'Diana Dors on house breaking charge'. 'Starlet Arrested'. Diana detested the entire matter especially because of its effect on her parents who were subjected to the side effects of disgrace and the inevitable 'tut tutting' by the good people of Swindon. She also feared a negative effect on her acting career. Dennis, on the other hand, applauded the windfall of media interest.

Dennis instinctively knew that the publicity generated by the arrest and court appearance – instead of causing public disapproval, instead of causing the big wigs in the entertainment industry to shun her, as Diana feared – would have the opposite effect; it would enhance her popularity. In keeping with his conviction that it didn't matter what the media said as long as they spelled one's name right; and Diana's name was spelled right, Dennis made sure of that; as long as a scandal wasn't the result of sexual abuse, especially child abuse, it was invaluable for creating intrigue, which was the forerunner of fame. Publicity was the oxygen on which celebrity status thrived and Dennis was an expert in its administration.

True to his credo the scandal did much to further Diana's career. Her name was on the tip of the nation's tongue. Film roles were offered, variety engagements, even a radio series, called *Calling All Forces*. Diana could hardly keep up with the offers. Work became the pervading reality to the exclusion of almost everything else. Although the money flowed, Diana's life was hardly fulfilling. Her film roles were mainly a means to an end, hardly what she had hoped for. Her relationship with Dennis had further deteriorated. Fun and excitement were a thing of the past, love and laughter were only memories.

Dennis's 'brainstorms' increased in frequency, intensity and violence. Once, during a dinner party at their home he suddenly began to shout at Diana accusing her of having an affair with Bob Monkhouse, the comedian and script writer she was working with on the radio series. His threats were fierce and graphic.

Waving a knife, he plunged it repeatedly into the air shouting, 'I'll get the fucker, then I'll get you, fucking slut! How would you like your lover with his eyeballs slit?'

Then, as though the insults and threats were not adequate to vent his rage, he began to smash the dishes and anything else he could get his hands on; lamps, chairs, ornaments, shouting obscenities, smashing, shouting, sweat streaming down his face, before he collapsed with exhaustion. The guests disappeared and Diana kept well out of his way.

Although by now there were numerous indications that something other than jealousy was seriously wrong with Dennis, was responsible for his erratic behaviour, his rages, his intense sweats, his, at times, distorted vision, the symptoms were overlooked, fobbed off as 'brainstorms' until eventually it became too late to address them. Meanwhile life continued without further investigation or concern; Diana's career was the all-consuming reality.

Diana's big break came when Sir Carol Reed chose her, over powerful competition, including such luminaries as Vivienne Leigh and Ingrid Bergman, for the leading female role in his film *A Kid for Two Farthings*. Reed, of *The Third Man* fame, a film considered one of the greatest of all time, was a distinguished film producer and one of the top film directors in Britain. Being awarded a role in one of his films was a great honour. It meant that an acclaimed film producer had recognised Diana's acting talent. It put Diana in a new league, a league she had yearned for; it at last established her as a serious actress.

Although Diana would have acted in the film free of charge, so important was it to her acting ambitions, the fee of £1,700 was a welcome bonus, allowing Dennis to engage in some lucrative property deals. The profits enabled him to buy a lavish five bedroom house in the country with a tennis court and a boathouse, and to hire a cook-cum-housekeeper. The initial period of country living was a happy one for both Dennis and Diana. Leaving a fraught London existence had a healing effect on their relationship. Dennis was far calmer busying himself with doing things he enjoyed like building an aviary, decorating the houseboat, and constructing a tree-house telephone box in the garden. Diana was basking in success and acclaim. *A Kid for Two Farthings*, her first film in colour, did wonders for her career. Offers poured in, money was plentiful and they both loved their country home. The tranquillity of the countryside was reflected in the serenity of their relationship. Dennis was affectionate and caring. He even took Diana to Paris; a gift for her 23rd birthday.

The following year, 1955, although one of the most successful career-wise, was a traumatic one for Diana. It began most auspiciously. J. Arthur Rank offered her a starring role in the film, *Value for Money* with a fee of £5,000, negotiated by Dennis, her highest fee yet. Dennis also finagled a lucrative contract whereby Rank would pay Diana £7,000 for doing one film a year. But, as usual, Dennis managed to poison the pleasure of success. He seemed unable to sustain the equilibrium of well-being and achievement.

That April, while filming *Value for Money*, Diana was invited to help judge a prestigious fancy dress competition in the south of England. Of course Dennis accompanied her. It was here that suspicions of Dennis's infidelity, aroused at Diana's 21st birthday party, were confirmed. Late one night, thinking Diana was asleep, Dennis took their car for a romp with a model staying at the same hotel. However, instead of being asleep, Diana heard them leave and waited up for their return. What she saw from her window made it obvious that the car had been used for pleasures other than joyriding. This time Diana confronted Dennis. The evidence was undeniable. Dennis, unable to deny her accusations, became aggressive. A bitter confrontation ensued, with the shouting and taunts escalating into violence. Dennis, cornered, was like a trapped animal. Wild with rage, he punched Diana in the face.

In the following days, Dennis was contrite, attempting to appease Diana with gifts and gestures of affection. But Diana was not to be appeased. She was so filled with hatred that she may even have taken steps to disentangle herself from Dennis if not for a shocking occurrence, so traumatic it eclipsed the Dennis troubles. Diana's emotional upheaval was compounded by an urgent message. Mary, Diana's mother was dead. She had had a heart attack after what was expected to have been a minor operation. She was 65 years old. Diana was devastated.

Ever since Diana was little she and Mary had had a unique mother-daughter relationship. When the plain mousey-haired child with a patch over one eye dreamed the impossible dream of becoming a film star, Mary shared the dream. Against the odds she provided the support and encouragement, the incredible faith in Diana's abilities, to make the dream happen. Indeed, if it had not been for Mary it is unlikely Diana Fluck would have become Diana Dors. For Diana, April was truly the saddest month.

At such a terrible time, Diana needed comfort and support, she needed someone to lean on to help her cope with the emotional turmoil. Dennis was more than happy to slip into that role. So, once again Dennis's abuses went unchallenged, confrontation was not an option.

Directly after the funeral Diana plunged into her heavy workload with renewed vigour. The concentration, long hours and intensity of the work demanded total focus and left little time for grieving, for being consumed by regrets, guilt and loss. But if her film work was a distraction from sorrow, the Venice Film Festival, coming only months after her mother's death, was a major diversion. And, if the festival was a blessing for Diana, it was heaven-sent for Dennis, providing him the opportunity to be his most ingenious, his most imaginative.

The Rank organisation, wanting to raise both their own profile as well as the profile of British films, decided on a high visibility approach. To this effect they planned an impressive grand entrance. A plane was chartered for their contract stars, complete with a publicity team, journalists and photographers. Upon landing they would be met by limousines and chauffeured to the Grand Canal, where motor boats waited to take them to the exclusive Excelsior hotel, the pivotal point of the festival.

Despite Rank's elaborate preparations to ensure high visibility, they were not high profile enough for Dennis. He wanted Diana's virtues to shine in the festival firmament, not dimmed by other stars. He wanted a sensational solo entrance on the Venice stage, not one obscured by a group scene. After all, it would not only be the Italian press who were on hand for photographs, but the world's press would be there, and Dennis was determined not to disappoint them.

As usual Dennis was right. Diana arrived in their new powder-blue convertible Cadillac, a queen waving to her adoring subjects. The press loved it. And Dennis did not stop there. Sensational gave way to spectacular when Diana sailed down the Grand Canal in a gondola, striking a provocative pose wearing a mink bikini. The photographers thought they had died and gone to heaven. The following day the photographs appeared in newspapers and magazines all over the world.

Meanwhile, back in London, *A Kid for Two Farthings* had received great reviews. On her return from the festival, Diana's Venice triumph was celebrated by a special showing of the film, attended by the Queen. Diana also discovered she had been nominated as one of the top ten box office draws; the only female to receive that honour. However the honour faded in comparison to the honour of being presented to the Queen and having a chat with her. As Dennis had predicted, Diana was now the top female British film star, confirmed by a cinema popularity poll, and the highest paid film actress. She was the hottest property in the business.

Chapter 12
Hollywood – The Dream Comes True

If 1955 began with a bang, with the highly paid film *Value for Money*, and the lucrative Rank contract, it went out with an even bigger sensation. J. Lee-Thompson, the noted film director, writer and producer chose Diana, against all predictions, for the leading role in his film *Yield to the Night*. The film, based on the story of Ruth Ellis, the last woman to be hanged in England, was a poignant outcry against capital punishment. It required an actress with serious acting ability. Diana had worked with Thompson before, both in 1953 in his film *The Weak and the Wicked*, based on his wife's prison experiences, and in *An Alligator Named Daisy* earlier in 1955. Although the latter was a slapstick comedy which didn't tax Diana's acting skills, Thompson must have recognised some quality in her performances to risk choosing her for a demanding role in a powerful drama which confronted highly controversial social issues.

Although Diana received excellent reviews for her performance in *A Kid for Two Farthings*, the film was essentially a light drama, and if Diana was not cast as the usual naughty, spicy seductress, she still provided the romantic interest. The stereotypical image of Diana as a blonde, sexy, lightweight actress, performing in B movies in B roles, mainly with comic overtones, persisted. Deeply embedded both in the national psyche and in the film world's appraisal it was difficult to dispel. True, she was certainly a talented all-round entertainer but just as certainly not a top dramatic actress. Thompson must have had every acclaimed actress, including Vivienne Leigh and Ingrid Bergman, salivating for the role but it was Diana who triumphed.

If the year 1955 ended with a bang, the bang erupted into an explosion in 1956. *Yield to the Night* was premiered to rave reviews, Diana was voted Variety Club's show-business personality of the year and the dream of a lifetime became a reality. Earlier that year Diana had participated in a Bob Hope spectacular, filmed in England but for U.S. audiences. The television show had brought spectacular results. The American company RKO Films offered Diana $85,000 to appear in a film called *I Married a Woman* with George Gobel, the biggest comedy star in America. Diana could hardly believe her luck. Since childhood she had waited for that invitation. It was accepted with a resounding 'Yes!' Diana had vaulted over the line dividing the starlet from the star with a tremendous leap. Her celebrity status was embossed in gold. After all, how many actresses were on chatting terms with The Queen?

However, Diana was never one to take celebrity status too seriously. Even while striving for its attainment, she knew it was an ephemeral condition, not to be relied upon. She was still the same person with the same goals, ambitions and talents as when the serious film world had shunned her as a blonde bimbo, when she was reduced to stealing a Christmas tree for lack of money. Being keenly aware of her weaknesses and failures, she did not allow fame to deceive her into thinking she was precious, divine, above the fray. But at the same time she took advantage of her celebrity status and the benefits fame offered.

Her posturing, her posing were tongue in cheek, performed with the attitude that if this was what was wanted, this was what she would give and she would enjoy giving it and enjoy the rewards it brought. If being a sexy seductress was necessary to achieve her goal of becoming a serious actress, than that is what she would be, it was easy enough, even fun. Fortunately she had all the prerequisites and was not averse to exploiting them.

She once quipped, 'I might as well cash in on sex now, while I've got it. It won't last forever.'

And she loved the resulting affluence. She knew how to enjoy the good life with the best of them. But she didn't dramatise herself, was devoid of airs and graces, was down-to-earth enough, wise enough, to know it was merely that: posturing and posing and in no way connected to what she really wanted or who she really was.

Diana had an earthiness, an empathy with ordinary people which saved her from becoming pretentious, from indulging in prima donna behaviour or believing her own publicity; something rare among today's fame-and-fortune celebrities some of whom are so enthralled by the illusion of omnipotence they believe that one kiss from them can solve the world's problems. Diana was generous with both herself and her money, never forgetting the Earls Court days when she lived on potatoes and onions. She was respectful and considerate of the people she worked with, be they acclaimed film director or tea boy. (Celebrity photographer William Carter, known as Billy Snapper, told me that whereas many celebrities he photographed were impatient, intent on impressing him with their busy schedules, Diana was easy and relaxed, sympathetic to the difficulties photographing presented, telling him to take all the time he needed). If luck was with her now she would embrace it with enthusiasm and appreciation, she would bless it, honour it, for she knew it was a fragile thing and easily broken.

As Diana moved from strength to strength in the film world, Dennis moved from strength to strength in the property world. Money was no longer a problem. Infatuated with the showy grand gesture he was keen on buying a new residence to reflect their wealth and status. 'Woodhurst' was the result. It was an impressive Victorian mansion in Maidenhead, about 25 miles west of London, alongside the River Thames. It had 23 rooms, two tennis courts, an indoor squash court, a stable and, most important for Diana, an indoor swimming pool, Roman-style with imposing marble columns. The roof was solid enough for Dennis to build a splendid penthouse atop the pool, with a huge stone fireplace and sumptuous furnishings and converting the squash court into a cinema with leopard-skin seats and a rock pool surrounding a fountain. In the spring of 1956 Diana and Dennis moved into their new fit-for-a-movie-queen home.

Before shooting had begun on *Yield to the Night*, Diana discovered she was pregnant. During her previous pregnancies she had dearly wanted to keep the baby. The abortions were the result of intense pressure, of being convinced that having a baby would end her career. Diana had reluctantly given in to the persuasions of others. This time, however, no one had to persuade her. Diana knew she was on a roll. *Yield to the Night*, a film she had waited for all her acting life, would be a casualty of the pregnancy. There would be other chances to have a baby, to become a mother, something she longed for, but only one chance to seize this acting opportunity. Without regrets or angst, indeed almost with relief, Diana had her third abortion.

When shooting began on *Yield to the Night* Diana was determined to give her very best performance, grateful for the opportunity to play a real human being instead of, as she said, 'a cardboard character with curves'; determined to emerge from the second-rate actress pigeon-hole, to shake the tarty, flirty, sexy image once and for all; determined to prove her acting ability. She was successful at all three. The film was a sensation and received the distinction of being chosen for the 1956 Royal Command film performance. This enabled Diana to meet The Queen once again and discuss the film and especially her reaction to playing a woman condemned to death, something which had intrigued the Queen when they had first met.

Yield to the Night was also selected for the Cannes Film Festival, the only British film to receive that honour. This time Diana attended the festival not as part of a group but singled out as one of England's leading film stars. The festival week was one of the highlights of her life. She stayed at the luxurious Carlton hotel and was chosen to lead the prestigious flower festival, a coveted trophy. Her name was up in lights together with all the world-famous film stars and she was photographed and feted to delighted exhaustion.

When *Yield to the Night* was premiered at the festival, Diana's very appearance was an award-winning performance. Wearing a strapless turquoise chiffon gown embroidered in silver, embellished with pearl sequins and trimmed with white fox, her shoulders caressed by a fox stole, dyed turquoise, she strode into the hall as though on a catwalk and took her seat with the tiniest of bows, amid enthusiastic applause. After the showing of the film the audience rose as one for a standing ovation. Diana had entered the magic circle of world-acclaimed film stars. It was everything she had wanted. Later, when *Yield to the Night* was premiered in London, fans lined the streets anxious to get a glimpse of Diana. And when she stepped from her powder-blue Cadillac, the police had to restrain the cheering, screaming fans.

One of the results of Diana's success was the profound effect it had on her relationship with Dennis. If the endurance of that relationship was a mystery to their friends and even to Diana herself, its dynamics had grown increasingly complicated by her newfound acclaim. From the very beginning of their marriage, Dennis had exerted complete control over Diana, not only of her career but of her life. Like a maestro with a compliant protégée he had orchestrated her career, directing it with a golden baton, whereas he ruled her life with an iron rod. He didn't let her out of his sight. He went shopping with her; wouldn't allow her driving lessons; even monitored her phone calls. He determined what she wore, where she went, what she did, constantly reinforcing her dependence on him.

'You couldn't get as far as the garden gate without me,' he would say, and because Diana never forgot, and Dennis never allowed her to forget, that it was he who had engineered her success had, in fact, created 'The Diana Dors', she believed this was true.

In his way, Dennis loved Diana, as one can love someone one holds captive. He cared for her needs both physical and emotional; fed her titbits of praise and admiration when she doubted herself; boosted her confidence when she was in despair about her career; buoyed her up when she was flagging. He understood that, like himself, Diana was easily bored, needed new sensations, constant stimulation and he was expert at fulfilling both their needs. Their relationship was entirely devoid of dull moments – all of which increased Diana's reliance on him.

Diana had always been in awe of Dennis, of the astounding effect he had on people, of how, like a snake charmer, he charmed others, including herself, into doing his bidding. And, of course, there were the good times, when they had fun, were happy together, when Dennis was affectionate, even loving. The threads that bound Diana to Dennis were like threads in a spider's web, beautifully woven, seemingly delicate, hardly visible, but unrelenting.

However, if Dennis had orchestrated Diana's initial success and was in control of her career, and indeed her life, now with her new star status she had graduated from that control. That status had been achieved through her own talent and hard work, recognised and paid tribute to by film critics, filmmakers and filmgoers alike. There was no longer any need to invent publicity stunts to attract media attention. Diana had made it on her own. She had slipped through Dennis's net.

Even before Diana's acclaim for her performance in *Yield to the Night*, Dennis was able to sense the writing on the wall. He was becoming irrelevant, was losing his grip on Diana, losing his command over her. The realisation made him increasingly desperate to prove, not only to Diana and to the film world, but to himself, that his power over her was intact. The necessity to prove this became more and more urgent as Diana became more and more independent and erupted into an ugly scene at a party one night.

Dennis adored giving parties and loved showing off their fabulous penthouse with its heated pool and dazzling extravagances and he especially loved the prestige of determining the much coveted guest list. The fact that Diana had been awarded 'Show Business Personality of the Year' was certainly grounds for a celebration and Dennis had invited a host of glittering guests to celebrate: film stars, producers, directors, and superstar musicians.

The award had been presented to Diana several days before the party at a special luncheon reported in the press. In the article, the journalist had referred to Dennis, as 'Diana's suede shod Svengali'. For Dennis the phrase was an outrage that seethed in his mind, an insult which his ego was incapable of tolerating. The night of the party, as the evening wore on and Dennis became increasingly drunk, he became obsessed by the thought of the insult.

'A suede shod Svengali,' he muttered over and over. 'I'll show him who's a suede shod Svengali, I'll stuff his fucking newspaper down his fucking mouth.'

Fermenting in alcohol, his insults and threats became more and more aggressive, more and more obscene. Diana, aware of Dennis's anger and fearing the results of its escalation, which inevitably became directed at her, escaped to bed.

About midnight she was awakened by Dennis bellowing, 'Dors, get down here!'

She slipped on a robe and looking down from the top of the stairs she saw two men.

'The press are here,' Dennis shouted, 'Get your ass downstairs.'

'At this hour,' Diana replied, 'Don't be ridiculous.'

Dennis stormed up the stairs, 'You'll do as I say,' he said between clenched teeth and spun Diana around by the arm.

The force of the spin caused Diana to lose her footing and she tumbled down the flight of stairs her robe flying open.

Looking down on her lying on the floor almost naked, Dennis sneered, 'There, now fucking well interview her.'

The journalists beat a hasty retreat; Dennis went into the kitchen to pour himself a drink; one of the guests carried Diana to bed.

Next day Dennis was in tears. He must have heard the death knell tolling for their relationship for he pleaded with Diana to forgive him, begged her to stay with him. Somewhere inside his addled brain he knew the balance had shifted and now he needed Diana more than she needed him. His ego, his prestige, his everything was bound up with Diana. She defined him. Her success was his glory. He was her satellite, it was her light he reflected. Without her he was reduced to darkness. Without him she was still a star.

In the following days Dennis was unusually contrite, trying in every way to make amends, attending to her bruises, smothering her with affection – incredibly there were no serious injuries. He even promised Diana driving lessons, his ultimate concession. Despite her threats, in the end Diana didn't leave him. However, in some way that incident freed her from the confines of Dennis and in her heart she knew their relationship was in its death throes. Nothing could ever be the same between them again. Meanwhile Hollywood was summoning and the lure of that call was so powerful it overshadowed everything else.

Chapter 13
The Hollywood Adventure

Because Dennis hated flying, the plan was to sail to New York in the luxurious Queen Elizabeth ocean liner and then fly to Los Angeles. The going away party in the grand state room of the Q.E. was a glittering affair. Everyone they knew wanted to wish them bon voyage: friends, colleagues, reporters, photographers, even Diana's father made the pilgrimage to Southampton to wave his daughter off and wish her success. The air was electric with excitement and the champagne flowed. Diana was thrilled. The trip was a culmination of a lifetime of wishing; of sitting cross-legged as a child with closed eyes in a special place for a special wishing ritual. The ritual had borne fruit as she had never doubted it would. Now, years later, when she opened her eyes she would be in Hollywood holding the cream telephone to her ear, living in the mansion and swimming in the giant swimming pool. The miracle had happened.

Her arrival in New York not only sustained the thrill of the departure but embellished it. Reporters and photographers rushed onto the deck as soon as the ship docked in a wave of cameras, tape recorders and notebooks, eager to catch a glimpse of Diana, to photograph her, to bid her welcome and to test her credentials. Diana was brilliant, impressing the journalists not only with the curves of her body but with the agility of her mind, with her quick wit, her humour and her style which had a touch of Mae West sauciness about it.

'Don't crowd me boys,' she admonished several photographers jostling for position, 'Or you'll cover up what I'm here to sell.'

They were unprepared for glamour armed with intelligence.

RKO studio laid the red carpet at her feet with an extra thick pile; chauffeured limousines, a grand suite at a grand hotel, almost a dozen public relation experts falling over themselves to cater to her every whim. And to top it off they arranged a lavish party in the hotel ballroom for the press and the New York elite to meet Diana. She shone. She was equally at home with dignitaries as with the press and chatted as easily with the VIPs as with the barmen.

The journalists' instant love affair with Diana was reflected in the excellent press coverage she received. The only irritation was being constantly compared to Marilyn Monroe as though she was in some sort of competition with her, despite pointing out that her career had begun well before Marilyn Monroe's and that in England Marilyn Monroe had been compared to her.

In late June, after a few heady days in New York Diana and Dennis flew to Los Angeles leaving behind a smile on the faces of reporters who were more inclined to frown, and taking with her the warm glow of success. Once again a lavish welcome greeted her at the airport with the head of RKO, William Dozier, heading a cast of well-wishers, journalists and photographers. And then to Hollywood and the world famous Beverly Hills Hotel. A reception was held the following day to introduce Diana to Hollywood. The star-studded guest list included the two terrifying gossip columnists: Louella Parsons, a militant Catholic with a chastity belt morality and the avid communist hunter, the bitter-eyed, acid-tongued Hedda Hopper, two arch rivals, either of whom could destroy a career or indeed a human being with the stroke of a pen and who took pleasure in the process.

Both Diana and Dennis had been warned of their killer reputations. Diana was suitably deferential, treading carefully. Dennis, however, was undeterred, indeed eager to take up the challenge, so assured was he of his ability to charm, especially when that charm was directed at the female sex. Armed with only an award-winning smile he rushed into a minefield where even angels feared to tread.

Confident of a big win he took Ms Hopper's hand like an admiring courtier and said, 'I can't understand, now that I've met you, how you can possibly deserve the reputation of being unkind to anyone.'

Pulling her hand away as though it had been caressed by a leper and with a look that could freeze the sun, she said, 'Alright Hamilton, don't overdo it' and turned away to engage elsewhere.

The snake charmer had been bitten by the snake. Dennis, probably for the first time in living memory, was struck dumb. That sort of direct bluntness, that kind of rebuff to someone just met at a social event in his wife's honour was entirely alien to him having been raised on the civility of English restraint and polite pretence. Hollywood was not London, it was not the pushover he was expecting. The rules were entirely different. The wining and dining, the champagne and flowers, the sugar and spice, concealed a hardcore cynicism, a ruthlessness where all but the highest and mightiest were disposable, where one had to learn one's place in the pecking order or die. In Hollywood he was a small fish indeed and could not flaunt his big fish style. The Hedda Hopper snub was the start of a lesson Dennis was not good at learning and which would have drastic consequences for both himself and Diana.

More than anywhere else in America, in Hollywood time was money, so as soon as Diana arrived preparations started for filming. Diana was impressed with the professionalism of everything and everyone involved in the preparations. Nothing was spared to achieve perfection. The level of skill and attention to detail was something she was unaccustomed to in England and something which meshed with her own professionalism and which she welcomed with obvious pleasure. If she was impressed with the studio, the studio was equally impressed with her. It wasn't long before Diana was rewarded by Dozier with the offer of a three film contract for the phenomenal sum of half a million dollars.

Dennis, still smarting from the Hedda Hopper humiliation, saw this as an opportunity for status enhancement. He would show these cocky Hollywood hot shots a thing or two. Who did they think they were anyway? Against Diana's wishes, he wasted no time in buying the most impressive mansion available. It had all the necessary accoutrements: guest house, tennis courts, extensive grounds, a swimming pool with five changing rooms, each with a shower, a sunken Roman bath adjoining the master bedroom, elegant furnishings and a five car garage with its own petrol pump. To complement the impressiveness of the mansion, he bought a new white Lincoln convertible, probably the most expensive car he could find.

'That'll show them who we are,' he boasted to Diana.

But it didn't show anybody anything.

Unlike England, which was still emerging from wartime austerity, from a grey post-war existence and where a display of wealth made people sit up and take note, California was awash with wealth and Hollywood was its wealth capital. An enormous mansion and a top- of-the- range automobile which would have excited the English press, guaranteeing photographs and articles, bringing admiration and fame to their owners, hardly raised an eyebrow in Hollywood. Dennis didn't ascend a single rung in the Hollywood ladder of estimation.

Whereas Dennis was failing to impress the Hollywood notables with money, Diana was succeeding in impressing them with herself. Bob Hope, whom she had developed a friendship with back in London, was filming close by and introduced her to the many Hollywood stars filming in nearby studios. With her warmth, good humour, intelligence and interest in others, Diana made friends easily. It didn't take long before she became a sought-after guest at the endless round of Hollywood parties. And parties were Diana's forte.

The first weeks of the Hollywood adventure were all that she had hoped for. Diana loved everything about Hollywood: the sunshine, the palm tree lined boulevards, the proximity of both ocean and mountains, the superb mansions where the stars lived which she was privileged to see from the inside instead of from a distance, the studios with their luxurious dressing rooms, more like an entire apartment with bathroom, kitchen and beautifully lit dressing tables, the parties which she often attended without Dennis, the opulence and glamour of the Hollywood scene. And she especially loved the air conditioned chauffeured Cadillac which drove her to the studio through sunlit avenues lined with flowers, in stark contrast to the dark cold London mornings when she had walked to the studio fearing for her life. The star treatment was so unlike the casualness of England. Hollywood stars were America's royalty and, in Hollywood, she was a princess, even a queen.

But most of all she loved meeting the people she had read about in magazines, admired in films and emulated in her own life. It was all hers now. She was suddenly on the other side of the silver screen and spent every spare moment feasting on the privilege. Like a kid in a candy store, she wanted to taste everything. All her life she had imagined Hollywood, dreamed Hollywood, talked Hollywood; now she was living Hollywood. The dream she had dared to dream really had come true. And she was still only 24.

Therefore, no one was more surprised than Diana herself when after the initial exhilarating flush of infatuation, the intensity of the love affair began to wane. The diet of incessant luxury and glamour began to lose its charm. The bright Hollywood colours began to fade in the unrelenting California sunshine. Suddenly everything seemed too big, too overstated, too excessive. To her utter surprise Diana began to have pangs of homesickness, began to miss her friends, miss the familiar, the ordinary, like a pub evening with her mates. Even shopping with a friend was a pleasure which was now denied her. In Hollywood anyone caught walking ran the risk of being stopped by the police and charged with vagrancy. She was all too aware that close friendships were forged through shared experiences, recollections, reminiscences, trust, all of which take time to develop and although she had met many warm and hospitable people in Hollywood, there was no real intimacy, none of the intensity she had shared with her close friends in England.

Diana even began to miss the clouds and the rain. Every day was the same as every other day with bright skies and hard sunshine which blotted out nuances, subtleties of colour, even shapes. She missed the softness of England, the muted colours, the lack of aggressive sunshine. Besides, Diana had moments questioning her future. She was famous, she was rich, she was in Hollywood. The dream of a lifetime had become an everyday occurrence. Where was she to go from there? She had outgrown Dennis, her relationship with him had lost its sparkle. They had different objectives, different desires, different intentions. He wanted to remain in Hollywood because he was so excited by the financial rewards. He even wanted to become an American citizen. She had dared to oppose him. She wanted England to be her home and money was not a primary consideration. She needed friends to confide in, to discuss her concerns, to share her good times. So, when her close friends, Raymond and Jennifer Bessone who had followed her success in British newspapers, which delighted in reporting Diana's state-of-the-art lifestyle and had listened to glowing reports in long phone calls from Diana, decided to visit, she was delighted.

Although Raymond, nicknamed Teasy-Weasy, was a successful London hairdresser, he had his eye on bigger things. He desired fame. He didn't see himself as a hairdresser but as an artist. He dreamed of creating hairstyles that would transform women, glorify them, revolutionise the beauty industry. What better place to fulfil his dream than in Hollywood. Like every child reared on Hollywood films he dreamed the Hollywood dream as fervently as a nun dreams of heaven. If he could establish himself as a hair stylist catering to the rich and famous, he'd become 'Hairdresser to the

Stars'. Diana could provide the introductions. Hollywood loved her and loving her they would love him. He could step into his dream through her footsteps. Diana encouraged him. She would do everything to help, thrilled by the possibility of her friends coming to Hollywood.

To initiate the plan, Dennis and Diana decided to host a party both to introduce Raymond to the Hollywood set and as a house-warming for their new Beverly Hills home, as well as to repay the abundant hospitality that had been showered on them. Dennis had other motives. He had not yet learned that a display of wealth did not impress the super-rich. In an attempt to stand shoulder-to-shoulder with the elite of the film world, he would make a party the opulence of which would dazzle Hollywood. Neither expense nor effort would be spared. Raymond was so excited by the idea of a Hollywood party in his honour and foreseeing the possibilities of achieving the fame he yearned for, he volunteered to fund it. The stage was set.

In mid-August, only two months after arriving in Hollywood, Diana and Dennis hosted what was to be a Hollywood extravaganza. Great hopes rested on its success: Teasy-Weasy would begin his climb to fame; Dennis would astound the elite of the film world in a grand statement of redemption and for Diana it would be the jewel in her Hollywood crown. The guests were an all-star Hollywood cast, including Lana Turner, Greer Garson, Doris Day, Eddie Fisher, Debbie Reynolds, Zsa Zsa Gabor, Ginger Rogers, Dinah Shore and Liberace, who remained a lifelong friend. And, of course, there were the top reporters, photographers and magazine columnists poised to feature the party of the year. It was a tribute to her popularity that after so short a time in Hollywood Diana was able to muster such a glittering ensemble.

The great day arrived. The garden was a fairyland with Japanese lanterns hanging from trees. A centrepiece of flowers spelling Raymond's name floated in the pool surround by blue carnations, Raymond's favourite colour. Musicians strolled through the garden serenading the guests. The smell of flowers perfumed the air. Champagne flowed.

There were well over 200 guests. Aside from the movie stars and media elite they included celebrated film directors, producers, agents and screenwriters. Everyone anticipated a gala occasion which would be talked about, written about, photographed. Everything began well. Film personalities posed for photographs, some with Raymond, some alone or in groups. Friends met friends, talked about the latest films, who was in which film, who wasn't – favourite Hollywood topics. People wandered through the garden, sat under the trees, feasted on the barbequed steaks and chicken served to them by the caterers. When the sun began to set the guests gathered around the pool. The band played, people danced. Everything was perfect: the garden, the stars, the music, Diana, Dennis, Raymond, the photographers, the journalists, the dancing, the drinking – all of them together.

Suddenly chaos erupted. Diana and Dennis were standing by the pool having a cosy chat with Diana's agent, Louis Shurr, who Bob Hope had introduced them to, and Howard Shoup, a well-known dress designer. Diana and Dennis had their backs to the pool facing the other two. One of the photographers probably seeking his claim to fame by scooping the photograph of the year, surreptitiously approached the foursome. Diana witnessed his approach from the corner of her eye. But what happened next was so unexpected and happened so fast she was unable to sound a warning. The photographer lunged into Louis and Howard with such force that they fell against Diana and Dennis. All four were thrown off balance and unable to regain their equilibrium plummeted into the pool.

Dennis, enraged, pulled himself from the pool and pounced on the photographer knocking him down. In a crazed fit of fury he began punching the man in the face, blow after vicious blow, shouting obscenities and punching. Someone screamed. Several people tried to pull Dennis away but he hung on, raging, kicking, pounding. When the photographer was finally extricated from Dennis's hold he was carried away unconscious and bleeding. Meanwhile Diana had struggled from the pool sputtering and gasping, her sapphire-blue silk blouse clinging to her, wet and transparent, her hair plastered against her face, demolishing Teasy-Weasy's showpiece creation. Louis and Howard emerged from the pool dripping wet and bewildered. The police came. The guests slipped away anxious to dissociate themselves from anything with even a whiff of negative publicity. Suddenly the party was over.

Next day the newspapers viciously attacked Diana and Dennis. The journalists tore at them like an incensed pack of rottweilers. Stewart Sawyer, the United Press photographer, attacked by Dennis, was one of their own. They closed ranks condemning Diana and Dennis. They accused them of setting up the whole thing as a publicity stunt, although no one could explain why Diana would want to be photographed looking in need of resuscitation. Diana and Dennis became 'hooligans', Sawyer 'an ordinary citizen just doing his job and struck down in the line of duty.' The party was described as a 'drunken orgy'. There was no let-up. Each day the newspapers vied with each other to malign, to vilify. If adoring a celebrity was good copy, crucifying one was even better.

The gossip columnists, rubbing their hands in glee, joined forces with the journalists. Such a windfall was their bread and butter. The love/hate relationship they had with celebrities registered hate, big time. Diana and Dennis were described as 'a bizarre boisterous couple', 'two publicity-seeking degenerates'. And if this wasn't enough they hit on the ultimate indictment. Diana was accused of having communist affiliations. Although a ludicrous claim, it was embraced by the press. One headline read, 'Up the hammer and sickle girl and gather those Yankee dollars while you may.'

The McCarthy era was in full swing and the determination to eradicate the communist enemy was a patriotic obsession. The communist virus was considered especially rampant in Hollywood, Hedda Hopper's turf. She outdid them all in exterminating the infection by hunting down communist infiltrators polluting the film world. She delighted in denouncing anyone on her hit list. With a single stab of her toxic pen she could kill a lifetime of dreams. A self-styled keeper of the faith, she was at the head of a right-wing crusading army ridding Hollywood of subversive elements and now she had her sights set on Diana. The communist stigma was the poisoned arrow in an arsenal of crippling weapons. It was the deadly missile which had hounded Charlie Chaplin out of America. And now it was pointed at Diana.

The publicity machine which Dennis and Diana had used in their favour in England had turned violently against them in America. Raymond and Jennifer were glad to return to England appalled by the injustice of the assaults on Diana, the Hollywood dream in tatters. The backlash from the ill-fated party was so effective that RKO, terrified of bad publicity which could drive away audiences, considered cancelling Diana's contract. They would have done so, using the 'morals clause' except they could not hold Diana responsible for her husband's actions and the communist allegation had no basis in reality. In the end Bill Dozier summoned Diana to his office insisting that she phone all the journalists to apologise, explaining that she had not planned the incident, agreeing that Dennis's behaviour was out of line, and denying any communist association. Although she hated the humiliation, especially when she considered it was she who had been wronged in the first place and then treated disgracefully by the very journalists she had to apologise to, she agreed to comply with Dozier's demands. Dennis was unrepentant and it was up to Diana to appease, to apologise, to eat humble pie.

But if Diana's love affair with Hollywood had begun to wane and if the recent onslaught had dealt it a near fatal blow, it was a mere lover's tiff compared to what happened next.

Chapter 14
Fallen Idol

Before the fallout from the ill-fated party struck with full force, RKO had already begun preparations for Diana's next film, a drama called *The Unholy Wife*. So, although Bill Dozier was knee deep in flack generated by the swimming pool fiasco and Diana was upset because no one would believe that the 'incident' wasn't a Dors ploy to obtain international publicity, there was no turning back.

Just weeks after the disastrous party a disgraced Diana, a disgruntled Dennis and a displeased Dozier, nursing serious misgivings, set off to Napa Valley, the wine growing area north of San Francisco, where the film was set, to shoot on location. Diana knew her honeymoon with Hollywood was all but over. Dozier must have wondered why he ever got involved with people who were hell bent on creating havoc. But money had been invested, equipment had been transported, actors and crew had been hired, venues had been booked, so despite personal grievances, reservations, even forebodings, the show had to go on.

The director of the film, John Farrow, had the reputation of being a terror to work with, feared more than respected by actors and crew members alike. Diana had been warned against him and in her vulnerable state she was nervous about meeting him and dreaded working with him. Both concerns proved groundless. They took to each other immediately. Once again her warmth, her good humour, her genuineness and her lack of self-obsession made a positive initial impression on Farrow. And later he found her easy to work with, responsive to direction and never late. She found him kind, helpful, considerate, at least to her. As a special vote of appreciation he even hired a guitarist to play for her during breaks.

Diana was soon into her stride. The filming was going extremely well, Dozier was about to count his blessings when once again calamity struck. However this time it was more insidious, not as immediately evident and even more damning. Diana fell in love with her leading man, Rod Steiger. RKO management had been so preoccupied addressing the damage to her reputation and building up her profile in anticipation of the film's release, that no one had realised anything was amiss. Dennis, however, with a suspicious eye trained on Diana and accustomed to detecting romantic liaisons where none existed, knew immediately that this time one did exist. However he suspected the wrong man, actor Tom Tryon, a typical heart-throb, tall, dark and handsome. He watched the decoy relationship so intensely that he failed to detect the genuine one.

Diana had been immediately drawn to Rod Steiger. She admired his acting style, the thoughtfulness with which he approached his role, the in-depth study of his character. He was the most impressive actor she had ever worked with. Besides, he was not only sophisticated, intelligent and inspiring but he made her laugh, a big plus. Admiration quickly became infatuation.

Steiger was equally taken with Diana. She was beautiful, sexy, fascinating. He was one of those special men in tune with the female psyche and had an intuitive affinity with women. He was quick to realise that beneath Diana's cheerful, good-humoured exterior, there was an undertow of unhappiness, of disappointment, both with her Hollywood experience and especially with her marriage. He too was undergoing marital difficulties. He was separated from his wife who was in New York performing on Broadway. The chemistry between Diana and Steiger was augmented by problematic personal circumstances. The die was cast.

Steiger wooed Diana with poetry, with romance, with admiration. He made her feel wanted, loved. Diana was enchanted. Since the age of 19, barely out of adolescence, she had been saddled with Dennis who treated her like a cross between an incompetent child who needed his hand to cross the road and a jumped-up fruit machine spewing out money. Steiger was all Dennis was not. He treated her like a woman, sensual, desirable. He was tender, passionate, adoring. He loved who she was, unlike Dennis who loved what she earned. He was not concerned with selling her to the highest bidder, only with loving her.

Diana had been aching to fall in love. She longed for romance, for dancing in the moonlight, for making love under the stars, for being looked at with eyes filled with desire instead of dollars, for magic. And now it had happened. She was in love. She threw herself into the relationship like someone dying of thirst come upon an oasis.

As her relationship with Steiger grew more compelling Diana found it impossible to behave normally at home with Dennis. She was so besotted with Steiger, so obsessed by him that the caution with which she had managed their initial contact became impossible to maintain. The charade of her marriage became intolerable. She resented Dennis's presence, made excuses not to be with him, couldn't bear any physical contact, drew away when he so much as touched her, was irritable, short-tempered, moody. Diana's behaviour was indisputable evidence for Dennis that she was having an affair with Tom Tryon.

One night during a vicious argument with Dennis who was badgering her about Tom Tryon, she became so incensed, so exasperated, so overwrought that before she could stop herself.

She burst out, 'I'm in love with Rod Steiger.'

Dennis was incandescent with anger. In a demented rage which made his previous rages look like endearments, he smashed dishes, furniture, windows, demolishing anything in sight, screaming, 'I'll kill the bastard. He won't live to see another day. You'll be fucking a corpse.'

Next morning he stormed into Steiger's dressing room waving a knife. Fortunately Steiger was not there. But the scandal was set in motion.

In Fifties' Hollywood the sin of adultery was only equalled by the sin of communism, both spelling death to a career. The gossip columnists acting as moral police had the power of judge, jury and executioner. Under the rule of people like Louella Parsons and Hedda Hopper they created an atmosphere of fear which hung over Hollywood like a toxic cloud. Hedda Hopper called her home 'The House that Fear Built'. Diana was a married woman, Steiger a married man. Their blasphemous affair could damn both them and their film to hell.

Dozier had to do something and do it fast. He summoned Diana to his office.

'Don't you know what this means, how serious this is?' he said, 'We're talking adultery. The press will slaughter you. RKO can pull the morals clause and cancel your contract, especially considering that last stint of bad publicity you put us through.'

He looked at Diana with a look of total incomprehension. 'I thought that at least Steiger would have more sense if you don't. If anyone approaches either of you, deny everything, and for god's sake, keep a low profile, both of you.'

He paused to allow Diana to absorb the full impact of the situation then said, 'The first thing we have to do is head off the gossip columnists before the story hits their columns. You have to call Louella Parsons immediately and say whatever it takes to convince her that your marriage is as solid as a gold brick. Tell her you're outraged by the insane rumour that you and Steiger are having an affair. Tell her the rumour is press hype, something the journalists have cooked up to get back at you and to get themselves a lucrative scoop.'

He threw up his arms, 'Be indignant, angry, insulted – you're the actress.'

Dozier wrote the script, Diana performed it and Louella bought it.

Dennis, however, in an attempt to punish Diana and prove to her how much she needed him, decided to return to England convinced that she would be lost without him and fall into his arms when he returned. His calculations, an indication of how little he understood Diana, seriously misfired. Diana was so eager to see him go that she drove him to the airport and helped him onto the plane. His absence was a blessing for her relationship with Steiger, which she had no intention of ending. On the contrary, she moved in with him and without the impediment of Dennis the romance flourished. They became so entranced with each other that despite vigorous denials that they were having an affair, they neglected to hide the evidence that an affair was exactly what they were having. They even drove to the studio together oblivious of the fact that photographers, like wolves stalking their prey, were crouched behind every bush, ready to pounce. So much for the low profile.

Unlike in today's England where even photographing a celebrity shopping in a public place is penalised by the courts on the basis of privacy; in yesterday's Hollywood newspapers vied with each other to publish photographs of celebrities, the more compromising the better. Photographers were unfettered, indeed they were encouraged to expose sexual indiscretions and substantially rewarded for their efforts.

Also, unlike in today's England where even describing the decor and layout of someone's house is considered private and a basis for suing, there were no such restrictions in Fifties' Hollywood. Celebrities could not conceal sexual escapades, orgies, adulterous antics, on the basis of privacy. They could not use their wealth to pursue newspapers in expensive court battles and win cases on the basis that these activities were private. Journalists were intent on exposing exactly those activities celebrities were intent on covering up.

Despite Diana's denials about an affair and her assurances that Dennis had gone to England for business reasons, and not because of any marital problems, the rumours about her and Steiger had flown across the Atlantic. Dennis arriving on the other side of the ocean was accosted by the English press, who had been reporting Diana's every move in Hollywood to a public eager for news about her. Dennis assured the press that he and Diana were happily married; that he was in England purely for business reasons; that Steiger was a good friend of Diana's and of his as well; that, of course, they were photographed in close proximity, after all they were acting together. It was 'utter nonsense' to accuse them of having an affair. But if he managed to convince the English press, he certainly didn't convince the Hollywood press. In Hollywood whispers became rumours and the rumours began to circulate, photographs began to appear. With an eye on the 'morals clause' which could end the good times, Dennis decided to return to Hollywood to quell the mushrooming scandal.

Upon his return both he and Diana were once again summoned to Dozier's office. This time Dozier took off the gloves. Compromising photographs had surfaced. The press was eager to provide evidence of an affair.

'I don't give a damn what's happening between you,' he said, 'That's your business, my business is to produce a film and make sure it has an audience. As far as the press is concerned you are happily married and it's up to you to prove it, I don't care how.'

He demanded public shows of affection, appearances together where they could be photographed, anything to stave off the press. Steiger was whisked off to a hideout, far from the eye of the camera. Diana was forbidden to see him when they were off set.

Dennis tried, once again, to win Diana back with the old techniques of flowers, jewellery, charm. But nothing worked. Although Diana made a public effort, in private, even being in the same house as Dennis became unbearable. She longed for Steiger, couldn't wait for the time they would be together again. What was there to stop them? She knew his marriage was ailing; her marriage was dead. They just had to wait until the filming was completed and everything had blown over. She dreamed about Steiger, fantasised about their reunion. Even in Hollywood couples divorced and married someone else. Why not her and Steiger?

But meanwhile the press had to be dealt with. Fortunately director John Farrow and Louella Parsons were good friends. Farrow had converted to Catholicism which endeared him to her. She was the godmother of his daughter Mia, one of his seven children who became a celebrity actress. Farrow undertook the formidable task of deflecting the hatchet. This time both Diana and Dennis would have to grovel. They were to meet with Louella and persuade her that despite some hiccups and minor wobbles all was now well with their marriage. Even if it meant Diana getting on her knees, weeping, beating her breast, it was vital for her to secure Louella's forgiveness and convince her that this time she was being truthful.

Louella reluctantly agreed to see them although infuriated that Diana had deceived her when she phoned pretending her marriage was all it should be. Louella held Diana's Hollywood career in her hands and Diana knew it. She was faced with the most difficult acting role in her life.

In subdued tones, as though she was in a confessional, seeking absolution, Diana said, 'Dennis and I were going through a rough patch in our marriage. Rod Steiger was a temporary diversion. I'm sorry I lied to you but I was trying to save our marriage. I know it was wrong and we both ask your forgiveness.'

Dennis bowed his head in contrition.

'But now we have worked things out and are happily reconciled and we want to make a fresh start.'

Dennis nodded in agreement.

'Please help us. I beg you to accept my sincerest apology and to find it in your heart to forgive me'.

Louella said nothing, her back rigid, her expression stern – a pious priestess sitting in judgment, enjoying every moment of Diana's torment.

Finally, after a few moments of silence when punishment and redemption hung in the balance together with Diana's fate, she allowed a magnanimous expression to replace the virtuous, unrelenting one.

'I can see you have realised the errors of your ways and that you want to make amends. As a Catholic I believe that anyone who confesses their sins and promises to right the wrongs they have committed, deserves another chance.'

She extended a wrinkled hand and Diana managed a grateful clasp. In the end the pretence succeeded and a stay of execution was granted but not before Diana promised that if anything changed, Louella would get an exclusive before her rival Hedda Hopper.

Both Diana's career and the film had been rescued, but nothing could sweeten the bitterness between Diana and Dennis. Life at home became unbearable; work in the studio, a torment. Diana and Steiger were forbidden to communicate for fear cast members would reignite the rumours which had been so difficult to quench and were still smouldering. Diana, madly in love with Steiger and forced to return to Dennis each night, was in despair. Something had to give and that something was Dennis's decision to leave Diana and return to England.

This time Diana did not drive him to the airport. By now the filming of *An Unholy Wife*, an apt title reflecting her own situation, was winding up and Diana found herself with time on her hands. People who had previously sought her out now avoided her fearing to be associated with even a whiff of scandal. There were no more invitations and even a friend who was visiting from England, moved elsewhere. It was as though bad publicity was a contagious disease and Diana was its carrier. She found herself alone in a huge silent house. The mansion of her dreams had become a nightmare mausoleum.

When the filming finally ended, Diana and Steiger conducted a cloak and dagger routine in order to be together. Waiting for the cover of darkness, Diana would be driven by a friend of Steiger's to an appointed place, transferred to Steiger's waiting car and whisked off to a 'safe house'. However the arrangement was not only cumbersome but dangerous as Hollywood was awash with spies. A solution was hit upon. Steiger had a beach house in Malibu, some distance from Hollywood and it seemed unlikely they would be discovered there. Eventually the clandestine manoeuvre was abandoned and Diana and Steiger took up full-time residence at the beach house.

The weeks that followed were the high point of their romance. Diana, wrapped in Steiger's arms, shielded from journalists, photographers, gossip columnists and especially from Dennis, was blissfully happy. She had escaped into the arms of passion, cosseted by love. She was deaf and blind to everything outside the beach house. Intimate photographs of her and Steiger appearing in newspapers, did not reach her eyes; being proclaimed 'a wanton hussy' by the Women's Catholic Guild did not reach her ears. Everything was perfect; the champagne, the music, the poetry, the moon on the sea, the lovemaking, all of them together.

Meanwhile, in England, Dennis was engaged in a whirlwind of revenge. The pretence about his happy marriage to Diana was over. Dennis was prepared to tell all. After a true-confession style revelation to the press, which included a blow by blow description of Diana's affair with Steiger, he proceeded with a she-devil, poor-me account of their marriage. Diana had been an unfaithful wife; she had lied to him, deceived him, betrayed him. After all he had done for her, devoting his life to her, giving her everything she had wanted this was how she had repaid him. In his role as victim the Diana Dors story became all about him. The media couldn't get enough of the drama. Even their housekeeper, Sholly, who had spent some time with them in Hollywood was interviewed on television to provide spicy insights into their marriage and, no doubt with Dennis's coaching, to blame Diana for its break-up.

Dennis played the role of the poor deceived husband with soap-opera intensity. Of course there were episodes he left out, facts he neglected to include, like the fact that he had managed Diana's money so that he had most of it while she was in debt; that all those wonderful things he had given her had been paid for with money she had earned. However, he was not satisfied that the newspaper reports of her treachery would reach Diana. But he knew what would. As further punishment for her and ego-boosting for himself, he embarked on a wild sexual rampage. If manipulating the press was easy for Dennis, seducing women was even easier. He had had a great deal of experience on both fronts. He was greatly assisted by the fact that he didn't care who he hurt or whose marriage he trampled on. He even seduced his friend Teasy-Weasy's wife Jennifer.

As it turned out Dennis had a powerful accomplice in punishing Diana for her affair with Steiger – Steiger himself. In order to sort matters out with his wife, and Diana hoped, to arrange a formal separation, Steiger had left for New York. Diana waited in the beach house for his return. But there was no return. Instead Steiger phoned from New York.

In a monologue that sent Diana reeling he said, 'I'm confused...You're confused... Live your life and enjoy it.'

The message was clear. The affair was over. Just like that. For Diana, possibilities, hopes, excitement, life itself seemed to end with that phone call.

There was no point remaining in the beach house, there was no point even remaining in Hollywood. But she hung on, returning to the mansion, comatose, in a kind of limbo, waiting for she knew not what. When Dennis had first returned to England and the rumours of a marriage break-up had hit the grapevine, various men had made amorous moves towards Diana. Even Frank Sinatra had approached her for a date. But her eyes had been only for Steiger. Now Steiger was gone, but the others were still there. It was public knowledge that her marriage to Dennis was over, she had even announced it to the press. The phone began to ring, with propositions and offers of dates. She tried to find some relief in dating. But it was useless. The dinners were tasteless, the men insipid, the kisses revolting.

Hollywood had lost its sparkle. Whereas before she had seen beauty everywhere she went – palm trees, flowers, fountains – now she saw miles of nothing. The mansions were invisible, enclosed by electric fences; the gates were barred against people; the gardens hidden from view. Hollywood had become a city of cars and concrete where the air choked and the heat melted and nothing human was visible. She hardly dared leave the house. She had no friends. She hated living in the mansion Dennis had bought. There was silence concerning the third film in her RKO contract. So, in early November, a dejected Diana returned to England, as she said of herself, 'a fallen idol'. There was no vestige of the bright-eyed, bushy-tailed hopeful who had left for Hollywood only five months earlier, with eyes filled with wonder.

London journalists who greeted her at the airport were confronted by a much-sobered Diana dressed in a black suit, unwilling to play along with glamorous poses and witty banter. After a few terse replies to their questions she left for London and the prestigious Dorchester hotel where she had rented a suite and arranged a press conference. Diana was keen on presenting a new image of herself to the press.

'Diana without Dennis is going to be a different girl,' she told the journalists. 'I'm putting an end to the publicity stunts, the practical jokes, the mink bikinis. In the five months I've been in Hollywood I've grown a lot wiser. My whole outlook has changed. I've had a very hectic and exciting five years with Dennis and I've made a lot of money. But money hasn't given me happiness.'

She was open, honest, answering questions frankly, intent on introducing the new Diana.

Meanwhile Dennis had arranged for a Rolls Royce to pick Diana up at the Dorchester even before he had phoned her and had convinced her to come to the penthouse in Maidenhead for 'a quiet talk'. And, of course, he had informed the press. When Diana arrived at the penthouse, journalists and photographers were already stationed outside the premises eagerly awaiting the next instalment in the Dors saga.

Dennis had set the scene for Diana's arrival with meticulous cunning. The house was filled with flowers. A log fire glowed in the living room. Platters of her favourite foods stayed hot on special heaters. Friends, delighted to see Diana, greeted her with embraces and toasted her return with champagne. She had been sorely missed. Diana didn't return to the Dorchester that night although she insisted on sleeping in a separate room.

Diana and Dennis talked for the next 36 hours. The press stood by, day and night, waiting in shifts for the crucial episode in the blockbuster drama. Dennis pleaded with Diana, he promised, he implored, they would make a new start together, he would do everything to make her happy. Diana was not taken in by his promises, she had heard them all before. She knew all too well that his main concern was holding on to a lucrative property called Diana Dors, but she was physically weary, psychologically depleted and emotionally exhausted.

Finally a jubilant Dennis rewarded the press with an announcement. 'My wife and I have agreed to reconcile.'

He took Diana's hand and lifted it high into the air in a gesture of victory. Diana managed a smile. The cameras clicked furiously.

Chapter 15
Exit Dennis Hamilton

Coming from sunlit California to damp dark England is an unusual choice for a honeymoon. But for Diana it was like being sentenced to indefinite internment. The transition from the beach house in Malibu with Steiger to the penthouse in Maidenhead with Dennis was a transition from freedom to subjugation, from enchantment to despair. With Steiger Diana had tasted bliss; every flower had been in bloom, every ripple etched in silver, every touch ecstatic. With Steiger she had flown to the gold of the sun. Now, back with Dennis, even the daylight was grey.

The promises Dennis had made were rapidly torn to shreds once Diana was back in his control. He even continued the affairs he had begun during their break-up, blaming his infidelities on Diana, justifying them because of her affair with Steiger. While Diana was left to contemplate the injustices she had inflicted on Dennis, Dennis occupied himself by entertaining his male buddies and lady friends with lavish parties where they enjoyed the heated swimming pool, rounds of champagne and each other. Suitably impressed by his generosity, his style, his charm, they sang his praises to a cynical Diana. Trapped in a series of re-runs played over and over, Diana dreaded waking up in the morning.

In between the parties and the 'brainstorms', which had grown not only more frightening but more frequent, Dennis occupied himself with various business ventures. He opened a trendy club which he called 'El Dors', always eager to cash in on Diana's name; he travelled to various tax havens where he set up companies to avoid paying tax; and he converted 'Woodhouse' into luxury flats. Woodhouse was the enormous mansion he had bought which included the roofed swimming pool over which he had built the penthouse where he and Diana lived. And he kept tabs on Diana, checking her every move through a network of informers, to be sure she was suitably miserable.

So when Diana was offered the lead in a film called *The Long Haul*, co-starring Victor Mature, at a fee of £20,000, she eagerly accepted. While Diana was filming in the studio, Dennis and his cohorts entertained a bevy of ladies-of-the-night who were not averse to operating in the day and who waived their fees in the hope of furthering their film star ambitions. Dennis maintained the secrecy of his 'playboy' diversion by dismissing everyone before Diana returned home. However, even while he was indulging in erotic adventures, he was plagued by the suspicion that Diana was having an affair with Victor Mature who had a reputation as a lothario. As it turned out, he needn't have worried. Although Diana was fond of Victor, after being involved with an actor of Steiger's brilliance and complexity, Victor seemed a lightweight whom she could not possibly fall for. However much Diana missed male attention and companionship and was in need of an antidote to the confidences of so-called friends who beguiled her with stories of Dennis's shenanigans with women, she couldn't force a liaison when there was no chemistry to ignite it. But although she wasn't attracted to Victor Mature, she gradually found herself responding to the attentions of his stunt-man, Tommy Yeardye. They began spending time together, first on set during breaks, then off set going for walks or drives.

Once again, Dennis had got it wrong. Irish-born Tommy was exceedingly good-looking, tall with dark hair, green eyes and a superb body. Diana always had an eye for good-looking men and the fact that Tommy wasn't an ego-obsessed actor was a big plus. She found his modesty, his humility, endearing. For Tommy, Diana was a precious gift he unwrapped gently and with care. He treated her with politeness, respect and a sense of awe. Tommy was exactly what Diana needed to heal a bruised ego.

One weekend two close friends were staying at the penthouse, the comedian Jon Pertwee and his wife Jean Marsh. On the Saturday evening Jon left to perform at a club some distance away and Dennis went out with a friend for a pre-dinner drink. Finding themselves alone, Diana and Jean indulged in intimate woman-to-woman talk. Jean and Jon were having marital difficulties and Jean confessed to Diana that she had fallen in love with someone else. Diana told Jean about Tommy, how handsome he was, what a stunning body he had, what a good time they had working on the film and how much she enjoyed his attentions.

'You know Jean,' she said, 'Knowing Tommy has made me feel alive again.'

What Diana didn't know was that Dennis, always on the alert to detect possible assignations had switched on the tape recorder and had recorded the conversation. Dennis returned with several guests he had invited to dinner. But instead of going to the dining room with the others he mysteriously disappeared. Suddenly a deafening crash came from the drawing room, followed by more crashes. Rushing to the drawing room Diana was confronted by a shattered glass coffee table and smashed statues and ornaments. Dennis was out of control, cursing, shouting obscenities, demolishing everything in sight. Nothing and no one could stop him. He screamed insults at Diana and Jean calling them whores, sluts, fucking schemers, and in a fit of hysteria he threw them both out of the house. A trembling Diana drove to London where they stayed in Jean's flat.

After a few days Dennis phoned asking Diana to return to the penthouse promising to put the tape recording incident behind them. Dennis could evoke his practical business side when it suited him. And it suited him not to hold up the filming as his management fee depended on Diana completing the film. Besides, he was busy sorting out complications resulting from his affairs with other women which required his undivided attention if he was not to be knee-capped by irate husbands.

Diana returned and enjoyed a period of relative quiet. Dennis even surprised her one night, telling her he was taking her to the theatre. But instead of watching other actors, Diana found herself the star of the popular television show *This Is Your Life*, hosted by Eamon Andrews. Diana couldn't stop the tears as her father, her aunt Kit and her first elocution teacher were brought on stage. Even Stewart Sawyer, the photographer who had pushed Diana and Dennis into the swimming pool had been flown in from Hollywood.

'I've come 6000 miles to shake your hand,' he said.

'If I'd known you were coming I'd have worn my swimsuit,' Diana replied.

The weeks that followed the television show were tense with unspoken grievances. Despite his promises, Dennis was rude and offensive at every opportunity, unable to restrain a seething hostility, pacing the floor, punching the air, banging his fist on the table when Sholly was slow dishing up the food. He was like a powder keg about to explode. Diana feared for her safety and Tommy feared with her.

But the explosion instead of erupting with a bang, erupted in a cool pronouncement.

One morning as Diana was leaving for the studio, Dennis stopped her at the door and with a calmness he rarely exhibited, said, 'I'm leaving you. I've fallen in love with someone else. I won't be here when you get home.'

Diana could hardly believe her ears. Did Dennis actually say those words or had she imagined them? And did he really intend to leave or was this another one of his ploys to unnerve her? When Diana returned home that night she found Dennis's clothes had gone along with several antiques and ornaments which had escaped his fury. He had indeed spoken those words. She later discovered he had moved into one of the luxury flats in Woodhurst. To Diana's surprise Dennis had not taken Sholly with him. She didn't suspect Dennis's cunning arrangement. Knowing he would not be there to operate the recording devices, Dennis had engaged Sholly as a live-in spy.

Diana was overjoyed. It was as though the prison gate had sprung open and she could walk free. She experienced an exquisite sense of liberation. Aside from the brief time with Steiger she had been constricted by a domineering Dennis, shackled to his agendas. Now she was free. She had to mark the occasion. She phoned Tommy telling him the good news.

'This calls for a celebration,' Diana said, 'We're going to have a party tomorrow to celebrate my freedom.'

Tommy had never been to the penthouse and Diana was delighted that now she could have him with her. The party continued late into the night. Several guests stayed over. Next afternoon Tommy, Diana and two friends went for a drive in the country. By then Dennis had received a report of the penthouse activities. When Tommy and Diana returned early that evening an agitated Sholly rushed over to Diana.

'Mr Hamilton is here,' she said nervously.

An expression of fear must have crossed Diana's face for Sholly said, 'It's all right. Mr Hamilton's not in a temper. He just wants you to sign some papers.'

Diana was relieved. Signing papers was one of her main marital duties.

Tommy, concerned about Diana's safety wanted to accompany her into the penthouse but Diana knew the sight of him would induce yet another a brainstorm and she wanted to avoid a violent encounter at all costs. Besides, it was Dennis who had walked out. It was he who announced he was in love with someone else. He had done what he wanted. What was there to fear? Convinced there was no cause for alarm, Tommy waited in the car. Diana mounted the stairs to the penthouse alone.

Dennis stood at the top of the stairs his face contorted with rage, his hands clenching a shot gun. Diana's heart raced in terror. Trying to control her trembling and pretending a nonchalance she didn't feel, she headed for the drawing room. Dennis followed her. Through the stain glass window she could see Tommy waiting in the convertible. If only she could signal him.

'I want you to sign this, Dors,' Dennis said gruffly, pointing to a piece of paper.

'What is it?' Diana asked, hoping her voice didn't betray the fear in her heart.

'It's a list of all the men you've had during our marriage.'

Dennis proceeded to recite a litany of men's names, some of whom she hardly knew. Then he indicated another paper for her to sign. It would give him possession of all the property, the cars, the money, even her dog, Crackers. Diana made an instant decision. Her life was more valuable than her possessions. With a shaking hand she signed both papers and started to leave. But Dennis had no intention of allowing her to get off so easily. A deranged anger had taken hold of him and he intended Diana to be its victim. Blocking her exit he caught sight of Tommy through the stain glass window and with an expression like thunder he smashed the window with his gun yelling, 'I'll kill the bastard!', then whirling around he punched Diana hard on the head. With a scream Diana fell to the floor, pain raging in her head.

Tommy, hearing the commotion, rushed to the penthouse. Finding the door locked he put his fist through the window and raced up the stairs. Oblivious of the gun, he jumped Dennis wrestling him to the floor. Dennis, unaccustomed to being the vanquished rather than the victor, remained on the floor sobbing with humiliation.

As Tommy lifted the crying Diana from the floor and ushered her from the room, Dennis wailed, 'How could you do this to me? I loved you so much.'

Tommy took Diana to his parents' house in London, gave her painkillers and tucked her into bed. She later discovered that her eardrum had been punctured.

Diana was able to rent a friend's house for a month but eventually legal matters to do with the properties had to be sorted. Because Diana had signed away the properties under duress, new arrangements were made. Diana got possession of the penthouse and the Cadillac. Dennis got everything else. Although Diana was reluctant to move back to the penthouse with Dennis living only yards away in 'Woodhurst', the fact that Tommy would be with her made the move less threatening.

Things went well for a while although Diana was subjected to journalists, eager to report every sordid detail regarding her tumultuous relationship with Dennis, and Dennis was equally eager to provide blistering copy. The story of Diana, Dennis and Tommy – riddled with sex, adultery, passion, violence – was headline news.

After filming *The Long Haul*, for which Dennis gave Diana £1,000 from the £20,000 he received, Diana was scheduled to film in Italy. The film, called *La Ragazza Del Palio*, meaning 'The Girl who Rode in the Palio', was about an American girl who wins a trip to Siena, rides in the famous horse race called the Palio, and falls in love with an Italian prince. After the ordeal with lawyers, journalists, and especially with Dennis, Diana decided to treat herself and Tommy to a much needed holiday. Dispersed with the long arduous days of filming, they spent a relaxed time visiting Rome, Florence and Siena. Tommy was easy to be with and at first Diana was able to lean into his strength, his tranquillity, his gentleness to find the serenity she longed for. But even before the holiday was over she began to grow restless. Despite the romance of Italy, the moonlight dancing, the aura of sensuality, Diana found herself dissatisfied. When everything should have been perfect, she had become disenchanted. Something was lacking and she realised that the something was her relationship with Tommy. The very qualities she had found so attractive in him had begun to pale.

Tommy was dependable, down-to-earth, predictable. Whereas at first she had needed those qualities to heal, to feel grounded, they had ceased to be enough. Although she and Tommy were doing and seeing wonderful things, going to wonderful places, the wonder came from the external, not from any enchantment between them. There was no gaiety, no abandonment, no fun in their being together. Diana needed sparkle, exhilaration, excitement, highs, even madness. Dennis had understood this about her and had always provided giant helpings of what she needed, what they both needed. Tommy was solid, dependable, steadfast, but there was no mystery, no surprises, no drama. There was no 'edge' to Tommy, and Diana needed edge. Tommy was safe and Diana needed danger.

All her life she had shunned the 'decent sort of chap' her father wanted her to wed; she had been repelled by that chap, hated the idea of that chap, now she found herself living with him. Italy ignited in Diana a small burning of dissatisfaction in her relationship with Tommy. Diana longed to douse that burning, to find contentment with Tommy, but contentment was not something she knew how to live with. Instead of leaving Italy refreshed with renewed vitality, Diana left Italy with a nagging sense of discontent.

When Tommy and Diana returned to England and the penthouse, Diana encountered a disturbing situation. Living so close to Dennis, Diana had access to his lifestyle merely by looking out her window. She watched the goodtime girls come and go, the endless parties, Sholly serving champagne in the garden; she could hear the laughter, the hilarity, she could even see her animals, her magnificent cockatoo riding on the handlebars of Dennis's bicycle, her dog Crackers chasing his ball. Her life seemed dull, the house silent, lifeless without the pets, without Sholly, with just Tommy and herself. And something strange occurred, something she could not even begin to explain: she began to miss Dennis.

Dennis hadn't come near the penthouse since her return. One encounter with Tommy was enough to discourage him from inviting further humiliation. But, through a mutual friend, he had invited Diana to see the changes he had made in Woodhurst and once, when Tommy was away, she accepted the invitation. After that they had frequent telephone chats. Dennis wanted her back. But no matter how tempting his offers of reconciliation were, some neglected instinct of self-preservation managed to kick in at the last moment. Diana resisted.

Not long after returning to England Diana left for New York to appear in the prestigious Perry Como television show. It was a relief to be away from both Dennis and Tommy. She was riddled with confusion and decided to spend several weeks in New York to give her the space and time to sort out her concerns, to think about who and what she wanted. Rod Steiger knew she was coming to New York and was eager to see her. They arranged to have dinner together and Steiger picked her up in a chauffeur driven limo. However, dinner turned out to be an unremarkable love-making session in a friend's apartment. Diana was not impressed.

Next day Steiger visited Diana at her hotel bearing gifts. Aside from the red roses, he had a very special offering. He proposed marriage. But instead of being overwhelmed with gratitude and excitement as Steiger had anticipated, Diana refused the offer. It was the very offer she had craved when they were together in Hollywood. But now the magic was gone, its disappearance hurried along by a chance incident.

Several months earlier, during a casual conversation with an acquaintance Diana was surprised to discover the woman knew Steiger. Upon prompting from Diana she confessed that she had had an affair with him, and upon further prompting revealed some intimate details of that affair. She told Diana how romantic Steiger had been, how he had read poetry to her in an alcove under the stars, some of which he had recently composed. It turned out these were the very poems with which he had wooed Diana and the very alcove where the wooing had been consummated.

Steiger did not take rejection lightly and in an attempt to change Diana's mind exhibited great passion, declaring great love, falling on his knees, even threatening to throw himself out the window. But to no avail. Diana was not moved and considered the dramatic display of his heartbreak merely a superb performance by an accomplished actor. After the poetry humiliation she would not believe anything Steiger would say or do.

Following the exhausting episode with Steiger, the emotional drain of being subjected to the dramatic antics of a brilliant actor, Diana had a flash of appreciation for Tommy. Tommy was straightforward, uncomplicated, devoid of acting skills. Unlike both Steiger and Dennis, she could trust Tommy, rely on him. In a moment of clarity Diana made some difficult decisions.

Since she had come to New York, Dennis had been sending roses imbued with messages of love and phoning her regularly in an attempt to persuade her to leave Tommy. Her first decision was to phone Dennis and tell him she could never again live with him. She must have been convincing because Dennis had an instant change of tone, the melodious sweet-talking turned to shards of ice so frosty that even the roses wilted. Her next decision was to phone Tommy and tell him all that had happened even admitting her temptation to reconcile with Dennis. Tommy, wary of further temptations threatening their relationship, flew to New York. Diana was surprised and grateful. After the cold shoulder from Dennis and the run-in with Steiger, Tommy was a blessing, even if only a temporary one. They spent a week together in New York and then returned to England and to profound changes for Diana, both with her career and in her personal life.

Chapter 16
Dickie Dawson

Diana's return to England and the Penthouse was not a happy homecoming. Her arrival was widely reported in the press which in turn gave rise to a favourite press preoccupation: *The Intriguing Life of Diana Dors*. Adverse publicity filled the columns of newspapers, with a rehash of Diana's personal life, focusing on the salacious bits: her breakup-reconciliation-breakup with Dennis; her affair with Tommy; fallout from the Steiger episode which the press kept chewing over like a dog that won't let go of a mangy bone; even re-runs of the pool disaster. Diana was beset by reporters lying in wait to hurl questions at her whenever she left the premises. There were also financial difficulties to contend with. Dennis had accrued large tax bills which she would have to pay. Besides all this, legal disputes with Dennis were an ongoing torment.

And if her personal life was fraught with anxiety, her professional life offered no solace. Her latest films, including *The Long Haul* with Victor Mature, received at best indifferent reviews. *The Unholy Wife*, her Hollywood film with Rod Steiger, was so badly edited she hardly recognised it. Yet, throughout all the difficulties she managed to complete a new film, called *Tread Softly Stranger*. She was never late on set, never missed a cue and was always ready to laugh.

However, if filming provided a temporary reprieve from her troubles, there was no reprieve from a vengeful Dennis determined to wreak havoc in her life. Living in such close proximity to him was becoming impossible. Mutual friends carried tales from Woodhurst to the Penthouse and back again provoking ugly scenes which the press leapt upon. Like the time Dennis's expensive yacht was set on fire, for which he blamed Diana, and which generated press headlines. Revenge inevitably followed: bricks thrown through Diana's windows, her phone tapped, and a break-in which left the Penthouse in chaos; a virtual press bonanza. It was time to move on.

Tommy had spotted a rather grand 15th century oak-beamed farmhouse called Palmers, and had his heart set on moving into it. It was in the countryside south-west of London, had six bedrooms, three bathrooms and came with 50 acres of land. Diana loved it and the thought of escaping from the frenzy of Woodhurst into the peace of the countryside was irresistible. She sold the Penthouse and with the money from the sale, combined with her earnings from *Tread Softly Stranger*, she bought Palmers. In the spring of 1958 she and Tommy moved in.

However, the peace of the countryside wore thin after several months. Film work had dried up. Producers avoided Diana, swayed by the relentless bad publicity: stories about fires, fights, adulterous behaviour, by rumours of divorce, which was still frowned upon at the time. Diana found herself isolated on the farm, confined to Tommy and the animals. After the first flush of farm life, the newborn calves and the sprouting cornfields ceased to excite her. Living with Tommy was dull and disappointing. In Italy there had been the excitement of travel to enhance their being together, to fill the gaps, the empty spaces in their relationship. But the farm offered no such diversion. She was reliant on Tommy's partnership for making country life all she had hoped for. Her expectations had been high. Living in the country with Dennis had been the happiest time of their marriage.

However, whereas Dennis loved classical music and poetry, writing poetry himself, and always had some interesting idea to discuss, some hilarious tale to tell, something exciting on the horizon, some unusual construction to work on; Tommy's interests were limited. Even sustaining a conversation with Tommy was hard work. There was little of interest or significance on offer the morning after. Although he had been enthusiastic about displaying his talent as a farmer he did little except sunbathe and maintain 'the body beautiful', hardly engaging with the farm or even with Diana. As much as Diana appreciated 'the body beautiful' at night, its repertoire was limited in the day. So when she was offered a supporting role in *Passport To Shame*, a film about prostitution, she enthusiastically accepted, despite the fee which was half her normal rate. She was pleased to escape the tedium of farm life with Tommy and the chickens.

Filming was completed towards the end of July but the fallout from bad publicity had not yet run its course, keeping film producers from making offers. Diana was desperate for work. She urgently needed money. Maintaining the farm and the animals was an expensive venture requiring experienced staff. Diana knew nothing about farming and Tommy was no help, preferring the barbells and the sun lounger to farm work, or any work for that matter.

Then, as had so often happened in Diana's life, when the situation was at its worst, there was a sudden turn for the better. The agent Joe Collins, father of Jackie and Joan, made a compelling proposal. He suggested a cabaret act based on the old *Diana Dors Show*. It would be an eight week event touring seven cities in England, as well as Dublin in Ireland. Diana eagerly accepted. Her talents shone in cabaret, she could act, sing, dance, and wow the audience with glamour and charisma. Besides it was fun and she could do with a little fun. She would revamp her old variety act, make it more upmarket, spice it up, make it more glamorous, more sexy. She knew what the audience wanted and she would give it to them. There was also a major publicity opportunity. Diana had been booked for a cabaret act in Las Vegas beginning in October, and that news would be a great boost for the current show. All that was needed was a comedian to perform with her and act as compere. Tommy, perhaps with a sense of foreboding, didn't like the cabaret idea, he was perfectly content with things as they were. However, he surprisingly came up with a suggestion: a comedian called Dickie Dawson. They had seen him perform at the Stork Club, and he had been a guest at one of Diana's parties. Ironically, as it turned out, Diana was opposed to the choice. However, in the end she acquiesced and they settled on Dickie Dawson.

The tour was scheduled to begin at the end of July. By then Diana and Dickie had been working together, developing the script, rehearsing the jokes, the anecdotes, the songs and dances. The more time they spent together, the fonder Diana became of Dickie. He was attentive, clever, entertaining, a treat to work with and, most importantly, he made her laugh. They bounced off each other, and roared with laughter at their hilarious creations. Dickie was just the tonic Diana needed. After the sparkle of being with Dickie, returning to Tommy was like entering the gloom of a mausoleum.

Diana had been growing increasingly unhappy with Tommy. She resented his lack of interest in his career, his willingness to live off her. He had no focus, no drive, no ambition. Whereas at the beginning he was a welcome contrast to Dennis's hyper-energy and relentless buzz, now he seemed so relaxed he was almost indolent, happy to do nothing, to go nowhere. Dickie Dawson was more her kind of man, ambitious, urbane, sophisticated. Soon they began spending time together even when they were not performing or rehearsing.

The tour was a great success with standing ovations and wonderful reviews. Diana and Dickie were formidable together and the shared success brought them even closer. It didn't take long for the inevitable to happen. Before the tour had ended Dickie professed his love to Diana and Diana realised she was in love with him as well. For Dickie, Diana was not only interesting, talented and sexy, but a major step up in his career and a great boost to his driving ambition to become a star. For Diana, Dickie provided the way out of a relationship that had run its course. Besides, and most importantly, Diana relished the high of being in love, the excitement, the adrenaline rush. It was the oxygen of her survival.

The only problem was telling Tommy. Diana was aware her attraction to Tommy had been that of a one-night-stand that went on for eighteen months. The relationship was well past its sell-by-date. But she hated hurting him. She knew how it felt to be informed by telephone that a relationship was over. Hadn't Steiger inflicted that very anguish upon herself? However, she also knew it was imperative to tell Tommy before the press did it for her. With Dickie's encouragement and enthusiastic support she phoned Tommy while still on tour. Tommy was devastated. He was sad, bitter, hurt, confused, he predicted disaster, all at the same time. He accused Diana of wasting eighteen months of his life. Diana offered no defence to his hostility and anger. It was the least she could do. Then as gently as she could she told him he could stay at the farm until the tour ended but he would have to leave after that.

Diana's initial feelings of guilt and sadness were quickly overridden by the deliciousness of being in love, enhanced by success and acclaim and reinforced by Dickie's efforts at distracting her. He made all the right moves. He made sure to keep her laughing. He entertained her with jokes, with impersonations of Hollywood stars; she was especially delighted by the one of Rod Steiger. The scripts were brilliant, performing with Dickie was fun, being with him was exciting. Diana felt she had finally met her match. The warnings of friends that Dickie's motives were suspect, his agenda devious, that he was using Diana, capitalising on her fame, went unheeded. Diana could hardly wait for Tommy to move out and Dickie to move in.

For a while all went well. Dickie liked living on the farm. And why not? The house was idyllic, everything was provided for and

Diana was besotted with him. Meanwhile, Diana had resumed contact with Dennis when mutual friends told her Dennis was seriously ill with a heart problem. She visited him in hospital and remarkably, Dennis congratulated her on her choice of partner. Diana was pleased, perhaps one day they could even become friends.

Financially matters were much improved. Diana and Dickie were booked for a cabaret act in South Africa in December and also contracted to appear in the very popular Steve Allen television show in New York in early 1959. Dickie was elated. He had always wanted to perform in the U.S. His liaison with Diana was paying off big time. There was only one tiny fly in the copious ointment of success. Diana detected the occasional twinge of jealousy in Dickie. But she chose to ignore it, dismissing it as a temporary blip, an adjustment to her high profile lifestyle and star status which at times required Dickie to share her with an adoring public.

Once again Diana was enjoying the good times. The South African performance went well and Diana and Dickie managed to extend their stay for a week's sunshine holiday. They were both excited about going to New York and performing on television for an American audience. Before leaving for the U.S on January 3ʳᵈ, Diana made sure to phone Dennis who was once again in hospital. The call was upsetting. Dennis seemed much worse. He was both agitated and depressed, convinced he was going to die before Diana returned to England.

'I'll bring you something from New York to cheer you up,' she promised.

'Yeah. Flowers for my funeral,' he replied.

Although Diana was disturbed by his deteriorating condition, she consoled herself by dismissing his doom-laden utterances as attention seeking – one of his many skills.

The Steve Allen show was so successful that Diana was offered three more appearances at $7,000 each as well as additional club dates. The audiences loved her. Things were going so well that Diana and Dickie decided to extend their American stay and fly to California. Dickie was especially eager to see Hollywood. At first Diana was apprehensive. Her time in Hollywood had been traumatic and she hadn't been back for two and a half years. She was reluctant to resurrect disturbing memories. Besides, she didn't know what kind of reception she would receive. Was she still considered an immoral wench, a 'wanton hussy', someone to avoid for fear of being tainted by association? But Diana was so keen to show Dickie Hollywood she decided to chance the visit.

As it turned out Diana had nothing to fear. She was warmly received by friends who were living there like Liberace and Roger Moore. However, if the visit to Hollywood was not marred by an unwelcome reception as Diana had feared, it was marred by a jealous Dickie. The twinges of jealousy contracted in England developed into a full-scale affliction in Hollywood. Instead of spending time enjoying Hollywood, Dickie spent it focused on Diana, obsessing about her contact with friends, resenting the time she spent with them, becoming possessive, petulant, suspicious. Liberace was the saving grace. Dickie had met him previously and when Liberace invited them to his Palm Springs home, Dickie welcomed the invitation, pleased to be away from Diana's Hollywood friends, most of whom he disliked. The time they spent with Liberace turned out to be the highlight of the trip.

Then, suddenly, just as things were going well, the holiday was brutally interrupted. Diana received an urgent phone call. Dennis was dead. She was stunned. He was only 34. How could this happen? He seemed so powerful, so indestructible, so imbued with life, so much larger than life. The holiday was over. She and Dickie returned to England immediately. Upon her arrival she was once again accosted by the press. 'Had she intended divorcing Dennis?' 'Could they have reconciled?' 'Would she marry Dickie?' 'Was she now a wealthy widow?'

Diana mourned Dennis quietly and alone. He had been such a major influence in her life, such an integral part of who she had been and who she had become. He had kept his promise. He had made her a star. Despite the bad times, and there were very bad times, she felt a terrible sense of loss. She would miss him enormously. She couldn't even conceive of life without Dennis somewhere within her orbit, somehow involved in her life for better or for worse. She needed Dennis even if it was only to reject him, to assert her independence from him. There had been no satisfactory completion of their relationship, there were issues left in abeyance, matters to resolve, to understand, to one day sort out. Now they would never have that opportunity. It was as though some crucial part of her self was no more.

Dennis's funeral was just the high profile, publicity ridden, star-studded event he would have loved. The obituaries were glowing.

The funeral parlour was mobbed both inside and outside. The street was lined with mourners, women sobbing uncontrollably, men surreptitiously wiping away the tears, starlets pretending grief while posing for the cameras. In death Dennis had become the well-loved, much admired, glorified figure he had never been in life. The media-circus funeral was a fitting farewell to someone who was an expert in manipulating the media and was doing so even in death. Diana's wreath was a cross of flowers with the simple wording 'To my darling Dennis with loving memories that words can never express. My love always. Diana.'

It wasn't long before Diana discovered what Dennis had bequeathed her: two bombshells. The first exploded with the reading of Dennis's will. It was expected he would leave millions with all his businesses, his club, his coffee bar, his properties, his expensive possessions. Even the tax inspector eagerly awaited the revelation, rubbing his hands in anticipation. In fact, the sum total of everything Dennis owned amounted to £800, which he left to his parents. Instead of leaving Diana the fortune everyone assumed he had, she would have to pay a fortune to sort out his debts, his unpaid taxes, unpaid bills, and the tangle of foreign investments the creditors were screaming about, threatening legal action.

But the biggest bombshell was still to come. Diana discovered that Dennis had not died from a heart condition. He had died from syphilis. The disease, in the last stages, had affected his brain, his eyes, his heart, gradually destroying his organs and finally killing him. After absorbing the shock, aspects of Dennis's behaviour began to make sense to Diana: the brainstorms, the sudden heat waves, the blurred vision, the demented behaviour, the violence; all were typical of the disease. If only Diana had known sooner Dennis's life may have been spared. Fortunately she had not been infected.

But if Diana grieved over the loss of Dennis, mourning his death; for Dickie that death was little short of a blessing. For some time he had been pressuring Diana to get married. Diana had been reluctant to make a commitment so early in their relationship; they had been together less than a year. She had used her marriage to Dennis and the prospect of an ugly divorce, with negative media coverage which Dennis would have delighted in procuring, as a justification for waiting. She had said she longed for a hassle-free period without the trauma of a messy divorce before she would consider marriage. But now her justification was no more. Dennis was dead, and Dickie was quick to seize upon the advantage. He wanted the marriage to take place as soon as possible, the sooner the better.

Diana and Dickie were scheduled to fly to New York several weeks after Dennis's funeral to fulfil a television engagement and Dickie wanted them to get married in New York. Diana wasn't keen on the idea. She needed time. She didn't feel right marrying Dickie while she was still mourning Dennis. She felt too raw, too unsettled to celebrate anything, let alone her own marriage. Besides, when the time was right she wanted to marry at home, in England, and for their wedding to be a celebration shared with friends. But Dickie was insistent. He had already planned everything, made all the arrangements, had even purchased the ring. And, as so often happens in relationships where one partner has a clear, determined agenda and the other partner is unsure, vacillating, preoccupied; the clear, determined agenda wins out.

Suddenly Diana was caught in a whirlwind of activity: flying to New York; performing in the Steve Allen show: preparing for her wedding, all at the same time. On April 12, 1959, directly after her television performance, with hardly time to change from television attire to bridal splendour, she rushed to the home of her American agent where the marriage ceremony took place, just as Dickie had planned. It was attended mainly by the agent's business associates. Diana had only two friends present: Jean Marsh, whose intimate conversation with Diana had been recorded by Dennis that terrible time back in England, and the actor Jean had confessed to being in love with. Coincidently they were now living in New York.

Later a reception was held in an exclusive club attended by showbiz celebrities, journalists, and Steve Allen, the one person Diana knew. In less than two months Diana had run the gamut of being an estranged wife, to being widowed, and then to being married again. Dickie had officially changed his name to Richard some weeks earlier. Suddenly, just like that, Diana was Mrs Richard Dawson. And Dickie, who had been a struggling, little-known comedian less than a year before, was now the husband of a national icon. It was a lot to take in.

Chapter 17
Motherhood

Returning to England as Mrs Dawson brought dramatic changes for Diana. Dickie, having achieved his goal of marriage, quickly abandoned the niceties of courtship. There was no longer the need to display colourful feathers and perform courtship dances like a peacock wooing his lady love. Gone were the jokes, the side-splitting sketches, the hilarious impersonations with which he had enticed Diana. These were only on offer when there were others to impress. Diana no longer had a personal jester to entertain her. The high-spirited jester slowly, almost imperceptibly, metamorphosed into a sullen malcontent who had to be approached with caution before noon, who disliked Diana's friends, who was stricken by moods of gloom and despondency. Gone was the sparkle, the fun, the laughter. Diana found herself living with someone she hadn't known before. And, as with Dennis, it was mainly her earnings which had to sustain their lifestyle.

In August 1959, barely four months after returning to England, Diana made a surprise announcement which made press headlines. She was pregnant. The baby would be born in February 1960. Becoming a mother was the fulfilment of Diana's greatest desire. She was overjoyed, as was Dickie, who unlike Dennis didn't consider motherhood an impediment to her career. They decided to put the farm on the market. It was a great financial drain and besides, Diana was tired of country isolation and wanted to be closer to London. She bought a lovely five bedroom house in Virginia Water, Surrey, within easy reach of London, which she called 'Springwoods'. Renovations were planned; an extravagant nursery for the baby, a glass-enclosed swimming pool which could be entered from the living room and a cinema.

As with her previous pregnancies, Diana had a difficult time, especially in the early months. She suffered from debilitating nausea, exhaustion, both mental and physical, and ached everywhere. However, aware that having a baby would curtail her earning ability and involve extra expenses, which she would be mainly responsible to cover, she agreed to take on several cabaret performances. Before the pregnancy became visible she performed in Cannes, Italy and

Spain, willing herself to appear on stage when all she wanted to do was remain in bed.

Before becoming pregnant Diana had been approached by a music publisher to record an album and had worked with the talented arranger, composer and band leader Wally Stott. Diana had a strong, sweet voice and Wally Stott knew how to make the most of it. Diana was delighted with the result. The album, *Swinging Dors*, had an elaborate pink vinyl cover featuring a double door which opened outwards; Diana loved it. *Swinging Dors* was to be released in February, the same month the baby was due. Diana had much to look forward to. She had no way of knowing that her joyful expectations would be obscured by nightmare realities.

Diana's successful sell-out cabaret appearances in the U.S meant she was much in demand for additional engagements. Diana's agent and Dickie planned to fly to the U.S to arrange a contract for Diana to appear in lucrative shows in Las Vegas and Palm Springs beginning in March until mid-April. This meant Diana would have only weeks to recover from the birth and to bond with the baby. Diana hated the idea of leaving the baby so soon. But due to a sudden disaster which resulted in a devastating attack on her character, and in turn threatened any future employment, she felt compelled to take anything on offer, especially something that paid $7,000 a week.

The press initiated the onslaught. Journalists had made Diana's pregnancy a national concern. Now they featured news of the impending tour and with stinging disapproval dubbed the unborn baby the 'Cabaret Orphan'. However, this was a minor blip compared to a major scandal centred on Diana. Some time before Dennis died he had arranged for the News Of The World to buy Diana's life story. The newspaper now approached her for permission to begin working on the project. It was to be ghost written, containing input from so-called friends, and released over the course of a twelve week serialisation. Although Diana felt that, at 28, she was too young for a memoir, the gigantic sum of £35,000 was too tempting to resist. She agreed. This was to be a near-fatal decision.

The serialisation of the memoirs, released when Diana was in the final months of pregnancy, turned out to be mainly an account of her life with Dennis, focusing on every sordid detail, delighting in every perverse disclosure the journalist could unearth, both real and imagined. The two way mirrors whereby selected guests watched couples making love, unaware they were on display, received much attention as did the sex parties, and the blue movies. Every salacious incident was elaborated upon, every sexual aberration revealed with relish. Readers were invited to revel in a voyeuristic extravaganza hosted by Diana Dors. It was the next best thing to being there.

Diana was mortified. Her life had suddenly become a cheap soap opera and she blamed herself for not being more vigilant in the writing and editing phases. She said it was as though she had 'sold her soul to the devil for money' and was now being made to pay the price. She was especially concerned and embarrassed about the effect the revelations would have on her conservative Victorian father. He would be stricken with shame. Besides, what child wants their parents to know the intimate details of their sex life, especially when that sex life includes highly unusual practices which are splashed across the pages of a tabloid newspaper. The readers, on the other hand, enjoyed every shocking moment, and, although condemning Diana for allowing such a sordid story to be made public, couldn't wait for the next scandalous instalment. Diana, her pregnancy, and her sex life became not only a public issue but a national disgrace. In former times she would have been burned at the stake, but in a more liberal, more generous climate she was merely held up to public scorn and ridicule.

The 'Swinging Sixties' and the permissive society were still only a glimmer in the eyes of English society. England was in the throes of repressive, straight-laced morality. And the guardians of that morality rose up to crucify Diana. The archbishop of Canterbury denounced her as a 'wayward hussy' in echoes of the Hollywood denunciation, only more fierce. The Press Council described the memoirs as 'grossly lewd and salacious' and the newspaper as 'debasing the standards of British journalism'. Diana was even the subject of the popular BBC panel show *Any Questions*. Baroness Stocks, a high-profile crusader, a champion of virtue and decency, and a panellist on the show stated that the best thing Diana could do for the child was to have it adopted. The righteous defenders of morality were unforgiving. There would be no more presentations to the Queen.

Today, in all probability, Diana's memoirs would register only the slightest of raised eyebrows, as is evident from a recent court case. When ruling on the outing of a leading, well respected member of society who had orchestrated a masochistic orgy, the judge accepted that the orgy had incorporated 'bondage, beatings and domination', which he pointed out was 'typical of S&M behaviour', but even so he was in no way critical of the orgy, despite its alleged Nazi overtones, although he conceded 'that such behaviour is viewed by some people with distaste and moral disapproval'. Apparently he was not one of those people. The best he could do was label a sadistic sex orgy with Nazi nuances, whippings, humiliation and subjugation merely as 'unconventional'. Compared to what's on offer now, Diana's participation in Dennis's sex games would be considered child's play.

Standards have changed so radically since the publication of the derided memoirs, that, in a recent national election, one of the mainstream political parties selected as a parliamentary candidate a female film producer who has produced around 300 pornographic films. But in 1959, the publication of Diana's memoirs was an affront to English sensibilities, deemed so obscene and so damning as to declare her unfit to be a mother.

In the midst of the gruelling ordeal resulting from the publication of her life story, the humiliation, the grief, the worry that her film career was over, or at least severely damaged, Diana went into labour. In the same hospital where Dennis had died the previous year she endured 27 hours of excruciating pain before Mark Richard was born. But the joy of cradling her newborn son in her arms made the misery of the birth irrelevant. Oblivious to the vicious condemnations, the stinging disapproval, and the physical suffering, she was suddenly exquisitely happy.

* * * * * * *

Baby Mark was born in a blaze of publicity. Photographers awaited his arrival with the anxiety of expectant fathers. Journalists were at the ready, eager to be the first to dispatch the news of the birth to the nation. Diana was only too pleased to cooperate, anxious to score points with antagonistic journalists, hoping to reinstate herself with a hostile press. She presented Mark Richard to the cameras like a peace offering. Shortly after the birth the press enjoyed a bonanza. Photos of the baby on his own, the baby with Diana, the baby in his ornate cradle, appeared in newspapers throughout the country. For a brief moment the vitriolic words hurled at Diana turned to honey, but just for a moment.

Diana found returning home with a newborn baby overwhelming. The reality of caring for the infant Mark was entirely different from preparing for his arrival. Whereas the latter was an exciting event – choosing the nursery colours, coordinating them with the curtains, with the frilly cradle; buying the fluffy toys, preparing the layette, the tiny socks, the little mittens, the velvety hooded towels – changing nappies and cleaning bottoms was quite a different matter.

Diana's domestic skills had been grossly neglected to the point where they were non-existent. She had been spared the rigours of domesticity first by an overly indulgent mother, then by the accomplished Sholly, who performed so beautifully on every domestic level that when Diana and Dennis were living in Hollywood they flew her out with them, unable to cope without her.

If Diana was sorely lacking in domestic skills, she was hopeless at caring for an infant. Although she adored little Mark, she lacked the experience and know-how to cope with the round-the-clock needs of a newborn baby. One of her first postnatal priorities was to find a nurse/nanny to help with the baby. At first, she felt fortunate to have found Amy Baker, an unmarried, unattached woman with no children of her own, who could devote herself fully to caring for baby Mark. However, although Amy oozed reassurance and reeked of expertise, almost from the beginning Diana sensed disconcerting aspects in Amy's behaviour, but they were brushed aside in her relief at finding someone so seemingly ideal.

At first glance, Amy had the attributes and appearance Diana desired in a nanny, with her black hair tied into a tight bun during the day, indicating a no-nonsense efficiency which inspired confidence, and then falling to her waist in the evening, indicating a romantic wistfulness which Diana found appealing. Amy was not only efficient but caring, and that care, although lavished on the baby, was extended to Diana. She wooed Diana with lotions and potions to prevent stretch marks; with special energy drinks to inspire well-being; with the freshly laundered, sweet-smelling baby Mark, exquisitely dressed, presented to her like a gift, to fuss over and adore.

It was some time before Diana realised that Amy was one of those supremely capable nannies who, instead of just helping the beleaguered mother with the newborn baby, takes over the household. The takeover is so complete, so effective, yet so insidious, that the mother, although thankful to be relieved of mundane chores and new mother anxieties, and grateful that the baby is in competent hands, gradually finds herself excluded, even intimidated, and ultimately replaced. But that realisation didn't happen overnight. Since Diana left for Vegas when Mark was only two months old, Amy hadn't been employed long enough for Diana to feel its full impact. Although early on she did have an indication of Amy's fierce attachment to the baby when she overheard her say, 'I knew from the first moment he grabbed my little finger that he was mine.' However, Diana was willing to overlook any reservations regarding Amy's possessive inclinations because there was one major reservation she did not have. There was no doubt Amy loved Mark. Although Diana hated parting from her baby, she knew he was in loving, capable hands. 'I'll guard him with my life,' Amy promised, and Diana believed her.

Notwithstanding the sadness at being separated from her baby, Diana was probably happy to be leaving England and the furore caused by her memoirs, which was still an ongoing indictment. She had had an opportunity to restore her professional reputation which had fallen into disrepute. She had been offered the female lead in the film *Saturday Night and Sunday Morning* with Albert Finney, which would have won her respect as a serious actress and have gone some distance in blotting out the stain of the scandal. But because Albert Finney was an unknown and the part wasn't paying much, her agent refused the role. He was also to turn down the lead in Thomas Hardy's *Tess of the D'Urbervilles* for much the same reason. It seemed to Diana that sadly money was now the main motivation shaping her career, hence the eagerness for Dickie and her agent to accept the Vegas engagements on her behalf.

Diana's performances went extremely well, although she was plagued by exhaustion. This was unsurprising, as she hadn't yet fully recovered from the ordeal of a difficult birth, and was doing three shows a night. It was four in the morning before she could leave the stage, and hours before the adrenalin rush of performing had subsided and she could fall asleep. Vegas had turned her life upside down. In the clubs and casinos daylight was replaced by artificial light to encourage gambling throughout the night. There were no clocks to remind people it was time for bed. Diana found the bizarre situation making her ill. Besides, she was pining for baby Mark, saddened by being deprived of the initial months of a baby's astounding development. She was resolved to return to England as soon as possible.

Whereas Diana was feeling overworked and depleted, working seven nights a week, feeling unwell, struggling to stay awake between shows, Dickie was enjoying the Vegas high life, gambling, cavorting with fascinating people, meeting celebrities he had only read about, wining and dining in exclusive company, indulging in the exciting nightlife. Despite being exhausted, Diana's performances were so successful and the reviews so flattering that she was offered an extended contract for a further month. Knowing Diana would resist any attempt to prolong her U.S stay, Dickie made a stunningly clever move. On the pretence that her lawyer had come to see her he escorted Diana to an adjoining suite where the lawyer was supposedly waiting. But when she opened the door there stood Amy with the four month old, golden haired, blue eyed baby Mark in her arms. Diana melted and so did her resolutions. When the $7,000 a week contract was upped to $10,000 a week, she accepted.

After the extended engagement, Diana was determined to return to England. But Dickie was equally determined to remain in the U.S. Now that he had brought baby Mark to Diana he felt justified in prolonging their stay and accepting additional engagements. One of the offers he accepted on Diana's behalf was a prestigious two week stint at Ciro's, an exclusive Hollywood nightclub. Diana's success at Ciro's, where the competition was brutal, led to film offers, one with Jerry Lewis and another with Danny Kaye. Suddenly Diana's career was blossoming. Whereas in England the stigma of the memoirs had made her a leper to the film industry, in the U.S she was a star. Whereas England had turned its back on Diana, America embraced her and, to her surprise, Hollywood, which had all but driven her out, couldn't get enough of her. The fickle see-saw of success was tilted at a precarious high.

Although Dickie welcomed the money, Diana's success emphasised his lack of success. His big break had not come. Diana was effectively doing all the work. Dickie was just another Mr Dors, and whereas Dennis had thrived on the compliment, Dickie was infuriated by the insult. And there were no Vegas diversions to distract him. He became increasingly morose, withdrawing into moods of despondency and silence which could endure for days. As Dickie became more remote, Diana became more alienated. If the entertaining, amusing jester had gradually slipped away back in England, he had vanished without a trace in Hollywood.

Diana had been renting Greta Garbo's mansion for the family to live in. But paying the exorbitant rent together with ever increasing expenses both in the U.S and in England meant she had to accept engagements wherever they were offered. Although she performed in cities all over the U.S flying from one coast to another while Dickie sulked at home, financial problems kept mounting. In the end she decided to stay on in the U,S, where cabaret work was lucrative and plentiful. The decision to remain in the U.S involved selling their Virginia Water home and buying one in Los Angeles. Dickie experienced a rare moment of happiness. He flew back to England to arrange the sale. With the proceeds, Diana bought a splendid Beverly Hills house, although at $175,000 it was more than she could afford.

Then the inevitable happened. Diana fell in love. When performers are exerting the kind of energy Diana was emitting, dancing, singing, acting, being the focus of attention, performance after performance, night after night, leaving the stage high on adrenalin yet drained and depleted, they need some special something to feed that energy, to sustain the sparkle, to infuse the old, tired performance with new life, new magic. For some that special something is alcohol, for others drugs, for Diana it was love.

John Ashly was a young Hollywood actor Diana had met while filming a television series called *The Racers*. The timing was perfect. Diana had been feeling not only unloved but unwanted, even disapproved of. John took up the slack. He was smitten with Diana and Diana basked in the attention and affection he lavished on her. A torrid love affair was the result. When Dickie flew to England on business, John and Diana spent glorious times together at her home. As with the love affair with Rod Steiger, Diana was oblivious to everything except an overwhelming and delicious passion. She was totally unaware of Amy's disapproving eye. The affair, which began in Los Angeles, flourished in a perfect Miami setting, where coincidently an episode of *The Racers* was being filmed, while Diana was appearing as a guest in a television spectacular. By the time Diana and John returned to Hollywood John wanted Diana to divorce Dickie and marry him. Diana went as far as consulting a lawyer with a view to making this happen.

When Dickie returned to Hollywood Amy was quick to fill him in on the details of his wife's activities. Dickie was furious. But when Diana suggested divorce, reality came crashing down. He had no work, no money and nowhere to go. Diana was faced with a dilemma: on the one hand she wanted to leave Dickie, on the other she felt responsible for him, after all he was the father of her son. Since she was about to embark on a three week tour of South America she decided to hold off making plans with John until she returned.

All through the tour she longed for John and couldn't wait to see him. But when she got off the plane in Los Angeles it was Dickie, with baby Mark in his arms, holding out a rose, who greeted her. As Dickie no doubt had anticipated, Diana was very much affected by the welcome. Dickie and baby Mark were her family, a divorce would tear them apart. After a long talk with Dickie where he promised to be more attentive, more caring, Diana reluctantly decided to give the marriage another chance although in her heart she doubted its success. John, although hurt and saddened, graciously accepted Diana's decision.

It was almost a year before Diana returned to England. She had been offered top billing on the popular television show *Sunday Night at the London Palladium*. However, even a year was not enough time to forgive her memoirs. The newspapers were at her throat. When a journalist, resurrecting the old chestnut, accused her of being 'cheap' by selling her memoirs she retorted sharply.

'Listen, for £35,000, I don't mind being cheap... For a long time I didn't have any money... I was very famous and had trunks full of cuttings about the fabulous Diana Dors and I literally didn't know where my next meal was coming from. In this business it's very easy to be famous and broke, and I have been very broke,' she said, perhaps recalling the time she and Dennis had to steal a Christmas tree because they were too poor to buy one.

All this time things were becoming increasingly difficult with Amy. By now she was queen of the castle and full of demands and complaints. Even when Diana took her and baby Mark to Spain in September 1961 when she was working on a film, Amy could see nothing good about the country.

'They do nothing right in these countries,' she complained, when room service was a little late, and later, 'Why can't they have proper money instead of these potatoes?' disdainfully scattering a handful of pesetas, the local currency.

Diana was working nonstop and so desperately needed peace of mind that instead of challenging Amy, she did everything to appease her. Even when baby Mark clung to Amy's skirt, screaming when Diana tried to pick him up, she put the matter aside to be dealt with later. Shortly afterwards when Diana went to London for a small part in the film *From Dawn to Dusk*, and to perform in cabaret, taking Mark and Amy with her, she had to contend with Amy's moods and volatile temperament. Amy was becoming mother instead of nanny, even referring to baby Mark as 'my boy'.

That Christmas Dickie flew to London to join his family bearing surprise gifts. But Diana had the ultimate surprise gift for him. She was pregnant. Dickie was once again delighted. The baby was due the end of June 1962. Diana continued with her London cabaret appearances, helped by Dickie. But Diana wanted the baby to be born in the U.S and the family left for Hollywood on February 14, 1962.

'I certainly won't be back this year,' she told the press.

Gary was born on June 27, 1962. His all-star godparents were Steve Allen, Liberace, Terry Thomas and Pamela Mason, wife of James Mason and Diana's close friend. But once again Diana had little time to enjoy her new baby. Dickie had signed a cabaret contract for her to appear in Chicago and another in Vegas. Within 10 weeks Diana was back on the road. Dickie was still unemployed. Although he had done some bits and pieces here and there nothing had come of anything and Diana had to keep the money flowing mainly on her own. The expenses were enormous. Maintaining a mansion in Beverly Hills was a full-time commitment; the grounds had to be cared for, the swimming pool serviced, the staff paid, aside from Amy's wages, the children's expenses, Dickie's expenses and later on when Dickie's parents came to stay for a year, they were given a weekly allowance.

Dickie had once again retreated into moody silence, shutting himself in his bedroom, avoiding everyone and everything. Thinking a visit from his parents would cheer him up, Diana invited them to Hollywood. Dickie's parents were ordinary salt of the earth people, the kind Diana easily related to. She found it refreshing to have people in her home who preferred the simple life to the life of glamour and stardom. However, neither the birth of his son nor the visit of his parents helped lighten Dickie's dark moods.

In April 1963 while performing in New York, Diana was informed her father had died. Although she had never been close to her father as she had been to her mother, she had come to respect the values she had rebelled against in her teens. Now that she had her own children she understood a parent's need to protect them and keep them safe. What she had considered unfair rules and severe restrictions had been just that, protection, care, even love.

Diana's life now consisted mainly of work. Aside from cabaret work she had television guest appearances and a lucrative two month engagement in the musical *The Pajama Game* in New Jersey. Although she was sending money home to support her family, continuous work prevented her from enjoying the pleasures the money bought. She missed her sons, her home, her friends and a life with them. When she did get home Dickie hardly came out of his room, Amy made no secret of resenting her presence and for the boys she was at best a guest who brought presents, but it was to Amy they turned with their scrapes and bruises. Constantly on the road travelling from one engagement to another, living in hotel rooms, she felt deprived of what she most needed.

Since her early days in show business when she had flung aside the chastity belt mentality her Victorian father had imbued her with, Diana always had a passionate connection with a man. Men, love affairs, amorous encounters were a fundamental part of her being. Since the age of seventeen when she had moved out of the YMCA in London to a flat of her own, there were few occasions when she had lived on her own. She needed to be romanced, desired, admired; she needed the excitement of passion to feel alive and if a committed relationship failed to fulfil these needs, to provide these essentials, affairs would. There was always a lover waiting in the wings and although most of them continued to deliver the 'punch in the eye' syndrome, begun when she was still a child, her need was so compelling the pain did not deter her.

Once having started on the road to affairs with Tommy Yeardye when married to Dennis and again with Dickie Dawson when living with Tommy, and then again with John Ashley while married to Dickie it was easy to continue along that path. The second time one commits a crime it is no longer a sin.

She met Frankie Jacklone in New York, an Italian-American who was not only good-looking but massively rich and spent a hot summer in a romantic embrace enjoying the jet-set life, the novelty of someone else paying the bills and the affection and devotion Frankie showered on her. But Frankie had a drinking habit which Diana was wary of and when he insisted on marrying her, she beat a hasty retreat to Hollywood. And when he followed her there she was able to stall him with the promise of meeting him in Australia where she was booked for an extended tour. It's an indication of Diana's remarkable appeal that her lovers, rather than having an affair with her were bent on marrying her. Whereas men often shied away from commitment, Diana's lovers coveted commitment.

Diana dreaded the Australian tour, the eighteen hour flight to Sydney and then the six hour flight to Perth, her first stop on the tour. She dreaded going to a country where she knew no one, staying in anonymous hotel rooms, waking up in strange beds confused and disorientated. After a gruelling journey she arrived in Perth exhausted and miserable to a five star, red carpet reception, complete with journalists, photographers, a brass band, a parade of soldiers and a police motorcycle escort. Facing journalists, tour organisers, city officials and enthusiastic fans when all she wanted was sleep and solitude was a form of celebrity torture. Frazzled, fraught, bone weary and feeling so depleted she thought she would never smile again, she was finally allowed the privilege of being alone to nurse her misery.

It was when she first met Darryl Stewart, a singer on the Diana Dors Show, just days after her arrival, that the misery turned to ecstasy. If Diana was on a perpetual quest for love and yearned for the exquisite high of the first ten minutes of being in love, those minutes had made a sudden surprise appearance. Diana was in love. And, of course, Darryl was hopelessly smitten.

The intensity of that encounter grew into divine enchantment in the idyllic week they spent together unfettered by family, friends and any social commitment except to each other and their raging love. There was only one blemish to mar Diana's euphoria: Darryl was married with two small children. However, even that became a positive when the show moved to Sydney where Darryl lived with his wife and children. Their encounters became ever sweeter heightened by the excitement of the forbidden. After eight weeks of bliss, Diana and Darryl had to face the inevitable parting. Although Diana missed her boys and longed to see them she found it unbearable to be separated from Darryl. In a wild, reckless move, concerned for nothing but prolonging their love, she took Darryl back to L.A. and set him up in an apartment owned by her friend, Pamela. Although she hated and resented the deceit, the lies, the secret phone calls, at least they could be together.

Then, early in 1964, everything burst wide open. Darryl's wife sent a letter to Dickie detailing the affair and stating she was giving birth to Darryl's baby in two months. Dickie was beside himself. He followed Diana and Darryl to Darryl's apartment and confronted them with the letter. Diana, who considered herself basically a moral woman, had been harbouring guilt about having an affair with a married man, but the fact that Darryl had left a pregnant wife shocked her, and the fact that he had kept the secret from her shocked her even more.

An outraged Dickie first ordered Diana to leave the house. And then, unknown to Diana, he told Darryl about her affair with John Ashley and warned him he would suffer the same fate and be cast aside to make way for Diana's next conquest. Diana countered by beginning divorce proceedings and closing their joint bank account. When Dickie realised it was he who would have to leave the house and no money would be forthcoming, he did an about turn. During a tearful meeting with Diana he apologised for what he had done and promised not to contact Darryl again nor interfere in their relationship if Diana stopped the divorce proceedings and didn't force him out of the house. As had happened before, Diana agreed.

The excitement of spending time together without any deception overcame Diana's qualms about Darryl. They flew to Chicago, where Diana was performing, and enjoyed a repeat of their time in Perth, with no one to please but each other. However, as they both knew, parting was inevitable. But the thought they would never see each other again was impossible to contemplate. And so a plan was devised. Diana was due to appear in the film *Allez France*, and scheduled to return to London. She knew that Darryl had to be in Australia for the birth of his baby which was imminent. But after that he would come to London where they would live happily, if not for ever after, at least for the summer. They parted in Chicago with promises of undying love. Darryl flew to Australia and Diana back to Hollywood. For Diana, the only good thing about being home was seeing her sons. Dickie was sullen, bitter and remote. Amy had a long list of complaints and was eager to prove to Diana that it was she who had control of the boys' hearts.

Darryl wrote often, his letters full of vows guaranteeing eternal love. Once he even proposed marriage. Diana accepted. They outdid each other in fantasising about their reunion and their wedding. However unrealistic, they needed to sustain the romance and letters provided an easy option. So despite the heart-wrench of saying goodbye to the children, Diana was happy to be leaving Hollywood and flying back to England to be with Darryl.

By now things had changed radically in England. The Sixties were in full swing. The sexual repression of the Fifties, when only the privileged elite had access to sex parties, two-way mirrors, affairs, and mistresses, had given way to the permissive Sixties; open, unrepressed, waving banners of 'free love'. The music scene had also changed radically; the Beatles were all the rage, the youth culture with its sexual liberation prevailed; peace and love were the bywords, 'All You Need is Love' was the motto reinforced by the lovingness of marijuana, instead of the aggressiveness of alcohol.

Diana was fascinated by the change. She told a journalist, 'London has changed fantastically… people are so very much more on the ball, especially the youngsters – new waves of them setting the pace… It's the age of reality, of the Beatles, and a good thing too. They're the stars of today.' (The admiration was reciprocal as evidenced by her subsequence appearance on the cover of the Beatles' *Sergeant Pepper* album featuring the people they most admired).

Liberation had infiltrated many aspects of life. The gaming and licensing acts had become more lenient. When the Isle of Man opened its first legal casino, it was Diana who placed the very first bet. The legality of gambling caused a proliferation of cabaret work and, as usual Diana needed the money to support her growing list of dependants, which would now include Darryl. Before starting work on the film, Diana did a six week nightclub tour.

In anticipation of Darryl's arrival Diana rented a cottage in Chelsea, an upmarket 'swinging London' borough. The stage was set. Diana waited for the action to commence. But the curtain never went up. The leading man did not make an entrance. Instead Diana received a letter.

'My darling, I cannot come to England just now. But I promise that one day I will make it.'

Stunned, hurt, furious, Diana answered with a stinging alternative:

'Either you come now, or not at all.'

Darryl did not come at all. It took fifteen years before she heard from him again.

However, Diana was not one to bury herself in misery. That very night she threw a party. And that very night she met Troy Dante, the young, dark-haired, handsome, lead singer of a band called 'Troy Dante and the Infernos'. Diana was not only intrigued by Troy himself but by the ethos, the glamour he represented. It was no longer the glamour of the Forties and Fifties but the new glamour of the Swinging Sixties; the stove-pipe trousers; the long-haired men; the long flowing skirts; the bra-free breasts; the flowers. She knew her generation was passé and she welcomed the new generation, Troy's generation. Within a week Dante was ensconced in Diana's cottage, benefiting from all the goodies meant for Darryl.

Diana adored Troy's Cockney accent, his cheeky humour, and most importantly he had found the direct way to her heart – he made her laugh. Diana had slipped into the swing of the Sixties as though she had been born into it: the fun, the parties, the music, the hell-raising. And Troy made the ideal accomplice. However, not long after the first flush of romance, Troy made a confession. He was married. Diana was aghast. After Darryl, Diana had vowed never to so much as look at a married man. But, once again, caught up in the wild whirlwind of a besotted love affair, driven by intense emotions and a hot summer she was unable to stop herself. Troy remained. Diana was out of control. She even began to drink heavily, albeit temporarily, as she was never much of a drinker.

Meanwhile film work had dried up and in order to pay for the good times Diana accepted the only work on offer: working men's clubs. The clubs were not only hard work but demeaning. The soft-tinted lights of Vegas were glaringly fluorescent; the plush furnishings, beer-stained Formica; and the adoring Vegas audiences became drunks shouting "Get 'em off" or 'Show us your tits'. But Diana persisted, ignoring the humiliation because the reward of being with Troy and living the party life made paying the bill worthwhile. Between cabaret performances and anything else she could find, Diana made pilgrimages to see her boys, facing the heartbreak of parting from them. Then she would return to Troy, working to pay his gambling debts, the rent and expenses in England, and the rent and expenses in Hollywood. But Diana was on a roll, if not financially than emotionally and sensually. She was hooked on a wild passionate life with bottomless pleasure, addicted to the parties and the loving, and Troy and the 'Collection' were the fix.

The Collection was a group created in order to secure the good times. It was instigated by Diana and several other entertainment notables, including Jess Conrad, who was considered 'One of the most versatile British artistes to emerge from the 1960s,' and who played Jesus in *Godspell* and Joseph in *Joseph and the Amazing Technicolour Dreamboat*, and who not only looked like a pop star but was a pop star. The group was modelled after the American 'Rat Pack' headed by Frank Sinatra, Dean Martin and Sammy Davis Junior, whose motto described them as 'The hardest partying group in town'. It was a motto which could equally apply to The Collection.

Diana was known as the 'High Priestess', she ran the group and fuelled its activities. The emphasis was on parties, mainly at her home. The Collection had about six core members, all male except for Diana, and many peripheral members who came and went and who had to meet her criteria for acceptance.

'You have to be beautiful to sit at my table, or if not beautiful, then rich or famous and if you are neither, than fuck off.' she would say mischievously.

The group was revered all over London, its members even had their own named seats at choice clubs and discos. Visiting celebrities, such as Jayne Mansfield and Liberace made their way to Diana's home. Diana encouraged younger affiliates and as High Priestess, advocated her three rules for success to the aspiring celebrities who sat at her feet:

'One: Never use public transport. Two: Never carry money. Three: Always dress up, not down.'

In the entertainment circuit, Diana ruled the waves.

In all Diana's carrying-on, the singing and dancing on tables, the posing, the fun, the laughter, Diana had Troy by her side, providing impetus and inspiration for every mad leap into hilarity. Troy was her muse, her passion. Then, at the peak of the good times, Diana was overcome by emotional havoc. Troy's wife made a sudden appearance, demanding Troy back. And although Troy left Diana and returned to his wife, Diana was unable to give him up. She held on, hoping and waiting. She didn't have long to wait. Troy knew a good thing when he had one. He wanted back. And Diana eagerly took him back. So urgent was her need for him, that even after his wife was dismissed, she clung to Troy even more desperately, taking him to Los Angeles on one of her trips to see the children, and then to Europe, Turkey and South Africa for her cabaret shows, often performing in seedy places in order to fund her life with him. Then back to England and, of course, to The Collection.

It was during an engagement in New York that she discovered Dickie was finally earning money, although he never let on to her, to ensure that she kept paying the bills. He would go on to realise his dream of fame and fortune, first with a television series and then as the host of a popular television show. However, even though he had money he was not generous towards Diana, refusing her money when at one point she couldn't afford the fare to visit the children.

Meanwhile back in England, twin forces were tugging at Diana's life. She was facing ongoing serious tax issues dating from her time with Dennis. She owed so much money in back taxes that bankruptcy was breathing down her neck. However, this did not deter her from The Collection parties, at times with almost 100 guests, mostly celebrity actors and musicians. It was akin to fiddling while Rome burned.

Despite the parties, the pleasures and the loving, Diana must have been overwhelmed by a massive sense of insecurity. The see-saw of career success had plunged to a dangerous low; she was without her children; she was obsessed with a gambler; and she was 35, no longer a young in-demand star and sex icon. Even the indulgences of The Collection could not obscure the harsh facts. She urgently needed some form of stability, some rock she could lean against, something she could depend on and trust.

In England, owning property is equated with security. As the saying goes: 'An Englishman's home is his castle'. Every young couple's ambition is to get on the property ladder. Diana's parents had always owned their own home and one of her major objectives had been to own hers. Now, faced with bankruptcy, owing every penny she had and more, she found herself, incongruously, bizarrely, looking for property, desperate for the security of bricks and mortar in her unstable world.

She found exactly what she wanted in Sunningdale, a large village about 24 miles west of London. It was a magnificent mock Tudor mansion, called Orchard Manor, with three acres of land. The problem was obtaining the money to buy it. She could not sell the Beverly Hills house as any money she was seen to have would go directly to the tax man. Her lawyer thought the notion of buying a house not only impossible but absurd. However, Dickie conjured up a series of complicated financial and personal arrangements whereby Diana agreed to divorce him, give him the Hollywood house plus custody of the children, in return for releasing the children's trust fund and buying Orchard Manor in their name. In the end desperate for security, she agreed to the arrangement and bought Orchard Manor. Then a bit of luck came her way. She was offered a role in the film *Hammerhead* and was able to furnish Orchard Manor in the opulent style befitting a movie star. If she no longer had the reality at least she could have the illusion. Meanwhile The Collection was in full swing and the parties moved to Orchard Manor which became its temple.

The brightest aspect of 1968 was a wonderful holiday visit from Mark and Gary, along with Amy. The children loved Orchard Manor. Although she had long ago given up on the idea of having the boys living with her on a permanent basis, their great holiday time together sparked the thought they could live with her part of the year. She asked Amy to run the idea past Dickie. Amy, however, ran an idea of her own past Dickie. She told him Diana had tried to prevent her from returning the boys to him, and, if not for her, he would now be without them. Amy was so convincing and Dickie so enraged he vowed never again to allow the children to visit Diana. Added to this depressing news was news from the bank that money she had deposited in Troy's name, because of the bankruptcy proceedings, was gone. Troy had emptied the account. Now, at 36, she had given away everything she had worked for all her life and was virtually penniless.

Diana was forced to sit up and take stock. The picture was not pretty. It wasn't so much the imminent bankruptcy, the degrading litigation she was subjected to, the downfall of her professional life and the scandals that she despaired of, but the disaster she had made of her emotional life. Her marriages were failures, her affairs were in ruins, her four year relationship with Troy a disaster. Worst of all she despaired of ever having a successful marriage, a successful relationship, or even a successful love life. For Diana this was equivalent to saying her life was over. But how wrong she was.

Chapter 18
The Pot of Gold

Unknown to Diana, while she was in the depths of despair, a miracle was brewing. And then, with the mystery of a rainbow suddenly lighting a dark sky, the miracle happened. Far from her love life being over, she found the pot of gold.

It all began with *The Thief*, a play Diana saw on television. She was captivated by the principal actor, Alan Lake, not only by his acting but by the man himself. He was the devastating gypsy man of the songs and legends, the gypsy man for whom women abandoned their home, spouse, even their children. He touched every hungry nerve in her body. The impact was so powerful, it was as though he had written himself into her psyche.

Not long afterwards Diana was offered a guest-star role in a new television series called *The Inquisitors*. When she asked the identity of her co-star, the answer was 'Alan Lake'. It was as though she had rubbed the magic lamp. That night she dreamed she had fallen in love with him. Even before she had met him, the miracle had been evoked.

Alan, however, was seriously unimpressed at hearing the name of his co-star.

'Oh no, madam tits and lips herself,' he said disparagingly, dismissing her as a pampered, flashy, glamour queen, trailing mink and diamonds, relying on hip wiggling and cleavage, instead of acting ability.

But, on October 10, when he entered the studio for their first rehearsal, he found an unpretentious, modestly dressed woman, sitting quietly in a corner, reading her lines. And when their eyes met and she smiled up at him, the miracle happened. Some destined recognition passed between them. From that moment the angels sang.

Alan was in fact part gypsy, a man's man, an accomplished fencer, boxer, horse-rider and drinker, more comfortable in the pub with his mates than at posh nightclubs with the elite. However the raw, primitive maleness he exuded was tempered by a light brush of refinement, a quality he possibly acquired at RADA where he had studied and taught drama. Diana found the combination compelling.

The attraction between Alan and Diana was so immediate, so all-consuming that after only after a few days, Alan presented Diana with an amethyst ring given to him by an uncle.

'I promised I'd give this to the woman I wished to marry,' he told Diana. 'I've never been in love with anyone else.'

For Diana to be stricken by love was nothing unusual. 'Love' was her middle name. But for Alan, 'love' was not in his vocabulary. He had never been married, had never given himself to a woman. It was as though Diana had opened the floodgates to an entirely new ethos, to new sensations, new emotions, new desires and like a new convert to a religion he embraced the doctrine of love with divine enthusiasm. He wanted it all, commitment, assurance, dedication, vows, and he wanted it now.

And there was nothing to prevent him from having it now. Alan was unattached. Diana was divorced. Her relationship with Troy was over. Emptying her account had been the last straw. Troy had departed with a loud grumble, Diana's car and all her money. The reins were loose. Diana and Alan were engaged having known each other for three days. But the wedding, the celebration of their eternal union, had to wait. Diana had not only been given another chance at love, but another chance at serious acting, something she had waited for since *Yield to the Night* back in 1956. She was playing the role of an embittered, no longer young alcoholic in a BBC play called *Where Have All the Ghosts Gone?* as well as rehearsing for *The Inquisitors*. They wanted nothing to interfere with the public declaration of their undying love.

After seven ecstatic weeks working together in *The Inquisitors* and laughing together (Diana loved his sense of humour), their being together enhanced by poetry, by romance, by exquisite loving, Alan and Diana were married. The ceremony took place on November 23, 1968, one day before Alan's 28th birthday, in the same place Diana and Dennis had married seventeen years earlier; where Dennis had threatened to kill the unfortunate man performing the ceremony, and where one of Dennis's discarded lovers had threatened to kill herself. This time everything was dignified perfection. The bride wore white satin and lace, the groom black velvet. They were surrounded by family and friends. The mood was one of celebration. Even the journalists and cameramen gave Diana a reprieve. There were no provocative questions or allusions to her debts, now totalling £56,000.

That night Diana and Alan appeared on television, sharing their happiness with the nation. The reception lasted for two days. Diana was immersed in champagne, flowers and love, giving no thought to her dire financial circumstances. The journalists, too, chose to ignore the much publicised bankruptcy proceedings and horrendous court hearings, and reported only the celebration.

Alan was the man Diana had been seeking all her life. She had endured relationship after relationship, affair after affair, disappointment after disappointment and when she had given up hope, there he was. Alan was not only gorgeous, talented, fascinating and fun; he not only read Shakespeare, and wrote poetry; but he was working and paying bills, a first in Diana's relationship with men. The fact that Diana was nine years older than Alan was something she considered a plus. Women lived longer than men and their sexual appetites outran men's. A nine year difference put them both on the same level. It was all perfection.

The icing on the wedding cake proved to be Diana's discovery that she was pregnant. A child was the ultimate gift for their perfect union. Although Diana experienced the usual misery in the early months of the pregnancy, for the first time she was not pressured to return to work while feeling wretched, in order to pay the bills. Much of the time Alan was away, acting in Manchester in a new television series, returning on weekends to Diana's eager arms. Anxious to compensate for the enforced separation he treated Diana with such tender care and concern it was as though she was the first woman to have borne a child. Diana, beautifully indulged, basked in the luxury of being pampered until the sickness passed and they returned to the joys of their blessed life together.

Then early one evening when Diana, Alan and several friends were having a Polynesian dinner at Trader Vic's restaurant in the London Hilton, Diana went into labour. She was rushed to the Princess Charlotte Hospital. With Alan at her side, on September 11, 1969 she gave birth to Jason, a healthy seven pound fourteen ounce baby boy.

'He will be an actor like his father,' Diana said gazing into the eyes of her newborn son.

And if this wasn't enough happiness, two weeks later Alan opened in a starring role in the play *There'll Be Some Changes Made* in a major London theatre. The reviews were great, resulting in more acting offers including one at the prestigious Royal Court Theatre.

Diana had to pinch herself to be sure she hadn't dreamed up the wonder of it all. One of Diana's first considerations when she discovered she was pregnant was hiring a nanny. Her attitude to motherhood was one of ambiguity. On the one hand she fantasised about being a housewife, devoting herself to home, husband and especially to baby Jason. She wanted to do all the things for him she had not done for her first two children, which had resulted in her estrangement from them. At that time she had rationalised she needed to work to maintain the luxurious conditions they were accustomed to and work involved living in hotel rooms and constant travelling, a life of insecurity she could not impose on the children. She had left them in the hands of Amy, who had eventually replaced her as their mother. Although she deeply resented this, she had allowed it to happen.

Later, when she moved to England, she rationalised it was better to leave the boys in the environment they were accustomed to, in the sunshine of California, instead of the chill of London, with a mother working in clubs all over the country. Of course, all of this was true, but also true was the fact that Diana had not really wanted to be a full-time mother, had not wanted to give up the celebrity status, the exclusive designer gowns, the applause, the excitement, the red carpet treatment. She had not wanted to give up the John Ashlys, the Darryl Stewarts, even the Troy Dantes. She wanted to be free to 'seize the day', unconstrained by motherhood. She could not be a full-time mother, a full-time homemaker and a celebrity at the same time, and so she had chosen the latter.

Now with a new baby, unlimited motherhood had a second chance. But Diana was reluctant to renounce the parties, the clubs, the fun. She wanted to keep the good times rolling, especially as she could now share them with Alan. Also, although Alan was now a sought-after actor, he had not yet reached the star income bracket and there was a mansion to support as well as a new baby. A nanny was a necessity. Fortunately she was able to find a capable, experienced young nanny to care for Jason, the first in a succession of nannies he was subjected to.

For Jason's christening, Dickie relented and allowed Mark and Gary to come to England, of course with nanny Amy. It was a joyous occasion. The family posed for photographs to the delight of the press photographers. Mark and Gary were allowed to stay until Christmas. Diana was overjoyed to have them with her. She had not seen her children for two and a half years. With two nannies on call, Diana and Alan were free to focus on the boys, to take them to films, to the circus and to children's exhibitions. They had a wonderful time together. Alan adored the boys and they adored him. He devoted much time to playing with them, telling them stories complete with dramatic effects, inventing card games and teaching them to ride horses.

Thrilled with all the attention, Gary said, 'Dad never plays games with us like this. I wish Alan was our father,' a sentiment which did not play well with Dickie when the boys returned home, and Amy gave her damaging report.

Their departure was a sad time. The boys pleaded to stay but Diana had to refuse, having promised Dickie to return them. Suddenly there was a rift in the family; the children were gone and with them the childish laughter, the games, the jokes, the carrying-on. Of course, baby Jason remained, but he was only four months old.

* * * * * * *

The new year, 1970, was very auspicious for both Diana and Alan. It began with both of them acting in the comedy *Three Months Gone*, which opened on January 28 at the Royal Court Theatre. Diana played a tarty landlady with a ravenous sexual appetite. Alan played one of her lodgers. Diana had been both happy and fearful playing a serious role: fearful because it was something she hadn't done for almost fifteen years; happy because she saw the role as an opportunity to reclaim her status as a serious actress, something she longed for. Aside from the one hour television drama *Where Have All the Ghosts Gone?*, the few roles she had played in the last decade had been fluffy, lightweight ones, and her career had been sustained by cabaret acts, sometimes lauded, often degrading, but never dependant on her acting ability. For Diana, much depended on the success of this performance.

On the opening night of *Three Months Gone*, the journalists were present en masse, intent on writing Diana's financial and professional obituary; poised, pen in hand, to sound the death knell to her acting career. But a feisty Diana was determined this would not happen. To their amazement the applause was thunderous. Sir Laurence Olivier clapped the loudest and after the show rushed into Diana's dressing room eager to offer his congratulations, showering her with praise, complementing Alan's performance and predicting a successful acting duo. Diana was delighted.

'When you've done a lifetime of cheesecake,' she said, 'the status you get from a "well-done" kiss from Laurence Olivier is something special.'

Her performance won unanimous raves. It changed her image from a has-been sex symbol who had once starred in Hollywood, to that of a talented, versatile actress very much in the now. It ushered in a new career, with new possibilities. She was inundated with film, theatre and television offers. Instead of being consigned to the pages of history, Diana was making history. Her comeback was sensational. She became sought-after by the very journalists who had written her off, featured in newspaper and magazine articles. She could hardly keep up with the requests from photographers for posters, advertisements and magazine covers. Diana was back in her stride.

'Being a sex symbol made me and killed me at the same time,' she said. 'It was lovely, but it never led to anything else...Now I'm looked on as a theatre actress instead of the sexy joke I was for god knows how many years.'

The journalists were only too pleased to have her back. She had provided them with many years of good copy and would no doubt provide them with many more. By this time Diana's figure had mutated from model to matron but she was unconcerned about gaining weight.

'Contentment ruins your figure,' she said.

And for the nation she was still 'Our Diana'.

By the time the play transferred to the prestigious West End, the heart of London's theatre world, Diana's life was studded with blessings. Against the odds she had found her ideal partner in a marriage filled with love, and gifted with a beautiful baby boy. She lived in the mansion she had dreamed about since childhood; it even had cream telephones and an Olympic-sized swimming pool. Her career had made a dazzling recovery. And her husband was not only a successful actor but about to release a pop record; a special comedy series for both of them was in the process of being written, and Diana was about to fly to West Germany for a starring role in the film *Starting Out*, which would be renamed *Deep End*. The see-saw of success had rocketed to the sky. Happiness, something Diana thought had disappeared forever, was overflowing. For a moment Diana had it all. But once again it was only for a moment.

Chapter 19
Jason

Jason was born of a great love. Although he was included in that love, integral to it, he was frequently separated from it, denied its abundance. Both his parents, the source of that love, were absent for long stretches of time. Sometimes they were physically absent, performing in different cities, even in different countries. But often, although they were physically present they were mentally elsewhere, engaged in being someone else, somewhere else, involved in a stage life with its own sorrows and joys often more demanding than their own lives.

Baby Jason, gazing up at his mother's face, his tiny fingers entangled in her long blonde hair, was often torn from her arms and handed to the nanny, when an agent summoned, a performance beckoned, an interviewer waited, a camera call was urgent, or even if a performance of one of The Collection members necessitated attendance. It was an unwritten rule that members attended each other's performances and especially their celebrations.

Diana, more than Alan, was prone to long absences and Alan often took up parental duty on his own. He adored Jason and was delighted to be a father. But if by now Diana had mastered some skills of motherhood, Alan was a complete novice, and some of his improvisations would have raised the eyebrows of childcare experts. For example, although he loved taking Jason out in his pram, proudly strolling down the street, usually in the direction of the pub, initially he was all at sea if Jason grew tetchy. But it didn't take him long to devise his own technique for re-establishing harmony. He would dip Jason's pacifier in champagne and if this wasn't effective he would replace the milk in Jason's bottle with a dose of champagne, a device which worked wonders in restoring peace.

Although both Diana and Alan were thrilled to be parents, and although Jason added a new dimension to their happiness, his arrival sometimes caused a dent in that happiness. The first such dent occurred when Jason was only months old. Diana and Alan were engrossed in the run of *Three Months Gone*, basking in its success, working flat-out in nightly performances plus two matinees, when suddenly Jason's nanny handed in her notice. Diana was frantic. After her experience with Amy, who managed not only to alienate Diana's children but to instil negative feelings towards Diana herself, she was wary of nannies. Fortunately for Diana and Alan, but perhaps less so for Jason, friends and relatives offered to care for him until Diana found a replacement nanny. This involved shunting him from one situation to another, one set of carers to another. Alan's parents took Jason for several weeks and he stayed with various friends – a few days here, a few days there – until Diana found someone suitable.

The first dent in their happiness was therefore repaired without too much anguish. The next one occurred when Jason was almost a year old, and had dire consequences. However between the two Diana experienced a period of supreme happiness. Diana and Alan were magic together and that magic was reflected not only in their personal lives but in their professional lives as well. They both received excellent reviews and were inundated with offers of work.

Married to Alan, for the first time in her life Diana was entirely fulfilled, entirely content. Of course she was subjected to external pressures, especially the pressures involved in being an actress – deadlines, learning lines, rehearsing, performing, but she found these pressures easy to handle. She was a professional, always knew her lines, was never late, was on stage even when she'd rather be in bed and was a treat to work with. Alan relieved her of the much more difficult emotional pressures. She felt well-loved and could relax into Alan's caring and support. She no longer had to seek love, she was surrounded by it. She didn't have to deal with paranoia as she had with Dennis, who would always be watching her, always suspicious; or with boredom, as with Tommy; or with a brooding, sullen self-absorption as with Dickie. She was spared the anxiety of wife problems, as with Darryl, or gambling problems, as with Troy. She didn't even mind gaining weight, Alan loved her as she was. She enjoyed emotional peace and inner stillness the likes of which she had never known before, and she leaned into it with great thankfulness.

In the throes of such happiness, Diana, who was a modest drinker herself, and who had never lived with a man dependant on alcohol, was not aware of Alan's growing alcoholism. She had been with drinkers before, even back in her LAMDA days when drinking was all the rage, and thought nothing of Alan's alcohol consumption, considering it par for the course in the acting profession. Besides, alcohol had no visible effect on Alan, not on his work nor on his behaviour. But Alan began drinking more and more and by the end of the theatre run of *Three Months Gone* he was slipping off to the pub during intervals, unable to wait until the play was over.

Alan came from Milton, a village not far from the town of Stoke-On-Trent, in the middle of England. Village life was simple and predictable with limited choices, far from the sophistication of life in London with all its diversity and abundance. A night out for Alan had been drinking with his mates at the local pub; a family night out was a sing-song at the same pub. He was a back country boy with a back country accent, which he had to get rid of when he came to study drama in London, and which he always regretted. But although he got rid of the back country accent, it was far more difficult to obliterate the back country boy. He was something of an outsider in Diana's circle, never entirely comfortable with many of her celebrity friends or with the celebrity culture itself, and was especially uneasy with The Collection devotees and their get-togethers, the quips, the fast banter, the references to people and places he knew nothing about. Often when they were engaged in some hilarious antic, he would stand apart. Diana, aware The Collection wasn't quite his style, would say, 'Let him be, let him do his thing' when he would wander off or sit quietly reading.

Basically Alan was a shy man from a village background, suddenly thrust into a fast-talking, fast-living, top-of-the-range, celebrity-studded milieu. And being the husband of Diana Dors added to the difficulties. Diana was public property, loved and admired not only by her friends and colleagues but by the nation. It was something Alan had to get used to; the constant attention, the glaring limelight, the adoring men, even the unspoken accusations. Many of Diana's friends thought he was using her, riding on her coat-tails to achieve success as had happened with most of her previous relationships. His friends were equally disapproving, critical of the world he was now part of, accusing him of abandoning his roots. Besides, he was still not a hundred per cent confident of his acting ability, and was just finding himself as an actor. Actually it had never been his intention to become an actor, his ambition had been to produce and direct his own company, and acting had initially been a step in that direction. For all these reasons and more Alan found consolation in alcohol, needed it to boost his confidence, to make him feel adequate to face the multiple challenges being the husband of Diana Dors involved. Although Diana began to notice him slipping out to the pub with increasing frequency when they were acting together, she had no idea how seriously dependant he was on alcohol.

Unsurprisingly, the second major dent in Diana's happiness which involved Jason concerned alcohol. One of Diana's good friends was Leapy Lee Graham, a successful pop singer with a hit record. When Leapy Lee bought a house close to hers, he and Alan became buddies. Leapy Lee was Alan's kind of man, someone he could easily relate to, someone he felt entirely comfortable with. He was like his mates back home with whom he had cavorted in his bachelor days, mates who appreciated good old-fashioned pub life, which Alan missed. They had a similar sense of humour, enjoyed the same slap-on-the-back jokes, loved raucous laughter, playing darts and especially drinking.

One Sunday afternoon Diana invited Leapy Lee and his wife for lunch. As usual, before lunch the boys went to their local for a pre-lunch drink, and then again for a post-lunch drink, and again for an early evening drink, as well as all the drinking with lunch. The previous day Alan had been to the pub with Jason in his pram. The manager, who Alan knew well, was on holiday and replaced by a relief manager. When Jason became restless, instead of giving him his usual champagne soother, Alan, probably on Diana's insistence, gave him sparkling water ordered from the bar. Although not yet a year old, Jason knew the difference. Refusing to be fobbed off with an inferior product, he howled in protest. Somewhat flustered, Alan left the pub, giving not a thought to paying for the water.

On the Sunday in question, July 13, 1970, the day after the Jason incident, the same relief manager was in attendance when Alan and Leapy Lee arrived for their evening drinking session. After a few hours of uninterrupted alcohol consumption they were about to depart when the manager reminded Alan he had not paid for the sparkling water ordered the previous day and asked him to pay up. Insulted, Alan refused. After all the money he and Leapy Lee had spent in the pub that day, and on all the previous days, he felt entitled to a small bottle of water. But the manager insisted. An argument broke out. Leapy Lee joined in. Insults were hurled back and forth growing increasingly vicious.

When an angry Leapy Lee emptied his beer glass on the manager's head the insults and swearing escalated into violence. A fight broke out, several pubgoers happy to join in. Alan was knocked to the floor by someone. Leapy Lee punched that person in the face, breaking his nose. Then the fight really got going. Glasses were broken, chairs smashed, windows shattered. Leapy Lee was hit on the head with a heavy object by the furious manager. He jumped the manager, cutting his arm with a knife, causing a wound which required eighteen stitches. The police were called. The following day Alan and Leapy Lee were taken in for questioning, then released. A month later they were charged with 'grievous bodily harm and causing malicious damage'. Leapy Lee was charged with stabbing, and Alan with being an accessory. They were fined, and a court date was set for September. The problem for Alan was that witnesses had told the police it was Alan who had handed Leapy Lee the knife, with the instruction, 'Here use this'.

Diana was extremely upset both by Alan's drunken behaviour and by its consequences. Aside from the bad publicity it would generate, she had arranged with much difficulty for Dickie to allow Mark and Gary to visit England on their summer holidays, and was worried that if Dickie heard about Alan's behaviour and the impending court case he would cancel the visit. The newspapers had a field day reporting the pub incident and it was little short of a miracle that Dickie had not been made aware of it. Mark and Gary did in fact come to England, and with *Three Months Gone* concluded, Diana and Alan were able to devote a lot of their time to entertaining them. Once again, the boys did not want to return to Los Angeles. However, Diana promised that she, Alan and Jason would visit them very soon and this lessened the trauma of leaving England.

The authorities allowed Alan to leave the country on bail for three and a half weeks. Looking forward to a holiday and a respite from the worry of the court case, Diana and Alan set off to California with Jason and his nanny. The trip was remarkably successful. Alan had never been to the U.S and the boys enjoyed showing him their favourite haunts like Disneyland and the best beaches. Even Dickie behaved beautifully, inviting Diana and Alan to the house and fussing over Jason.

By now Dickie was rich and famous, and success had made him affable and accommodating, helping to wipe away the bitterness and resentment of the Diana years. For Diana it was strange and disturbing visiting her former home; seeing the bits and pieces she had once so carefully chosen, some dating back to the Dennis days, which were no longer hers. Every item of furniture, every gift, every painting she had loved, evoked memories of a past life filled with joys and torments, which she recalled with a wistful mixture of pleasure and pain.

The only major blip in the visit was that Diana found Mark and Gary too adult-like, concerned with issues which were not only beyond their comprehension but none of their business. For example, Amy had not only turned the boys against her but against any woman who came into Dickie's life. The boys seemed too eager to find fault with the women Dickie dated, deriding them and their relationships with Dickie in language which Diana found disturbing.

After several weeks of holiday time with the boys, the memory of the court case had faded, but on returning to England its full impact was inescapable. Lawyers had to be consulted, statements prepared, legalities adhered to. As usual, the press were at her door wanting interviews, taking photographs. Not only was Diana confronted by the worry of the approaching court appearance but by a more immediate worry. Jason's nanny announced she was pregnant and was leaving. This was especially bad news because both Diana and Alan were about to star in a new TV series, *Queenie's Castle*, for Yorkshire television, written expressly for Diana. Once again Alan's parents agreed to care for Jason while the hunt was on for a new nanny – the third in Jason's short life.

Alan's court case was fast-tracked, with the court taking into consideration the fact that he was due to begin work on *Queenie's Castle*. To speed up court proceedings his lawyers advised him to plead guilty. They assumed that since Alan had no previous convictions, the worst that could happen would be a suspended sentence. They assumed wrong. The case was heard on October 16. Yorkshire Television had a car waiting to whisk Diana and Alan away for filming as soon as the hearing was over, so certain was everyone that a prison sentence was not a possibility.

When the judge announced the verdict there was a gasp of disbelief in the courtroom. Three years imprisonment for Leapy Lee, and eighteen months for Alan. It took Diana several minutes to absorb the information. Several curt, cruel sentences uttered by an aging man in a preposterous wig had suddenly shattered her life. Her head dropped as though she could no longer sustain its weight and she burst into tears. A traumatised Alan was led away to the cells. After much negotiation by the lawyers, Diana was allowed a three minute visit with him. The one ray of hope was the immediate decision to appeal the verdict; the lawyers confident the judge's decision would be reversed by an appeal court.

A distraught Diana was driven to Yorkshire without Alan to begin filming the next day. Sustained by the sacrosanct entertainers' adage 'The show must go on', an unwritten obligation as strictly adhered to as the sworn Hippocratic Oath, Diana somehow managed to complete the filming. Everyone working with her was amazed at her resilience and lack of self-pity.

Despite glowing character references from Sir Laurence Olivier and other notables, Alan's appeal was turned down. The wonderful, expansive happiness Diana had experienced in her marriage to Alan was now reduced to a pinpoint – a monthly three hour visit in a remote prison which necessitated a six hour return journey. Their five-star Orchard Manor lifestyle had suddenly dwindled to a depressing, crowded room, shared with other convicts and their tearful relatives. Diana and Alan held hands across a stained, chipped, Formica-topped table, talking over the buzz of conversations emanating from the other tables, their precious moments together inhibited and cramped, overlooked by the entire visiting prison population. It was impossible to be private, let alone intimate. The visits were especially difficult for Diana with prisoners, their visitors and even the guards anxious to catch a glimpse of the famous celebrity. Some people even approached her for autographs.

Once the appeal was over and nothing more could be done, Diana and Alan resigned themselves to serving the prison sentence determined to make the most of their time apart. Alan was a model prisoner. He got along well with the other prisoners and spent much of his free time working on dramatic productions which became so popular they were attended by members of the Women's Institute and other non-inmates. Eventually his sentence was reduced to a year for good behaviour. Diana ticked off each day of that year in her calendar.

Fortunately Diana had been able to find a nanny she could trust to care for Jason, which enabled her to continue working. She was determined to earn sufficient money to repay her debts, according to a repayment schedule which had been set by the court. Her goal was to eliminate the debts and to save as much money as she could for Alan's return.

Even more fortunately she had as much work as she could handle and threw herself into it to the exclusion of everything else. She acted in a film with Raquel Welch in Spain, performed on location in Germany, in cabaret up and down England, and was in various television shows, while making sure to be free for her precious monthly visits with Alan. Her recreation was planning a gala celebration for Alan's release, inviting more than a hundred guests. Each time she returned to Orchard Manor she would sit with Jason, holding him for hours at a time – he was all she had of Alan.

Prisoners regaled Alan with tales of being abandoned by sweethearts and wives who were unable, or unwilling to wait for their release. Not surprisingly, Alan worried about Diana meeting someone else. But there was not the remotest possibility of that happening. On the contrary, being separated from Alan made Diana increasingly aware she had never loved any man the way she loved him. She desired no other lover. Alan had stilled that restless pursuit forever. He was her man and there would be no other. She was fully aware his terrible behaviour had caused the grief they were both now suffering and she certainly did not condone his irresponsibility. But she loved him, loyally, devotedly, through the grief, through the irresponsibility. She yearned for October 16 when he would walk through the prison gates a free man and their happiness would be forever. But, once again, that was not to be.

Chapter 20
The Accidents

At 7am on October 16, 1971 the prison gates opened and Alan Lake walked through them a free man. He looked exceeding handsome, fit and healthy. He had spent a year without alcohol except for the monthly treat Diana managed to smuggle past the guards – vodka mixed with orange juice – still unaware that Alan had a serious alcohol problem. Diana's chauffeur-driven Rolls Royce was waiting to drive him to a friend's nearby house where Diana had arranged a private champagne reception. Alan's release was primetime news and reporters were eager to report his first words as a free man. Alan was only too pleased to oblige.

Before stepping into the Rolls he said, 'It's marvellous to be free again. The first thing I want to do is see Diana and hold her in my arms. Then I'd like a really good breakfast... without porridge.'

Reporters were also waiting at the reception house eager to witness the reunion, the first embrace, the first kiss. Looking her glamorous best in white knee-high boots and a clingy thigh-length dress, Diana willingly posed for photographs with Alan, but refused an interview.

'Sorry boys, no talks,' she smiled.

This was the best day of her life and she wanted to share it with Alan without further delay. Waving goodbye to the reporters, she closed the door and drew the curtains. Finally alone, Alan and Diana toasted Alan's homecoming and their future happiness with an ice-cold bottle of champagne.

On their arrival at Orchard Manor Alan was greeted by a 'Welcome Home' banner spanning the entrance gate, and by his parents, Cyril and Millicent Lake, standing at the gate. Waiting by the door to the house was Jason, in his nanny's arms. Alan was thrilled. When he had last seen him Jason had been just one year old, now he was two. The changes in that year had been spectacular. Jason had been a baby, not yet able to walk. Now he was a little boy and when the nanny set him down, he took a few steps toward Alan.

'He's walking!' Alan exclaimed delighted and scooped Jason up in his arms, beaming with pleasure.

Diana had a surprise present for Alan to welcome him home. She had bought him a splendid grey mare called Sapphire. Diana's plan was to lead Sapphire onto the floodlit lawn on the night of the welcoming party and have her waiting for Alan as his special guest. The plan was a winner. Alan was so overwhelmed he could hardly speak, instead he embraced Diana, holding and kissing her with such tenderness and affection it seemed nothing could ever diminish that love. Friends, gathered on the lawn, clapped and cheered. Emotion ran so high that some of the guests were in tears. The nightmare was over. The lovers were reunited. Alan was handsome, Diana – beautiful. The ever-after fairytale happiness was of mythic dimensions. No one could have anticipated the terrible darkening, the wasting away of such happiness.

* * * * * * *

Almost as soon as he was home Alan got a role in a television drama, acting with Diana. After a year in prison his acting confidence had been severely dented. However, his performance was excellent and fears in that department proved unjustified. But there were other fears to deal with. Alan's resistance to alcohol had been weakened after a year of enforced abstinence. Diana, in her eagerness to indulge him after their long separation, was happy to buy him the finest champagnes, the best whiskies, wanting every blessed moment they had together to be a celebration. The result was to kick start a habit which was to become a merciless addiction.

On February, 1972, just four months after his release from prison, Alan was out riding Sapphire at a nearby park. He loved his early morning rides and, deliciously invigorated, he was heading back to Orchard Manor when calamity struck. He was suddenly confronted by a partially fallen tree with a low overhanging branch. He bent down to avoid his head being struck by the branch only to be struck in the back instead. The blow was so severe it wrenched him off the horse. He fell crashing on to a tree stump breaking his back, shoulder and ribs. To make matters worse, other horse riders tried to help by pulling Alan to his feet and encouraging him to walk, instead of making sure he did not move until the ambulance came. By the time Alan arrived at the hospital he was barely conscious.

Diana received a phone call telling her Alan had been in an accident. When she got to the hospital she found him in a room reserved for the dying. The doctor told her even if he did survive he would never walk again. Diana stayed by Alan's bedside all through the night, willing him to live. She talked to the unconscious Alan, caressing his face, stroking his hair, kissing his eyes, telling him how much she loved him, how much she needed him, how much Jason needed him, massaging his hands, whispering her fantasies into his ears.

When the sun rose, Alan opened his eyes and smiled.

'I made it' he whispered. 'Darling, I made it.'

Then, attempting to turn towards Diana, he winced, his face contorted in pain. Overjoyed and perturbed at the same time Diana called for painkillers. The pain was agonizing, and even the morphine injections administered at regular intervals eased it only for a short time.

When Alan had arrived at the hospital in a semi-coma, he had heard the directions given to the staff:

'Put him in a side ward, then when he pops off he won't disturb the other patients.'

From that moment he was determined to recover. The doctors were astounded by his progress. They had told him he would be confined to a wheelchair for the rest of his life, would never be able to stand, let alone walk, and would lose the use of his right arm.

To this Alan replied, 'Have you ever seen a one-armed wheelchair man? They go around in fucking circles.'

And when the doctor suggested an electric wheelchair, he said, 'That'd be great. I'd be halfway to the pub and I'd run out of battery juice.'

Alan was resolved to confound the doctors. When he stood up for the first time the doctors were amazed and when he took several steps around the bed, they were speechless. After only three weeks he was allowed to leave the hospital in a wheelchair. He still suffered excruciating pain and needed an extended period of rest to make a full recovery, but he was alive and even walking, although with difficulty.

Diana's greatest joy would have been to care for Alan and nurse him back to health. But this was not possible. She was now the sole breadwinner and had to be constantly employed to keep them afloat. She would creep out of bed for an early studio call, trying not to wake him. But no matter what the hour, Alan would not allow her to leave without a kiss and a blessing. While Diana was out working,

Alan was confined at home with Jason and the new nanny. For a while he was able to entertain himself, reading, writing poetry and entertaining Jason. Jason, now close to three years old and just about able to hold a conversation, revelled in his father's attention. Alan played with him and read him stories, acting out different characters, changing his voice for each character to Jason's delight. Jason began to imitate him and they acted out scenes together, Jason squealing with pleasure. If Jason benefited from Alan's convalescence, Alan himself grew increasingly impatient and discontent.

1972 was a difficult year for both Alan and Diana. Diana worked hard, making three films while having to contend with Alan's enforced inactivity and growing restlessness. The one thing that pleased her was acting in *The Amazing Mr. Blunden*, a family ghost drama. She was delighted to be working with her good friend, Lionel Jeffries after a break of 20 years. The film was one of the highlights of her acting career. She played the horrid Mrs Wickens, an evil, repulsive woman, grotesquely ugly, her face disfigured by a large wart on her nose. She had never played such a role and worked hard to get the character just right. Diana was certainly not wed to her image, that of a glamorous sex icon. On the contrary, she enjoyed dismantling that image, grateful to be given the opportunity to portray a character that would dispel it and allow her a serious acting role, something she always hoped for.

As days turned into weeks, and then months, the situation at home deteriorated. Fearful of becoming addicted to morphine, Alan relied more and more on alcohol to ease his pain. With increasing frequency Diana would return from a difficult day at the studio to find him drunk and belligerent, resentful that she was working while he was unable to do so. Frustration and inactivity worsened Alan's drinking. As his body grew physically stronger, his will grew weaker and his dependency on alcohol increased until it began to seriously affect their lives. On a brief holiday to France, Alan began hallucinating and later, in Canada, where he accompanied Diana for a television show, he was constantly drunk, and behaved abominably. On the way back to England after an appalling weekend in New York because of Alan's drunken behaviour, Diana had to plead with the airline staff to allow him on the plane – his reputation had preceded him.

By now, although Diana had enough evidence to convince her that Alan was addicted to alcohol, she resisted acknowledging this, excusing his drinking as a temporary situation, blaming it on his recent misfortunes – his prison ordeal, his horrendous accident, and his terrible pain. Although her friends, aware of the anguish Alan's drinking was causing Diana, tried to convince her to leave him, she loved him unconditionally and was prepared to see him through what she considered was just an extremely difficult period. But she was beginning to worry about the effects Alan's drinking would have on Jason. She was anxious to avoid subjecting Jason to their arguments about drinking, often bitter, often loud. When he was sober Alan agreed with her, he promised to stop drinking, for Jason's sake, for Diana's sake, for his own sake. He would vow to quit, apologise for his behaviour, behave rationally, convincingly. But, in the grip of an uncontrollable craving, the promises were soon broken, the vows consigned to the bottle bin.

Diana was delighted when Alan began working again, thinking work would cure his drinking, or at least curb it. She was especially pleased with his starring role in the film *The Swordsman*, which gave him the opportunity to utilise his amazing fencing skill. Although he managed to stay sober when he was actually working, he began drinking as soon as he was not. Diana found him impossible to deal with when he was intoxicated. He was rude, he ranted, he raved, he created frightening scenes, he hallucinated, he didn't know who he was and neither did she. The day after a drunken orgy he could remember nothing and was humiliated when Diana recounted how obnoxious his behaviour had been. On the rare occasions they visited friends for an evening out, the next morning Alan would ask Diana, 'Did I have a good time?' Finally Diana was forced to recognise that Alan had graduated from a heavy drinker to an alcoholic and that professional help was needed.

It was about this time that both Diana and Alan became involved with Catholicism. After one especially harrowing night, Jason's nanny suggested to Alan that he go to church as a comforting experience. There was a Catholic church next door to Orchard Manor run by The Italian Brothers. Diana had already met one of them, Father Fontonari, who she was fond of. Alan found the church experience so rewarding it wasn't long before he embraced the Catholic religion. He discovered in Catholicism a faith he could submit to and in submitting he experienced a profound sense of tranquillity and peace, a haven from his chaotic alcoholic existence. He knew he was out of control and needed a centre, a focus to keep him from spinning into space and disintegrating into a thousand pieces; or being sucked into the dark hole of remorse and helplessness. The Church seemed to provide the centre of healing he so desperately needed.

Having found a restorative power in Catholicism he was eager for Diana to embrace it as well. Diana wasn't keen. She had always hated hypocrisy and found an abundance of hypocrisy in churchgoers, who preached one thing and lived another. She found Catholicism questionable in that it allowed its practitioners to commit any manner of sin as long as they confessed the sin to a priest. Her main experience with religion had been that of condemnation; first in Hollywood by the Women's Catholic Guild of America, and closer to home by the Archbishop of Canterbury; both upholders of religion, both denouncing her as a 'wanton hussy'. However, if religion helped Alan with his alcoholism, she would gladly become a Catholic.

Alan with his beautiful singing voice was a great favourite with the Brothers, and especially with Father Fontonari, who offered him reassurance that his life was a valuable one, even when he despaired of his worthlessness, and his destructive behaviour. He found a source of strength in the Church and in Father Fontonari, who had become a great friend and mentor to both himself and Diana. Under his guidance they studied religion, taking instruction for about a year. After crossing various hurdles, especially that of Diana having been divorced, divorce being anathema to Catholics, they were eventually received into the Catholic Church.

Then, as though Diana hadn't had enough to contend with in 1972, the following year she was performing a cabaret act in Wakefield, a town in Northern England, when she accidentally slipped on a stair and broke her ankle. This time it was Alan's turn to rush to the hospital. Diana required an operation to place a pin in her ankle and Alan arranged for her to be transferred closer to home so he could care for her. Diana was totally out of commission for three months, confined to bed, helpless and dependant. Her main consolation was Father Fontonari's visits, and managing to go to church pushed in a wheelchair. Later, she made good use of the incident in her cabaret shows.

'A little while back I broke my ankle,' she would say in a tone overflowing with pathos.'

The audience would respond with a sympathetic, 'Ah…'

'I did it falling off the bishop.'

While her ankle was still healing she was approached to do a film in Sweden. The producers were so keen to have Diana they were willing for her to act the part in a wheelchair. It was just what Diana needed to restore her spirit. Alan went to Sweden with her. Confined to a wheelchair she required his help for nearly everything. Despite undertaking the responsibility of caring for her and promising to refrain from alcohol, Alan was unable to do so. Diana had to deal not only with her injury and her acting role, but with his drunkenness.

In early 1974 Diana received a great honour. She was offered the much sought-after role of Queen Jocasta in the Greek tragedy *Oedipus*, to be performed at the prestigious Chichester Festival Theatre. King Oedipus was murdered by his son who then, unknowingly, married his mother Queen Jocasta. Diana was thrilled. It was the highest compliment her acting ability could have received, a supreme accolade. The critics were confounded by the choice. One said it was comparable to casting Laurence Olivier in the role of Peanuts. The opening performance took place in the summer of 1974, to mixed reviews, some highly complimentary, some not. Shortly after the *Oedipus* run she began work on a television drama, a thriller called *Nurse Will Make it Better*, in which she played a malicious, manipulating nurse, who annihilates an entire family, a role Diana could relate to after her experiences with nurse Amy.

Meanwhile, life at home continued as before. Jason was in the care of a new nanny while Diana worked. Alan worked intermittently and was usually drunk and difficult when she returned home exhausted after a late performance. That autumn, after *Nurse Will Make it Better* was completed, she insisted on spending time at home with Jason. Jason was now almost five and Diana felt she hardly knew him having spent most of her waking hours working, often far from home. She was determined to devote all her time and energy to being with Jason, making up for lost time. She discovered a bright, sensitive child who delighted her with his imaginative observations. She enjoyed being with her son, playing with him, reading to him, telling him stories, taking him on visits, sometimes with Alan, sometimes on their own, lavishing the love and affection he had been denied because of her heavy work schedule and long absences.

That November, with Diana at home, Alan was drinking less, and they enjoyed a semblance of family life, mainly centred on Jason. Diana and Alan had discussed the possibility of a celebration for their sixth wedding anniversary, as well as Alan's birthday, as both would come later that month. Alan had even planned a surprise dinner for Diana at one of their favourite restaurants. But none of that was to be. Instead, disaster struck once again.

One evening Diana went to bed early complaining of a terrible headache and pains throughout her body. Next morning the pain was unbearable. Her head felt like it was being drilled from the inside and pounded from the outside. She was both burning with fever and shivering with cold. The doctor was called and then the ambulance. Diana was rushed to a specialist hospital in London in a coma. Meningitis was confirmed, a killer disease that, at best, leaves one deaf, blind, paralyzed or all three. The doctor told Alan there was little hope of Diana surviving the night. Alan was in tears, beside himself with anguish. He sat by Diana's bedside hour after hour willing her to live, just as she had sat by his bedside, willing him to live less than three years earlier.

When Alan took a quick break at a nearby pub he was accosted by journalists waiting for news of Diana, but he had none to give. As he was leaving the pub glasses were raised in a toast to Diana's health.

Someone said, 'You go back there and tell her that we are all rooting for her. She's one of the all-time great birds.'

Around midnight Diana opened her eyes, reached for Alan's hand and said, 'Hello Darling.'

Alan breathed a sigh of relief and the entire nation breathed with him. The ordeal was over. Diana had survived.

Chapter 21
Innocence Lost

Diana opened her eyes to a room filled with flowers and cards from not only all across the UK but also from the U.S, Australia, even Japan. There were phone calls from Hollywood, from friends, from people she had worked with, from celebrities such as Joan Crawford and Myrna Loy. She was overwhelmed by the outpouring of affection and love. 'You're part of Britain, part of our bricks and mortar,' one message read. Another stated, 'Life just wouldn't be the same without you.'

After several weeks, on December 3, 1973, Diana was discharged from the hospital. Like Alan's amazing recovery hers was equally miraculous. Although not in optimal health, she had been spared all the usual afflictions of the disease. However, instead of taking it easy as she had been advised, within weeks she was rehearsing the play, *Murder Mistaken* in which Alan was to play the male lead. Diana hoped that working together would be a positive experience for both of them, helping him to drink less. She was wrong. If Diana's illness was the reason for Alan decreasing his drinking, her recovery was the reason for increasing it by way of celebration. He drank not only before the show, but during the show and after the show.

To add to her difficulties, only months after the meningitis attack Diana discovered she was pregnant. The doctors recommended a termination. The baby was due in October 1974, when she would be 44. Not only was her age an obstacle but she had just pulled through a serious illness and was not yet fully recovered. At first she agreed to the termination but when the day came she was unable to go through with it. Earlier that year, after much objection from the Catholic hierarchy, she had been officially accepted into the Catholic Church with its unequivocal anti-abortion stand, equating abortion with murder. A termination of her pregnancy would mean she could never again, in good faith, enter the church, and how would she be able to face Father Fontonari? In the end she decided against the abortion. In May of that year she announced her pregnancy to the press and, once again, the nation rejoiced.

The decision against termination had been a difficult one, but once having made it both Diana and Alan were delighted to be having another child. Diana felt it was important for Jason to have a sibling, remembering her experience as an only child and her longing for a brother. She decided to spend the months of her pregnancy at home preparing both herself and Jason for the new arrival. The nanny had left and Diana did not hire a new one. Jason would soon be five and she wanted to care for him on her own, a privilege they had both been deprived of throughout his babyhood. She felt blessed to be able to do so now.

'This wonderful, unexpected pregnancy is the greatest gift of my tranquil middle age,' she said. 'I truly believe that life for me is beginning at forty… well, nearly forty-four.'

The 'unexpected pregnancy' also allowed her to come to know Jason as she had never known Mark and Gary; to anticipate his tears, placate his fears, hold and console him, encourage his love of animals, to entice his appetite as he was a poor eater, take him to and from nursery school, and to protect him from the worst of Alan's excesses. She found great pleasure in just being with him, in just looking at him. He was a beautiful child with blue eyes sparkling with the promises of life, unruly blond hair that escaped the comb and lips like hers, generous and often in a pout, although for different reasons. They watched television together, read together, even baked cakes together. And when Alan was sober, a more frequent occurrence now that Diana was pregnant, they took Jason to the circus, to the zoo, to the sea, for picnics and were a family together.

Diana did her best to involve Jason in the baby's arrival. They went shopping for baby furniture, for a bouncer, for soft toys, many chosen by Jason; they bought yellow baby clothes, a neutral colour because Diana didn't know if the baby would be a boy or girl, although Jason was sure it was a boy. He wanted his own baby brother to tease and to play with like other children in his nursery school had. Jason helped to paint the nursery yellow and was consulted on its decorations. As the time drew nearer he grew more and more excited and began to include the baby in his life.

Jason had an amazing memory and was able to recite poems by heart. He would listen to the baby's heartbeat, stroke Diana's belly and recite poems especially for the baby. And when Diana told him stories he lifted her blouse so the baby could hear them too. His favourite stories, the ones he wanted to hear over and over again, were those Diana told him about the time she was a little girl and had wanted to become an actress although no one except her mother believed that would ever happen, and about all the secret things she had done to prove them wrong. And so the months went by.

Although Diana felt well during the pregnancy, her raised blood pressure caused some concern and was closely monitored. Then one day, toward the end of summer, she and Alan were relaxing together on the sofa when she suddenly felt a strange sensation convulse her body. It was so disturbing that she burst into tears. Alan covered her with blankets and calmed her down. She recovered quickly telling Alan that perhaps she had caught a cold when she and Jason had opened a country festival the previous day. But when she was next examined by her doctor he could not hear the baby's heartbeat, and he informed her there was a possibility the baby had died. However, since this could not be confirmed, a termination was out of the question. Diana went home to wait. The possibility of having a dead baby inside her was a terrible thing to contemplate but, with her usual positive approach to life she put the thought out of her mind and was optimistic and hopeful, eagerly anticipating the birth.

On August 28, she began to experience labour pains. Since her due date was less than two months away, she was prepared for a premature delivery and hoped the baby would be the girl she had long wished for, a sister for Jason. That day Diana was home alone. Jason had a great fascination for the sea and Alan, wanting to give Diana some time by herself, had taken him to the seaside. (Living by the sea was what Jason wished for when he came to emulate his mother's childhood wishing ritual.) When Alan and Jason returned home they found a distressed Diana waiting for the ambulance. Alan was at his best when coping with a crisis. He was reassuring, telling Diana he would be at the hospital just as soon as he arranged for someone to look after Jason, and would be at her side throughout the birth. He organised everything Diana needed for the hospital. He kept her calm, even cheerful.

Just as Diana was about to depart, Jason, with uncanny insight said, 'Are you going to lose the baby Mummy?'

The previous week Jason had an especially vivid dream about his baby brother. When he asked his brother, 'Will I have to be sharing everything with you?' The reply was, 'No, because I won't be there.'

Alan rushed to the hospital to be with Diana and experience the birth with her. But, alas, the baby was stillborn. It weighed just 3 pounds 2 ounces, a tiny, pathetic infant. Diana did not see the baby, but Alan, who did, broke down weeping uncontrollably outside the delivery room. The baby, a boy, looked exactly like the infant Jason.

The difference in the way Diana and Alan dealt with the tragic death of their baby was indicative of their emotional resilience, their inner strength. Although Alan was great in a crisis, where there was something he could do to make things better, he fell apart in a tragedy where there was nothing he could do. Although he had been a source of strength and reassurance when Diana was worried she was carrying a dead baby, he crumbled when the baby was confirmed stillborn. Although he had cut down on his drinking during Diana's pregnancy, he now rushed for the bottle. A drunken, hysterical Alan caused such mayhem in the hospital, cursing, raging against his impotence, banging the walls, accosting the staff with outbursts fuelled by maudlin self-pity, the staff insisted Diana get rid of him. Exhausted from the harrowing birth and terrible grief, she now had the embarrassing task of coping with Alan's drunken behaviour, eventually persuading a friend to take him home.

Diana, on the other hand, was anxious to avoid expressions of pity. Not wishing to be looked after, she discharged herself after a few days. Diana was from the school of 'pull up your socks and get on with it'. Alan was of the 'hit the bottle' school when things went wrong, and 'hit the bottle even harder' when they went very wrong. When Diana returned from the hospital one of the first things she did was to phone her agent asking him to get her some work. A few days later she was a guest on the popular television show *Celebrity Squares*. The very first thing Alan did when he got home was to get blotto drunk. He hit the pubs with such ferocity that a few days later he was found passed out in a ditch.

Things went from bad to impossible. Aside from having to deal with Jason's terrible disappointment, Diana had to cope with Alan's drinking problem which was spiralling out of control. She was at her wits' end, no longer able to cope with it. She had learned to tolerate waking up for an early call to overflowing beer-soaked ashtrays and whisky glasses containing twists of cigarette butts and to the reek of stale air, after Alan and his friends had spent the night on yet another drunken escapade; she understood how the tensions of the acting profession caused actors to become heavy drinkers; she understood Alan's vulnerabilities, his insecurities, his fears and the contrasting bravado drink gave him; and she certainly understood how the grief of the death of their baby had turned Alan to alcohol for solace and relief. What she did not understand and refused to tolerate was Alan's offensive, irrational behaviour, his rudeness to guests, his ignorance of how what he was doing had the potential of violence to herself, even to Jason; how he suddenly, without warning, became a dangerous Mr Hyde. His behaviour was so worrying, so erratic she feared leaving him on his own. But when she took him along to a cabaret performance he behaved so atrociously he was expelled from the club and Diana was told never to bring him anywhere near the premises again.

One of Diana's major concerns was the impact of Alan's alcoholism on Jason. When Alan was at his worst he was oblivious of Jason's presence, and unconcerned for his well-being. He would rant incoherently, hallucinate, swear; entangled in a world no one else could enter. Jason adored his dad, delighted in his company, found him hilariously funny, but there were times when he feared him, feared his wild, angry look, his stormy eyes, his dishevelled clothes and he hated the incessant bitter rows between his parents, often hiding away and blocking his ears. Something had to be done. Even Alan agreed. In his sober moments he was mortified by reports of his behaviour, but these periodic bouts of humiliation and remorse weren't enough to stop his drinking. He desperately wanted to put things right for Diana and Jason but was trapped in a cycle over which he no longer had any control. Finally, at Diana's insistence, he checked into a treatment centre for alcoholics.

After undergoing a nightmare of abstinence, painful vitamin jabs and heavy self-assessments, he was discharged in less than a month, completely cured. Diana hardly recognised him. She felt as though she was living with a new man, or more poignantly, with the man she had married, caring, kind, funny and with the bonus of being wonderful with Jason. Diana remembered all the reasons she had loved him and loved him still. Life returned to the blessing it had once been.

With Alan in a state of grace, Diana decided on a trip to Hollywood to visit Mark and Gary. She missed her sons terribly and the prospect of spending an entire month with them was heaven-sent. Alan had not seen the boys for three years. It was six years since they had seen Jason at his christening and, of course, Jason had never seen them. They were both teenagers now, good-looking, mischievous and confident. The holiday was a great time for everyone. Alan got along famously with both boys, Mark and Gary were delighted to meet their little brother, enjoyed playing with him, and especially enjoyed teasing him, inventing tricks to momentarily confuse and terrify him, revelling in all the big brother antics they had been denied for so long.

They spent a great weekend in Las Vegas, with Mark and Gary eager to see Jason's reactions to the wonders of that city, Jason following his brothers like an excited puppy, looking up to them as though they were the last word on just about everything, wanting to do whatever they did, and they in turn, although pretending annoyance, were amused and flattered. Even Dickie was amiable, inviting them to a dinner he prepared himself. Now wealthy, famous and with a lovely woman in his life he was willing to forgive the past, even if only temporarily. For Diana, parting from the boys was heart-wrenching, with promises of an early return the only consolation.

Then after months of bliss, months of the happiest times they had together, Alan relapsed. The news that his mother had cancer was a major contributing factor. But this relapse was more horrific than anything that had come before it. He picked fights for no discernible reason, 'I don't like your face. I think you're a cunt.' Cars were smashed, drunk and disorderly charges entailed court appearances, expulsions from clubs and restaurants after creating embarrassing scenes became routine, humiliating Diana to the point where she refused to be seen with him. Alcoholic binges became more frequent. Alan would disappear for days, sleeping by roadsides or in fields, found in a drunken stupor where he didn't know day from night. Once he was discovered with his hair and face frozen into the side of a ditch.

Diana, anxious to protect Jason from the terrifying behaviour of an alcoholic father, would often leave the house taking Jason to a hotel. The hotel escapes became more and more frequent and lasted longer and longer. In fact, Diana and Jason became regular guests at the luxurious Sky Line Hotel. Jason loved staying in the hotel, he loved the adventure, the thrill of calling for room service, of riding the elevators, but he especially loved having his mother in close proximity with all her attention focused on him. He was quick to suss out that hotel visits occurred after his father had numerous drinks. He would watch patiently as Alan's glass became empty and if the inevitable 'Jase, dear boy, pour me another,' was delayed, he would prompt, 'Same again, Dad?' eagerly anticipating another hotel adventure.

But if Jason had a love/hate relationship with his father's alcoholism, Diana's was one of unmitigated hatred. At one point after several especially bitter scenes, Diana took Jason to a friend's house in Brighton for an indefinite period.

'I don't care what you do with your life,' she told Alan, 'But you're not going to ruin Jason's'.

However, after several days she received news that Alan was seriously ill and required hospitalisation. Diana and Jason rushed home to find Alan so dehydrated he was at death's door. This time Alan was hospitalised for a month and vowed he would never again succumb to alcohol, a vow he was unable to keep. For a while all went well but then the inevitable happened, the stresses and strains of work, of lack of work, of his mother's incurable cancer, of the struggle to stay off alcohol, set the old pattern in motion; punch-ups, drunk and disorderly charges, wild all-night drug and alcohol sessions with friends like Oliver Reed and the rarely sober Richard Harris, hallucinations, a complete rerun of those places where Alan found his solace.

Despite advice from friends, who were fed up with Diana's patience in dealing with Alan's alcoholism, Diana would not leave him. After a drinking bout he would be on great form with an instant reversion to his better self: charming, loving, amusing, the ideal husband and father. There were no tell-tale hangovers. It was as though he had rid himself of the hostility, the terror, the acute frustration that lay buried somewhere inside him. He even managed to work when work was available. But only until the next alcoholic plunge into oblivion. Diana considered his alcoholism an illness and was determined to help him get through it whatever it took. She would not give up hope, would not abandon him to his devils. But she wanted to shield Jason from the rows, the upsets, the drunken episodes. So, with a heavy heart she sent Jason off to boarding school.

Jason hated boarding school. Discipline wasn't his strong point and sleeping in a dorm with early lights-out, strict clean-ups, and a punishment regime was not his idea of a good time. He was accustomed to being indulged, adored, loved unconditionally and he was especially accustomed to being with adults, even being treated like one by his parents' fascinating and exciting friends. As a matter of fact Diana, concerned about Jason's involvement in the adult world complained to Alan, saying, 'Jason should have more of a childhood, it's such a precious thing.'

But Jason, who saw no point in enshrining a childhood which curbed his freedom, parted him from his pets, and prevented him from watching his father's sex films, didn't take long to plan his escape from the dreaded boarding school. Dressed in a shirt and pyjama bottoms, because he was unable to locate his trousers as it was still dark, he walked eighteen miles to return home. But instead of being welcomed by comforting arms and exclamations of joy, there was no one to greet him as his parents were in Australia on Diana's book promotion tour – she had already written her first book by then. He tried to enter the house via the cat flap but discovered he was bigger than their biggest cat, Nick, a super-sized Siamese, nick-named 'Fat Ass'. Exhausted and hungry he sat on the doorstep to wait.

Eventually, Mr Howard, the headmaster, alarmed by Jason's absence, informed the police he was missing. But when the police came looking for him, he hid, fearing the consequences of his delinquency. However, after several hours of waiting in the cold, and not happy with the approaching dark, when the police came a second time he gave himself up. The offer of a Mars bar went a long way in convincing him to hand himself over to the police without a struggle. Instead of the punishment he feared, the headmaster, thankful to have him back without injury or trauma, which would have alerted the newspapers and given the school a bad name, merely said, 'If you have any problems, come and see me first before you run away again'. However, like everything else involving Diana, her son running away from school was splashed all over the newspapers, to Mr Howard's dismay. Although Jason detested boarding school he never ran away again. Aware of his mother's ambivalent relationship with the press he was determined to deprive the newspapers of further copy.

Throughout this period of upheaval Diana still had to work and earn money, burdened by tax debts and high maintenance expenses. She appeared on television shows, in cabaret acts, unenthusiastically guest starring in several unremarkable sex romps – film work was work and there wasn't much of it around at the time – and in a television adaptation of the *Just William* stories, where Jason, too, had an acting role, his first, as one of the gang members. She even wrote her first book, *For Adults Only* in 1978 and then her second *Behind Closed Dors* in 1979, and while Jason was still in boarding school she went on a promotional book tour, selling books to the shops with a value of £100,000, a most necessary supplement to her earnings, as film work was practically non-existent.

In the Seventies the British film industry experienced a severe dip, due in part to the advent of television with its big budget possibilities and exciting potential. Both in the U.S and in Britain the film industry was entering a period of recession. Rank, the dominant force in British film production was in the process of closing up shop. The few films being made were cheapies revolving around horror and sex. Diana was appalled by the film scene with its emphasis on sex and nudity.

In 1977 she said, 'I hate what is happening to British cinema today. I still get sent film scripts but I reject them with alarming regularity. They're nearly all pornographic. I never have taken my clothes off and I refuse to do so now.'

Diana's style was based on suggestion, tease, nuance, not outright brash nudity which left nothing to the imagination.

The incursion of pornography into Britain was highly influenced by the U.S where hardcore porn films were becoming practically acceptable. It's almost axiomatic that where the U.S goes, Britain follows. A repressed, moralistic Britain was not yet ready for hardcore porn films like the 1972 American film *Deep Throat*, but soft porn films were slowly becoming respectable under the guise of 'Adult Films'.

Mary Millington, an outspoken campaigner against censorship, was the British porn queen and 'sex superstar' of the Seventies. She acted in illegally made hardcore porn films sold under the counter, and opened her own sex shops which were continuously raided by the police. Although the permissive Sixties had set the stage for sexual freedom, Britain was not quite prepared for the Millington crusade, and she was always in trouble with the law. But that did not stop her assault on hypocritical morality and censorship.

'I love sex and I intend to carry on making a living from it,' she declared. 'I don't consider anything I do to be obscene.'

In 1978 Alan acted in a film with Mary Millington called *Playbirds*, a combination of violence and sex, with an abundance of naked flesh, titillating see-through negligees and culminating with Millington dead and topless in the bath tub. The film, whose virtue was neither acting, plot, direction or production was nevertheless a box office success and led to the follow-up *Confessions from the David Galaxy Affair* in 1979. This time the cast included not only Alan Lake and Mary Millington, the porn duo, but Tony Booth who was to become the father-in-law of Prime Minister Tony Blair.

Alan played a sex-obsessed, fraudulent astrologer who converts astrological readings into sexual encounters, his main achievement being his encounter with the frigid Millicent Cumming (Mary Millington), aptly named because he provides Miss Cumming with her first orgasm. Diana had a role in the film as Galaxy's landlady, but it was mainly to watch over Alan who seemed to be having too much fun. Whereas many actors reluctantly accepted roles in these cheap, often humiliating films to keep themselves off the dole, Alan revelled in them. Diana must have dropped her guard, because Alan, who was expected to keep his underpants on during filmed sexual encounters was discovered playing them blissfully naked.

'These sex scenes are a laugh,' he declared. 'You have five birds between the sheets and they're all trying to get you excited... It's a great feeling lying back with a line of women all queuing up to throw themselves stark naked at you. But they don't get very far. When it's over I'm Alan Lake again and then it's back home to the missus.'

Diana had to settle for the 'back home to the missus' assurance and the fact that Alan was at least earning money, a welcome boost to their finances, and, most importantly, with the knowledge that when he was working he wasn't drinking.

'I may be an alcoholic, but I'm an actor first,' he maintained.

Diana, whose pet hatreds were hypocrisy and lies, admired Mary Millington's honesty and her courageous stand against the hypocrites of censorship. Millington had originally become involved in the porn business to fund the expensive medication and treatment her ailing mother needed which further endeared her to Diana. The two women became good friends and Millington was a regular guest at Orchard Manor, invited to bring her girlfriends to spice up Diana's parties; parties which increasingly appealed to Jason as he approached puberty. When Mary Millington committed suicide in August 1979 at the age of 33, Diana and Alan were the only celebrities who dared to attend her funeral.

When Alan wasn't involved in acting, it wasn't long before he was back on the bottle. Although alcohol provided him with his choice intoxicant, drugs played an important role in his quest for the ultimate high, a quest which inevitably had its effect on Jason. At the tender age of five, Jason's nursery education was supplemented by an introduction to the joys of recreational drugs. Often, when Diana was away working, Alan and several choice friends would have a special party that went on all night and then some. Early one morning, on one such occasion, Jason was awakened by raucous laughter and wandered into the room where Alan and friends were still at it. The party was in full swing, several friends sprawled on Diana's cream sofa, some on the floor reclining amongst the satin embroidered cushions, and all of them falling about with laughter. The laughter grew even more hilarious at the sight of little tousled-haired Jason standing in the doorway, wiping the sleep and confusion from his eyes, wearing pyjamas featuring a grinning Mickey Mouse face with tiny dangling feet.

'Come to Uncle, Jase my boy,' said Andrew Ray, an intimate friend of Ronnie Kray, between gulps of laughter, beckoning Jason to the sofa and pulling him onto his lap.

Jason, suddenly wide-awake, watched with increasing curiosity and fascination as something that looked like a giant white jelly bean was circulated, then broken and inhaled, followed by fits of laughter. He didn't hear anything funny being said, as a matter of fact he didn't hear anything at all being said and worked out that the joke was somehow embedded in the sweet.

When Andrew was passed the mysterious sweet, Jason said, 'I want a funny candy too. Please can I have one.'

'No Jase,' Alan managed, convulsed with laughter enhanced by Jason's 'funny candy' observation, 'It's not for you.'

Unaccustomed to refusals and knowing that persistence was ultimately rewarded, Jason continued to beg and plead.

'Please...please...please.'

'Let the lad have some fun,' Andrew said, chocking with laughter. 'Here Jase, my boy, take a sniff of this.'

Alan either didn't hear or was too out of reach to care. And so Jason joined the party, laughing and screeching with delight until his belly ached. The only stipulation on offer was Andrew's warning, delivered between spasms of laughter.

'Jase, this is our secret, you must promise not to say anything to anyone about it.'

Jason promised.

After this early induction into the world of elite recreation, Jason had to wait until he was nine before he could explore the realms of drug-induced euphoria any further. During one of Alan's alcohol remissions, Diana decided the three of them would visit Mark and Gary. Several years had passed since their last Hollywood holiday. Although Diana had been to see the boys taking Jason with her in the interval, Alan had been working and unable to come.

That visit had been a brief, unfulfilled one. Diana had been aware for some time that Mark and Gary bore a grudge of resentment towards her. They were curt and uncommunicative when she phoned, rarely contacted her and never acknowledged the birthday and Christmas presents she never forgot to send. No wonder. She discovered in one of her rare telephone exchanges with Mark that he and Gary had never received the gifts. In an attempt to convince the boys their mother didn't love them, Amy had withheld everything.

'You see,' she would say, 'She couldn't even be bothered sending you a Christmas present.'

There were also other resentments, fuelled by Dickie, that Diana wanted to sort out. But mainly she wanted to express her love for the boys and explain away any reservations they had concerning that love. But that had not happened. Diana and Jason had stayed in a hotel, unable for various reasons to have the intimate encounter she desired. She felt thwarted. It rained. After a week they returned to England.

But this time things were different. Diana had rented Rod Stewart's sumptuous house for a month. The weather was perfect. Mark and Gary were welcoming having looked forward to the visit, and Amy was dead; she had died of cancer in the summer of 1974. Alan hardly recognised the boys, they had grown into young men; good-looking, witty, sophisticated. They were both involved in show business careers. Gary, whose idol was Mick Jagger, played the guitar and the piano and wrote his own songs. Mark was in especially good form, having broken up with his girlfriend he was now in love again. Both Mark and Gary were eager to spend time at the Rod Stewart house. They were both down on Dickie, complaining of constant arguments, fed up with his attempts to control their lives and were pleased to get away from Dickie and the house. The close relationship Alan had with the boys as children became even closer now. Perhaps too close.

Jason was thrilled to be spending so much time with his brothers, unlike the last visit when he was six, now at nine he felt grown-up and entitled to partake in everything they did. One day he returned unexpectedly from an outing to find Mark, Gary and Alan smoking a bong – a water pipe designed to give a superior cannabis hit. They were having a great time laughing and joking.

Jason watched the merriment for a few minutes and anxious to be part of the fun, said 'Let me have a go. I want to try that.' He pestered them until they relented, which didn't take too long. 'All we need now is the candy,' Jason said, recalling his first drug experience. However, 'candy' was a Hollywood synonym for cocaine and the boys fell about laughing. And so Jason had his second experience with the world of forbidden pleasures, and then his third, and fourth, and fifth.

Diana did not partake in the bong excursions. Although aware of their existence she chose not to be concerned. Delighted to have her sons with her, she was reluctant to rock the boat. Besides, in the hip, trendy circles, marijuana was preferred to alcohol, especially among the young who considered it part of the revolt against their parents' generation of double standards, pretence and subterfuge; far less harmful than alcohol and intricately bound up with the philosophical assertions of 'love' and 'peace'.

Not only did Gary become pals with Alan, he became especially close to Diana. Whereas he found it impossible to communicate with his father he found it easy to talk to his mother, who was in tune with the music scene, and a darling of some of the high-profile musicians like the Beatles, Elton John, Rod Stewart and many more.

Shortly before they were due to return to England, Gary said, 'I can't stand living with Dad anymore.'

Almost before the words were out of his mouth, Diana said, 'Then come live with us.'

The idea found favour with all concerned. Dickie, who had always been resistant to the boys living with Diana, even to them so much as visiting her, leapt at the opportunity to get rid of a worrying teenager who was already in difficulty with the law. Jason was delighted, Alan and Gary were by now buddies, and Diana was ecstatic, she would at last have one of her estranged sons living with her, something she had always longed for.

Diana's greatest sorrow had been her relationship, or rather her lack of relationship, with Mark and Gary. She had wanted desperately to be a mother to them, and knew she had failed miserably. She had rationalised that failure with elaborate explanations and excuses, but that didn't suffice. No matter how satisfied she was with various aspects of her life, the failure at motherhood gnawed at her, was always hovering, even in her most successful moments. Now she would have the opportunity to make amends, however modest, or so she thought.

Chapter 22
The Ultimate Punch in the Eye

One of Gary's main aims in coming to England was to further his music career and, he no doubt saw his mother, a five star celebrity with close connections in the music world, as a means to that end. Diana, on her part, anxious to make up for the years of neglect was determined to promote Gary's career with everything at her disposal. She enrolled the seventeen year old in a prestigious music school. She introduced him to her high profile musician friends who invited him to their studios for jamming and recording sessions. She initiated showbiz introductions. She took advantage of any publicity opportunity, not averse to concocting outrageous publicity stunts. One of the most audacious was choreographed with the help of her agent, the infamous Max Clifford.

One of the first things Diana did was buy Gary a car and one of the first things Gary did was crash the car into a parked vehicle. Thinking no one had observed the accident he attempted to make an unseen getaway. However, a passer-by had witnessed the hit-and-run incident and reported it to the police. Gary was arrested, charged with multiple offences and a court date was set.

The outcome could have had dire consequences as, aside from the hit-and-run and reckless driving charges, Gary was driving without a licence and without insurance. However Diana, together with Max Clifford, managed to convert a near disaster into a triumph. Taking advantage of the court proceedings with the attending reporters, photographers and packed courtroom they staged a cheeky publicity stunt.

After a series of pleas and defences and thanks to a sympathetic judge, Gary was released with a driving suspension and a fine of £140. Leaving the courtroom, he quickly discarded his conservative court attire and donned a flashy white outfit befitting a super star. He descended the wide polished staircase with the air of a celebrity making a debut performance. A fine-looking stallion was stationed outside the courthouse poised to receive him. Amid flashing cameras and an amused crowd of onlookers Gary mounted the stallion as though ascending the stage for a premiere performance, with bows to the audience and pop idol gestures. Then, with Diana walking alongside the horse, dressed in her glamorous best, they paraded down the bustling boulevard handing out copies of Gary's first record, a single containing two songs. *Dreamer*, the name of both the horse and one of the songs, was not a coincidence, but a carefully planned ploy in anticipation of intriguing newspaper headlines.

* * * * * * *

Ten year old Jason loved having Gary living with them. Gary's presence added a new dimension to his life. The 'best pals' relationship between Alan and Gary that had begun in Los Angeles blossomed in England, and Jason became a junior affiliate of that association. Gary and Alan were mates indulging in various adventures, often inspired by alcohol, and Jason was allowed to join in some of their escapades. He loved the excitement, the fun, the fast driving; Diana never exceeded the thirty mile an hour speed limit. However being party to that association meant being exposed to situations and activities which bordered on the perilous.

One of these situations began as a treat for Jason's tenth birthday. Diana persuaded Alan to take the boys to Blackpool to see the Blackpool Illuminations, a world-famous electric light extravaganza. Jason was delighted. He loved and admired his father who was full of wonderful surprises and he regarded Gary as an affectionate big brother whom he longed to emulate. Being included in activities with them made him feel grown-up and part of the adult good times.

All began well. Alan rented a luxurious suite in a five star hotel and treated the boys to an extravagant dinner with a surprise birthday cake twinkling with sparklers, delivered to their table by a trio of singing waiters, Alan joining them, harmonizing with his beautiful singing voice. Jason couldn't have been happier. It was his night.

After Jason had gone to bed Alan and Gary went out on the piss. Their first stop was the hotel bar. The bar was crowded with hotel guests, members of a trade union delegation who Alan for some reason took against, although when he was drinking he didn't need much excuse to take against anyone or anything. As he became increasingly drunk he began to hurl insults at the delegates, at the trade union, even at the bartender.

'Get back to work you lazy cunts and stop posing with your fancy pants,' he said addressing a group of delegates standing by the bar. 'You too cunt face,' he said, lifting his empty glass to the barman, 'Who do you think you are? Little Lord Fauntleroy? Fill my bloody glass.'

When one of the men made a surreptitious gesture, indicating that Alan was some sort of crazy, in a voice thick with alcohol Alan said, 'I saw that, cunt. You're about as subtle as a wet fart in a new pair of white trousers.'

Being ignored only made him more offensive. He became belligerent, berating, swearing, doing all he could to pick a fight. Finally, furious with the bartender who refused him any more alcohol he became aggressive. In a fit of rage he produced the knife he always carried with him and slashed the man's face. The police were called and Alan was arrested and locked up. Gary returned to the suite alone.

The next morning Gary and Jason had a late breakfast on their own. Jason assumed Alan was out on an errand. Some time later, Gary confessed to Jason he had had a speech prepared for him when Alan didn't return, explaining what had happened, preparing Jason for the fact that he may not see his dad for some time because he would be in jail. But before he could deliver the speech Alan appeared, looking exhausted and contrite. He had been released on bail. Not wanting to deprive Jason of his birthday treat, despite spending a sleepless night in a police cell he took the boys to Pleasure Beach, even joining them on some of the rides, and later that night taking them to see the illuminations. The hotel, not wanting to endanger its reputation, did not press charges. In the end, Alan was fined for possessing an offensive weapon. At least this once Jason was spared the consequences of his father's drunken behaviour.

One of Jason's main duties in his role as junior affiliate was to roll spliffs – marijuana cigarettes – and prepare the mixture of hashish and marijuana for the bong – duties he performed with the pride of a disciple become master. After his Hollywood initiation to the bong ritual he graduated to seasoned participant and then to connoisseur although his participation was limited to weekends as he was still attending boarding school. Diana was often away working and not party to the bong sessions. Jason became adept at distinguishing between slabs of Afghani Black, wrapped in cellophane printed with a golden eagle, gold Arabic lettering, and secured with a gold seal;

and slabs of Red Lebanese, with a PLO (Palestine Liberation Organisation) stamp and the picture of a girl wearing a mini skirt and pointing a machine gun.

Alan did not prohibit Jason from smoking marijuana. He thought it better for him to be smoking with family and friends than off with some unknowns. Unlike alcohol or tobacco he believed marijuana to be not only harmless but, under the right circumstances, emotionally and spiritually beneficial. His conviction of the benign effects of marijuana as compared to tobacco was evident when he caught Jason smoking a cigarette.

'Why are you smoking rubbish tobacco when there is a case of first class spliffs?' he scolded.

He considered marijuana a herb that made for calmness, peace, and well-being, unlike alcohol, which made for aggression, something he had first-hand experience with. After all it was as old as mankind itself, used for thousands of years by ancient societies for religious and spiritual purposes, considered by shamans to be 'the weed of wisdom'. Alan had a profound religious and spiritual leaning and a thirst for knowledge. He read books on Buddhism, on ancient religions, on philosophy; he read Plato, Jung, Nietzsche and was especially keen on the writers prominent in the counter-culture of the Sixties, like Gurdjieff, Carlos Castaneda and Timothy Leary, writers who described practices which enabled higher levels of consciousness and enhanced awareness.

Diana wasn't as erudite in these matters and voiced concern about Jason's marijuana smoking, not entirely happy with the bong sessions which she considered excessive. She leaned towards restraint

'Please don't smoke so much Jase, it's damaging your lungs,' she cautioned.

Alan agreed and added his concern, 'If you smoke too much, instead of flying with the angels you'll be fighting with the demons'.

But neither warning availed.

When Jason was about eleven he seriously overdid the bong. He began to hear weird noises, cries of pain, voices shrieking at him, and the unbearable screech of chalk scraping a blackboard. The sounds penetrated the din of trains racing through his brain and although he blocked his ears he was unable to stop them. His stomach knotted in pain and he was acutely nauseous. Diana was away working and Alan put him to bed but the noises in his head and the agony in his belly kept him awake. Next morning, exhausted, sick and with a head full of racing trains, he pleaded with Alan not to send him to school. But Alan insisted, determined to teach him a lesson. However, he was so ill that the headmaster sent him home. Jason gave up smoking for a year.

* * * * * * *

Even as a child, Jason's friends were the adults who frequented Orchard Manor, he found kids his age too childish. Being precocious and extremely bright, Jess Conrad called him 'The Brain'. At an early age he sussed out what was important to adults, what their concerns were, how their world worked, and was able to use the information to his advantage.

When Jason was about six, Leapy Lee was still in prison serving time for the infamous pub incident. Leapy Lee's belongings were stored in a small house on the Orchard Manor estate. Jason, always curious, always mischievous, managed to break into the house. Rifling through Leapy Lee's possessions, to his delight, he came across a stash of pornographic magazines. Hiding them from his parents he engaged in a little commercial dealing of his own. With the acumen of an under-the-counter salesman, and the shrewdness of a market trader appraising prospective customers, he approached 'Jerry The Shovel', appropriately named as he was the man filling the potholes on the estate. His choice was spot on. Jerry The Shovel jumped at the opportunity to acquire such sought-after merchandise, asked no questions, and gladly paid the inflated asking price and vowed secrecy. Jason had enough illicit sweets for months to come.

Because Jason was privy to the world of his parents, their concerns were his concerns, concerns which were often troubling, magnified in his child's mind. Although he didn't understand the ramifications, he feared words like 'bankruptcy', 'taxes', and 'court'. One of Diana's major concerns was evading the dreaded taxman, who Jason envisioned as an assassin, intent on robbing them of all their money and sending his parents to prison. In order to avoid their earnings being swallowed whole by the taxman, Diana and Alan had an emergency fund of between £20,000 and £30,000 concealed in a special case Alan named the 'Albatross' because hiding the case was a relentless burden. 'Where should we hide the Albatross?' and 'What should we do with the Albatross?' were recurring refrains as the house was open not only to guests but to guests of guests, who, with Diana and Alan's fascination for people on the slippery slope of the law were not known for their ability to resist temptation.

The Albatross was a constant worry, hidden in places so imaginative they were often forgotten, necessitating hours of searching. Once it was discovered in the freezer, Alan declaring, 'Voila! Our frozen assets!' On one occasion the Albatross accompanied them to a Chinese restaurant.

On the way home Jason suddenly panicked, 'The Albatross is gone!'

It had been forgotten in the restaurant. In a state of shock, Diana broke her 30 mile an hour speed limit and, tires squealing, raced back to the restaurant. Fortunately the case was exactly where they had left it.

The near disaster convinced Diana and Alan the Albatross needed its own permanent, secure residence. With this in mind Alan removed several floorboards in the utility room and tucked the Albatross safe and sound under the floor. All went well until the washing machine flooded and water seeped under the floorboards. An alarmed Jason rushed to inform Alan. The Albatross was rescued, its belly swollen with clumps of drowning pound notes in different denominations. Alan, Diana and Jason worked for hours peeling the notes apart and carefully sticking each one to dry on the tiled walls of the bathroom, where they clung in all their sodden splendour.

'So much for money laundering,' Alan said.

'The bathroom looks like an Aladdin's cave, I rather like it.' Diana said, standing back to admire the decor.

'That's because we didn't economise on the wallpaper.' Alan replied.

When the partly dried notes fell from the wall they were spread on a table where the radiator was set to maximum so they would dry completely, then bundled into separate piles and returned to their case. Once again the Albatross lived to see another day, its fate being ultimately sealed several years later.

* * * * * * *

In the three years or so that Gary was living with them, Diana was busy not only promoting his career but expanding her own. As well as performing in cabaret, acting in television plays and continuing to write books, she enthusiastically embraced other forms of entertainment. She gladly accepted the invitation by the pop star Adam Ant to appear in his video *Prince Charming* as a shimmering fairy godmother, the song becoming number one on the charts. She appeared on the popular television show *Top Of The Pops*, she became a frequent guest on chat shows, on game shows, on comedy shows, on any show that would have her. Little wonder she became one of the most popular television personalities.

She was so at ease on television, so warm, so endearing and so quick and witty that her wish to host her own show soon became a reality. The show was called *Open Dors*, a seven-part series, hosted by a local network, which received excellent reviews. It was lively, the topics intriguing, and the guests chosen by Diana were so fascinating that ITV, a national network, offered Diana a six-part series called *The Diana Dors Show*.

Diana had an instinctive sense of how to make a show vibrant and alive, part of her instinct as an entertainer. She knew how to choose subjects that would both interest and entertain, like the spicy topic 'what turns a woman on?' She was a natural host, perceptive, aware, sensitive, with the ability to create what seemed like an effortless flow, and most important, she knew how to listen. Her guests found her instantly likeable, she put them at ease, made them feel important, knowledgeable. She brought out the best in them.

Gaining weight did not deter her popularity, in fact it enhanced it. Instead of a remote glamour queen she became 'one of us', adding to her television appeal. It suited her image in her role as agony aunt, someone approachable, someone who understood, someone who had been there. She entered the nation's living room, both on television and in her newspaper columns as a sympathetic but honest friend. She was so popular, so familiar, that people had the illusion they knew her personally.

However, despite her career success, her personal life was in turmoil. Having Gary living with them did little to help Alan's alcohol problem. In fact it made it worse. Alan now had not only an in-house drinking companion but someone he could count on to pick up the pieces when he fell apart. And Diana had not only Alan's drinking problem to contend with and its effect on Jason, who fortunately was in boarding school during the week, but its negative effect on Gary who was right in the firing line.

Alan's mother died in January 1980. Her death plunged Alan into a black tunnel of despair where the bottle was his only light. The usually meticulous Alan stopped changing his clothes, stopped shaving, even stopped washing. He no longer cared what he looked like or what effect his drinking was having on Diana or Jason, and he had left Gary far behind. The situation became so unbearable that Diana finally had to admit there   was no alternative but to leave him. Her final act of compassion was to commit Alan to a rehab centre. By this time Alan was so comatose he didn't even object. In fact he hardly knew where he was. Diana was determined never to take him back. For years she had struggled with hope. Now she had nothing to wrestle with. Hope was no more.

But, once again, Alan rose from the dead. His recovery was little short of miraculous. After a month he was back to the very best of Alan: caring, loving, even funny; the perfect father and husband. It seemed the further down he went the higher up he rose. But Diana was adamant. His assurances failed to move her. She had been there before. Alan pleaded for one last chance. He was certain this time things would be different. For the first time he had faced the fact he was an alcoholic. For the first time he knew he could not be a social drinker or any other kind of drinker and for the first time he vowed never to take another drink.

He begged, 'Please don't deny me. Let me prove to you that I'm cured'.

He implored, he beseeched, he even prayed. Diana relented. Jason was overjoyed. His best times were with his dad. His mum was often away working but his dad was usually there for him, especially when he was sober.

This time Alan kept his word. He didn't touch a drop of alcohol and couldn't believe how wonderful he felt. He was a new man, not only reformed but reborn. He wanted nothing more than to be with his family and his love for Diana was celebrated with renewed passion. Alan's sobriety paved the way for the happiest family time ever. Diana was thrilled, it was all she had dreamed about. And Jason had a proper family with two parents. There were long walks together, picnics, drives in the country and Jason's favourite activity – trips to the seaside. Orchard Manor took on a new life with dinner parties, pool parties and celebrations even when there was nothing to celebrate. The parties resumed their 'talk-of-the-town' reputation from the Dennis days, but featured a quality of risquéness which left Dennis's two-way mirrors back in the dark ages. Diana was in her element. She loved the fun, Alan was really cured and the good times were overflowing.

Even Jason's school life, a hateful imposition, became if not a joyous occasion at least a tolerable one; the ongoing nightmare concerning his schooling temporarily resolved. Although he had left the dreaded boarding school and had been going to a private school closer to home, he had been no happier. He liked being closer to home, but disliked the school. It was a stuffy place for rich American kids and their arrogant American teachers. He didn't fit in. He was teased, especially by the boys, as 'his father was a jail-bird, his mother was overweight', but mainly because of his success with the girls who adored his accent. He managed to stick it out for a year but after a physical scuffle with one of the teachers, his parents received a letter telling them 'it would be better if Jason didn't return'. In the end Jason was enrolled in the local state school, a surprisingly happy move. He had friends there, the atmosphere was relaxed, and he didn't have to defend his parents. On the contrary he gained kudos because of them. He even began to enjoy his studies.

The good times not only included the happy family situation but the gratifying work situation. Not only was Diana working but Alan was working as well. A sober Alan was much in demand. There were appearances in television shows like *Doctor Who*, and good parts in theatre productions, one in which he had the leading role. Alan loved working in the theatre and was a fine actor. John Le Mesurier, the celebrated actor famous for his role in *Dad's Army*, the popular television series, and who had worked with Alan in various dramatic productions considered Alan, 'The most underrated actor in the U.K.'

It was during this period of the good times that one day Alan casually said to Jason, 'By the way, Jase, you have a sister.'

Diana had heard Alan rant and rave about a daughter whom he had never seen, 'My daughter. My beautiful daughter. I want my daughter'.

But Diana dismissed his daughter rant as another one of his drunken hallucinations. She had no idea that Alan did indeed have a daughter, resulting from an atypical brief encounter with a media personality many years before.

Katie was aware she had a biological father, the fact was not hidden from her, but she knew nothing about him and was not tempted to find out. Her childhood was a happy one and she loved her mother's partner whom she considered her dad. She was not curious about her real dad until she was about fifteen, when she was suddenly compelled to investigate. Discovering her father was an actor she sent a letter to him via his agent. Alan phoned the next day. He insisted on meeting her at once and turned up on her doorstep before she could catch her breath. They were bowled over by each other, fascinated by the similarities between them. They compared hands and feet and giggled over the sameness. They laughed, they cried, they hugged, they even danced, excited about finding each other. Alan impressed Katie by driving her to Orchard Manor in a Cadillac that same day.

Katie was welcomed into the Dors-Lake family, and embraced with open arms. Diana was thrilled to meet her, made special dinners for her, and Jason, who was now twelve, treated her to his unique form of welcome by tormenting her with teasing and pranks, like terrifying the life out of her by suddenly jumping out of a bush. He loved having a sister to play tricks on, and she loved having a brother to scold. One of their favourite activities was play-fighting. Katie was bigger and stronger than Jason, being three years his senior, and would pin him to the floor rendering him helpless. But Jason got his revenge in the swimming pool. Being a stronger swimmer he would pull Katie to the deep end of the pool and dunk her mercilessly.

Katie adapted to her new family with ease, taking their high-profile lifestyle in her stride and becoming a permanent feature in their lives.

Diana's 50th birthday in 1981 was the high point of the good times. Life had provided her with many gifts. Her autobiography *Dors By Diana* was published that year and quickly became a number one bestseller. Her bankruptcy was discharged – a law had come into force absolving anyone who had been bankrupt over ten years. Her career had taken wonderfully rewarding directions. Gary was living with her, she had a lovely step-daughter, and Alan was cured – the greatest gift of all.

The birthday celebrations were both private and public, and continued for several days. Diana's publishers treated her to a splendid lunch to celebrate both her birthday and the publication of her book.

When one of the guests asked how she felt about turning 50 she said, 'It's like waiting to go to the dentist. Once you get there it's alright and you feel just the same.'

A 50th birthday pool party was televised live on the Russell Harty Show, a star-studded event featuring a feast of names. But her favourite part of the festivities was a family treat. Diana, accompanied by Alan, Jason, Gary and Katie celebrated on their own in a private club. It was a superb occasion, the climax of which was Alan's presentation of an enormous birthday cake shaped like a heart. It was glazed in pink, Diana's favourite colour, and trimmed with enlarged breasts and inflated lips, immortalizing Alan's quip before he was introduced to Diana, 'Oh yes, Madam tits and lips.' Diana laughed until her sides ached. It was the best day of her life.

Then, like a sunset sky suddenly beginning to darken, everything began to change. Just as there had been a series of good things happening, in 1982 there began a series of bad things happening. The first was Gary's announcement that he was returning to California that summer. Despite Diana's best efforts his music career had not taken off and he thought Los Angeles would be more promising. Diana was devastated. Her heartache over her lack of contact with Mark, who never bothered to phone or write, was almost a constant in her life, and now she would be losing Gary as well.

Then in June of that year the downward cycle of health problems began. On June 24 she was due to preside over the opening of a hotel. Although she wasn't feeling well she honoured the obligation. Suddenly, in the middle of the ceremony she was consumed by severe stomach pains. Somehow she managed to carry on, smiling, shaking hands, giving an ace performance. But the effort cost her dearly. She hardly made it home before she collapsed and had to be rushed to the hospital. An emergency operation on an ovarian cyst revealed cancer. Diana and Alan were both terrified. Alan's mother had so recently died of cancer that her terrible suffering was fresh in their minds. However, after absorbing the initial shock, Diana, with her usual positive approach to life made an immediate determination. She would beat the cancer.

The doctor told Diana she needed total rest and that for two days each week she would have to be hospitalised for chemotherapy treatment. Diana, having resolved to get well, cancelled all engagements for several months. Alan, who was due to appear in the much loved television series *Bergerac*, cancelled, in order to spend time with Diana and stay with her in hospital while she underwent treatment. Diana reacted badly to the chemotherapy, constantly vomiting, even when there was nothing left to vomit and feeling dreadful. But she endured without complaints and even with a sense of humour. Once the chemotherapy was over, convinced she was cured, she experienced a renewed sense of vigour.

Several months after the operation she received a great honour. For the second time she was asked to appear on the popular television show *This Is Your Life*, featuring celebrities who are suddenly surprised with people from their past. The previous time she had been on the show some twenty-five years earlier, Stewart Sawyer, the man who had ruined her Hollywood career had been flown in from California. On this occasion, Desmond Morris, the renowned zoologist and Diana's first love, who she hadn't seen since they were teenagers, made a surprise appearance. There were tributes from friends including Bob Hope and Liberace. But the surprise of surprises climaxed the show. Thinking she was on the phone to Gary and Mark in Los Angeles, they suddenly appeared on the set. Diana couldn't hold back the tears.

* * * * * * *

It was during this period that Jason left the state school and enrolled in drama school, where half the day was devoted to the usual lessons, and half to acting. Since the school was in London, Alan drove him to the station each day to catch the London train. With Gary gone, Jason had become closer to his dad. They spent more time together, just the two of them, going for long walks, playing chess, Alan attempting to introduce Jason to books on philosophy, on poetry, despite Jason's resistance, which was fiercest of all when Alan attempted acting tips. Jason was determined to make it on his own.

Until the age of seven Jason had been intent on becoming a fireman, that is until he saw the film *The Towering Inferno*, after which he quickly changed his mind. Diana had always discouraged him from becoming an actor, considering acting an unreliable profession full of hurt. However when Jason was about seven, Diana was playing the mother in a television adaptation of the *Just William* books. Being between baby sitters, Diana took Jason along to the studio, and it so happened that additional gang members were needed, and so Jason was given his first acting role.

The die was cast. Jason loved every bit of the experience, loved having a dirty face, loved fighting with a wooden sword, loved the fantasy, and especially loved the £50 fee for doing something that was so much fun. That role set the stage for his subsequent decision to attend drama school. He did well at the school, acquired an agent, and was selected for the role of 'The Winslow Boy' in Terrence Rattigan's play of the same name, about an actual incident in Edwardian England. The play was performed at the Lyric Theatre in London and Jason received excellent reviews, both to his delight and to the delight of his proud parents.

* * * * * * *

After Diana's operation and the prolonged chemotherapy treatment she felt so well that in May of 1983 she accepted an offer from ITV to appear on a television breakfast show. The show became *Diet with Diana Dors*. Diana weighed 14 stone 3 lbs (199 pounds) at the time and her goal was to lose 52 pounds over a period of approximately 5 months; that is, before her 52nd birthday on October 23 – a pound for every year of her life.

Diet With Diana Dors began that summer. Each week Diana would be weighed, while both the studio audience and the home audience waited in suspense to see if she had met her goal. The format was incredibly successful. The show was lively, informal, and informative. Diana's special talent for keeping a show interesting and fun was at its best. There were not only jokes, anecdotes and laughter but discussions on health, on the diet Diana was following, and on her personal fight against cancer. Diana became a symbol to the nation of outstanding courage. Everyone was rooting for her to meet her weekly target, and unknown to the audience Diana had employed a little ruse not to disappoint them. Besides wearing heavy pieces of jewellery, she had sewed some weights into the hem of her kaftan and whenever it proved necessary she removed either one of the weights or an item of jewellery.

During this period, Diana went for regular hospital check-ups. Then one day calamity struck. In the course of a routine scan in early September an alarming trace of cancerous tissue was discovered. An operation was immediately scheduled. Alan was in

Greece at the time filming the television detective series *Hart To Hart* in which he had a choice role. Diana was reluctant to disrupt his work and tried to dissuade him from returning to England. But there was no way she could keep him from dropping everything and rushing home to be with her. He arrived at the hospital on September 3rd just hours before the operation. Despite her attempt at bravery, the terrified Diana was relieved to have Alan at her side.

The news was devastating: the cancer was back. Diana and Alan wept together but were determined to keep the news to themselves. They decided it was especially important to keep it from Jason, who believed his mother was in hospital for a routine operation. To sustain that myth Diana left hospital after only a week, against the doctors' advice, in order to celebrate Jason's 14th birthday on September 11th. Also, Alan returned to Greece to finish the shooting, telling everyone that Diana was fine. In a television interview at Orchard Manor shortly after her return from hospital, Diana told a concerned audience that yes she had been 'scared stiff', but the cancerous tissue had been removed and she had been given the all-clear. A week later she returned to her TV-am breakfast show, looking beautiful and radiant, having missed only one appearance.

Her fan mail expressing joy at her supposed recovery was overwhelming. The audience for *Diet With Diana Dors* hit the roof. Returning to the show, her desperate secret concealed, Diana the professional actress performed her ultimate role. She looked stunning. She was cheerful and funny telling her fans she couldn't have done it without them. At her last weigh-in, the nation held its breath. But Diana mounted the scale with supreme confidence. With the help of her little ruses she had not only met her goal, but bettered it. She had lost 54 lbs. The audience cheered. And the charade was over.

The slimming program led to a flood of letters by viewers inspired by Diana's fight against cancer; and the interest inspired a TV-am show called *Open Dors*, which aired a month after her operation. Diana discussed questions posed by viewers who admired her straightforward, honest answers and her genuine concern. Aside from the television show she wrote a newspaper column for the News of the World called 'Diana Dors... Straight from the Heart', dealing with personal problems, giving advice, and relating her experiences. It was her way of giving solace, of sharing her amazing inner strength.

Her illness had given her a unique perspective whereby she was able to relate to people's fears and concerns with a deeper compassion. It had given her a keener understanding of suffering and the importance of allowing that suffering to be heard and addressed. She had developed the special gift of giving comfort, of rekindling hope. Diana did not sink into despondency, she continued to find strength by giving strength. Instead of the cancer deterring her demanding workload, it gave it renewed impetus and purpose.

Alan on the other hand refused work, as he wanted only to be close to Diana; the thought of losing her was unbearable for him. He did not have Diana's emotional resilience; anxiety and worry depleted his health. He lost weight, he was unable to sleep, staying awake for days on end, he had psychotic episodes, talked to himself, hallucinated. He suffered from hyper mania – 'dry high', induced by giving up alcohol after years of abuse. Finally Diana persuaded him to seek medical attention. He was admitted to a special hospital for psychiatric disorders. Although it was Diana who had cancer and had to deal with the debilitating chemotherapy treatment, it was Alan who suffered the breakdown.

By now Jason had left acting school and had a private tutor. One day he had simply announced, 'I don't want to go to school any more. Can I have a tutor at home please?' There were no objections. Both Diana and Alan were pleased, they would be able to spend more time with Jason if he was at home. John Thoroughgood, one of his former teachers, was engaged. John came twice a week, and Jason learned more from him than in all the years of being in school.

Diana was busy attending to correspondence, filming at the studio and caring for Jason and Alan when she could fit them into her busy schedule. Alan was at home, with calm patches dispersed with fraught ones. For Jason it was normality as usual. Mainly he was left to his own devices. Sometimes he played chess with Rob Barker, the home help, or got stoned with his dad, during his good periods, or with anyone else who was around, during his bad periods. He did his schoolwork with John, continued the flying lessons he had recently begun, but mostly he was preoccupied with Michelle Morley.

Jason had secretly fallen in love with Michelle Morley when he was just ten, and was devastated when she moved away. Although she had disappeared from his life she had not disappeared from his heart and when she reappeared almost three years later he was bold enough to declare his love. They both became absorbed in, and dedicated to, the wonders of first love. Jason even reverted to reading the poetry books his father had unsuccessfully attempted to foist upon him. For both Diana and Alan, Jason's involvement with Michelle was a blessed relief. It provided him sustenance while Alan was preoccupied with despair and Diana with performances and fan mail.

Some time later, when Jason was offered a role in the play *Breaking the Silence* by Stephen Poliakoff, alongside the actress Juliet Stevenson, to be performed by the Royal Shakespeare Company, Diana and Alan temporarily abandoned their preoccupations to celebrate with him. Jason was concerned that accepting the role would mean seeing less of Michelle, but Diana assured him the time they had together would be even sweeter. With all the good things happening in his life, Jason was blissfully unaware that his mother was dying of cancer and his father was dying of heartbreak.

Diana fought the cancer all the way and for a while it seemed as though she was winning. She looked fantastic, slim, glamorous, and sexy. She abounded with life-affirming energy and enthusiasm. Alan and Diana breathed a sigh of relief, convinced Diana was on her way to a complete cure. Alan made an impressive recovery. Diana felt so well that in March of 1984, she accepted a role in the film *Steaming* with Vanessa Redgrave and Sarah Miles. Another miracle was in the offing. But it was not to be.

Although Diana knew the cancer had invaded her lymph glands, she didn't let on, believing she would get well despite the lymph glands.

She told Alan, 'I'm going to be better like I always knew I would darling, I'm too busy to be ill.'

She continued with the filming even though she was often in pain and nauseous from the new medication she forced herself to take, certain it was making her well. She asked for no special privileges. Each morning at 6am she was at the studio, never late – true to the expression she had coined, 'Early Dors'. She always looked lovely, was in great spirits on the set and even kept everyone laughing. In the film itself she looked at her glamorous best. But the filming had hardly completed when on April 28th she collapsed with agonising stomach pains and was rushed to hospital. Perhaps for Jason's sake, she refused a stretcher and walked to the ambulance. An operation revealed the cancer had spread so extensively that further surgery would be useless.

After the operation Jason was suddenly faced with the terrible realisation that his mother was very ill. There were news flashes on television and hourly radio reports on Diana's condition, and his dad didn't come home but stayed in the hospital both day and night. Then early on the morning of May 4th Alan returned to Orchard Manor and woke Jason.

In a voice hardly his own he said, 'I don't think your mother will last the day.'

'You're kidding,' Jason said.

'I wouldn't kid about something like that.'

But before Jason had time for the information to impact on his senses Alan said, 'I'm going back to the hospital,' and without another word departed, leaving a traumatised son, bewildered and alone.

When Alan returned to the hospital he was in for a surprise. The nurses had changed Diana's hospital gown into her favourite nightie. She was leaning against the pillows her blond hair newly brushed framing her face like a golden halo, her favourite gold necklace spelling DORS, removed only for the operation, resting reassuringly on her breast. Alan gasped. She looked sixteen and so beautiful it made his heart ache. He loved her more than ever, more than it was possible to love.

Alan spent the day holding Diana's hand as she drifted in and out of consciousness, repeating over and over, 'I love you'.

Sometimes she responded, 'I love you too'. Once she smiled and said, 'This isn't the way we rehearsed it.'

'No, my darling, it isn't, somebody damn well changed the script.'

Towards evening Diana asked Alan to thank everyone for the cards and flowers and for their concern and love, and made him promise to look after Jason and not let him fly until he was well qualified. Then she slipped peacefully into a coma. Alan knew it was the end but was unable to let her go, his need for her was so urgent. Suddenly Diana opened her eyes.

'Why did you call me back?' she asked gently.

'Because I love you so much.'

'I know,' she said and slipped away again.

A little before nine that evening, Alan was called away for an urgent phone call. It was Katie inquiring about Diana, wanting to convey her love. Alan was curt, resentful of the intrusion, anxious to get back to Diana. But when he returned, Diana was dead. He never spoke to Katie again.

Alan phoned Rob, asking him to tell Jason his mother had passed away, before he forced himself to confront the journalists waiting in the hospital, anxious for news. Alan was brief. He thanked the journalists for their patience and said simply, 'I have lost my wife and soulmate. My son has lost a friend and mother, and the world has lost a legend.'

Jason had spent the day sitting with the television waiting to hear the announcements about his mother. He was still there that evening. Someone was talking about her when Rob came into the room.

'Jason, I have some bad news for you,' he said as gently as he could. 'Your mum is dead.' He waited a moment before he said, 'Can I do anything for you? Shall I make you something hot to drink?'

But Jason didn't hear him. He had turned to stone. Only his brain was alive and the word 'dead' was whirling around inside it. Dead? How could it be? She was in hospital for a routine operation and now she was dead. Why hadn't anyone told him? His mother was dead. How could it be?

Jason was still sitting with the television when Alan came home. He couldn't think of what to say or what to do or even what to feel. Even though he hadn't left the sofa all day, he was exhausted. He knew his father was in pieces but although he loved his father dearly he was unable to rouse himself to comfort him. He felt numb. When eventually he fell asleep on the sofa, fully dressed, Rob turned off the television and covered him with a blanket.

The following day Alan was surprisingly together. There was much to do, forms to sign, arrangements to make. Diana's death was headline news in every newspaper. Knowing the tabloids would be competing for an interview, Alan headed them off by offering the *News Of The World* an exclusive. That same evening the newspaper sent two journalists to cover the story: Rosalie Shann, a senior reporter, and Maurice Chittenden, a young freelance journalist. Maurice was overwhelmed by the sumptuousness of Orchard Manor. For a moment he thought he was in Hollywood. He was so distracted by the aura of the place, by the headiness of Diana's almost palatable presence in her lovely pink and white living room, that it took him a while to remember why he was there. Jason was asleep on the sofa looking peaceful and angelic. But when he awoke and saw his father's distress at reliving Diana's death, for an article to be entitled 'My Darling's Final Hours', he lost his angelic appeal and said, 'My father and I would like you to leave now.' He spoke with such authority that the journalists departed without another word. It was at that moment that Jason – a spoilt, indulged child – became a responsible adult carer, a weight which was to prove too heavy for his fourteen years to shoulder.

Diana's funeral was held at the Church Of The Sacred Heart in Sunningdale, one week after her death. Lying serenely in her golden oak coffin wearing a gold lamé evening gown and matching cape, her gold necklace gentle on her breast, she was the ultimate beauty queen. Even in death she did not disappoint her fans.

The church was packed with friends, actors, directors, musicians, colleagues and celebrities, including Barbara Windsor, Danny La Rue, Shirley Bassey and Lionel Blair, come to pay their last respects. Charlie Kray was present representing the infamous Kray brothers, Ronnie and Reggie, who were in prison, but who had once ruled the London underworld, and who had sent an enormous wreath of flowers with the message, 'We'll miss you Diana.' Standing out among the multitude of floral arrangements was a beautiful display of white carnations and pink rosebuds, shaped like a cross, running the full length of the coffin, with the message, 'To my own sweet love, only a whisper away. Love always.'

A section of the church was reserved for journalists, photographers and filming equipment and a special section for close family members. Conspicuously absent were Mark and Gary. Alan had phoned them and they had promised to come. Jason had phoned as well begging them to come for Alan's sake. But at the last moment they had informed Alan they wouldn't be attending. Instead each sent a red rose covered with glitter. Both Alan and Jason were deeply upset.

The funeral service was broadcast to the many fans gathered outside the church. It was composed of eulogies, religious readings, poetry, music and Diana's favourite hymns. Especially poignant was *Amazing Grace*, the hymn she loved most. It tore the heart out of

Alan and he could not hold back the tears. The cameras, poised for just such a moment, began clicking mercilessly. Jason, incensed by the insensitivity and disrespect, glared so hard at a camerawoman about to snap a photo that she dropped the camera. He sat expressionless throughout the service determined to deny the press the satisfaction of capturing his grief for public viewing. He was angered by the press, by the galaxy of flashbulbs on the way to the church, in the church, out of the church, on the long walk following the hearse to the cemetery, at the cemetery, even as Diana's body was lowered into the grave. The clicks reaching a hysterical pitch when Alan, plucking a rosebud from his personal wreath, kissed it lovingly and let it fall into the grave: his final farewell.

The callousness of the press at that heartbreaking moment sent Jason into a spasm of fury which he held tight inside himself. Perhaps it was that very fury which shielded him from the terrible sorrow that lay concealed beneath it, a sorrow so overwhelming he couldn't allow himself to feel it. The fury gave his turmoil somewhere to go, somewhere to hide, it substituted for the grief he didn't know how to express. However that fury, that tight rein on feeling, on emotions, perhaps a necessary refuge at that moment was to become a terrible affliction for some time to come.

After the funeral there was a reception at Orchard Manor at which Alan performed his own private ritual. In a special corner of the garden where Diana loved to sunbathe, he burned the formal pin-striped suit he had worn to the funeral – his way of obliterating the funeral and with it Diana's death.

In the first few weeks after the reception Alan coped amazingly well. He seemed imbued with some hidden source of vitality. He was energetic, active, busy. Only days after the funeral he appeared in a difficult television role. Shortly afterwards he was in another television play. He insisted on fulfilling Diana's engagements. He designed a beautiful headstone for Diana's grave with the wording:

'Always Remembered
Diana Dors-Lake 1931 – 1984
Forever Loved
Only A Whisper Away'

During early summer Alan spent little time at home, occupied with television engagements, with substituting for Diana in charity events, with accepting the many invitations friends extended, with arranging Diana's memorial, a private service for family and close friends, to be held at Westminster Cathedral on July 24. Jason was left to manage the business of living, making sure bills were paid, wages were paid, necessary phone calls were made. Rob helped. There was no time, no opportunity and, most importantly no one, to console or comfort Jason. Distracting Alan, deflecting his grief absorbed everything and everyone, especially Jason, who was left to cope on his own. But gradually the flush of vitality vanished and the strain on Alan began to show. He became fraught, agitated, anxious. He began pacing, muttering to himself, he looked dazed, disorientated. Jason was familiar with the signs. He knew his father was mentally and physically exhausted and on the verge of collapse. After the memorial service he managed to convince Alan to spend two weeks on a Greek island for the tranquillity they both needed.

It was a good holiday and Alan seemed to be recovering his equilibrium. But returning to an Orchard Manor devoid of Diana set Alan on a path of despair. It was as though he suddenly realised that not only was Diana not there but that she would never be there again. The realisation was unbearable. It resulted in a swift, relentless deterioration of body and soul.

Alan found himself inhabiting a house warm with Diana's presence but without Diana. Each day became a living hell. He longed for Diana with every beat of his heart. He mourned for her in every room, sniffing the air, inhaling her scent. He saw her face in every mirror; heard her sound in every footstep. His heart ached at the sight of her beautiful dresses hanging in the closet, her shoes lined up in neat rows. In a moment of deep despair he burned all her clothes – a gypsy custom – because no one could wear them like she did. But there was no relief. If the days were unremitting wretchedness, the nights were unbroken desolation. Alone in bed, crazed with anguish he would reach for Diana but the bed was cold and empty. His grief was terrible.

He began to speak to Diana, both silently in his head and out loud, calling to her, 'You can't leave me; you've got to be here.' He couldn't do anything, couldn't go anywhere, not even to the christening at his dear friend Freddie Starr's house. Nothing helped, friends and family didn't help, drugs didn't help, prayers didn't help, his religion didn't help. He felt abandoned by God. He wasn't able to eat or sleep. He became so distraught, so confused that sometimes he didn't recognise Jason, other times he thought he was with Diana.

During his sane moments he knew he had to sell the house. With Diana gone there was no point keeping it. The realisation threw him into even deeper despair. He had lost his wife and now would be losing his home. He tried phoning friends. He called Max Clifford but was hardly able to talk. Finally he called Freddie Starr saying, 'I don't think I can go on any longer.' His anguish was heartbreaking.

Jason could do nothing to help. He longed to comfort his father but didn't know how. He tried smoking marijuana together, but it only made things worse. He became so preoccupied with his father's grief that there was no time or space to deal with his own. When he saw Michelle he would hug her so tight that once she cried out in pain. Jason's 15th birthday on September 11 was a joyless occasion. Alan barely managed to rouse himself to acknowledge it. The saving grace for Jason came with the beginning of rehearsals for *Breaking the Silence* at the Barbican theatre. He threw himself into the rehearsals with the intensity of a drowning man clinging to a raft. Rob would take him to the station to catch the London train and he would have a day of respite from his father's torment.

October 10th was the day Alan had met Diana. Special days like birthdays and anniversaries were especially difficult for him. That day Alan made a point of driving Jason to the station.

'See you later dad,' Jason said as the train approached.

'Yeah,' Alan replied.

But Jason heard something in that 'Yeah,' some dullness, some utter depletion, which was chilling.

Jason was engrossed in rehearsing for that night's performance when he was summoned to the office. Two policemen were waiting. Jason knew immediately something was very wrong. Probably it was a dope bust – the police had found the marijuana stash. Or maybe it was a driving accident, his father was known as a 'speed freak'; sometimes even his mum had refused to drive with him and now his driving was especially erratic.

'Your father has had an accident,' one of the policemen said.

So that was it, Jason thought, it was the driving, and he felt a stab of guilt for having enjoyed the speeding, indeed for having encouraged it. The policemen ushered Jason into the waiting police car without another word, and drove him to Orchard Manor. Jason said nothing, asked no questions, sitting quietly, promising himself to look after his dad no matter how serious his injuries. How lucky that he had learned first aid, how to bandage wounds, how to stop bleeding, his dad himself had taught him about artificial respiration, how to restart a heart that had stopped beating. Everything would be fine. He would never let his dad down.

But as soon as they entered the gates of Orchard Manor Jason was overwhelmed by panic so intense it was as though his heart froze and he could hardly breathe. The scene was one of pandemonium. His home had been invaded by a host of strangers. Police, cameramen and journalists were frantically setting up equipment, taking notes, filming. An ambulance, its doors opened wide was parked outside the front entrance, a stretcher abandoned by its side while agitated paramedics rushed medical equipment into the house. Before Jason could comprehend what was happening or go to his father, the police car reversed and sped away, a stunned Jason trapped inside.

Jason sat bolt upright in the car, stiff. No explanation was asked for and none was given. But instead of taking him to the hospital to see his father, he was deposited at the home of Susan and Alan Blackburn, close friends of his parents who lived in Bray, about 20 miles from London. Without a word and remembering his mother's insistence on politeness and good manners, Jason shook the hand of each policeman, thanking them before turning to the house.

The door was open. Susan and Alan were waiting for him.

'Will you take me to the hospital please to see my dad?' was the first thing Jason said. 'He's been in an accident'.

'Sit down for a minute Jase,' Susan said.

A reluctant Jason sat on the edge of the sofa without removing his jacket. Susan sat beside him, Alan on a chair facing him.

'Take off your jacket,' Alan said. But Jason didn't move and Alan didn't insist.

After a moment of silence, Susan said, 'You know Jase, your dad loved your mother very much.'

'I know,' Jason replied.

'And you know better than anyone else how hard it's been for him since she died, how ill he's been, how terribly he's missed her, how much he's suffered.'

Jason nodded.

'Today is the anniversary of the day your mum and dad met.'

'Yes, I know that.'

'Jase, your dad just couldn't go on living without your mum. He just couldn't go on living without her, he was in too much pain. He wanted to be with her so much... that he shot himself.'

Jason flinched as though he had felt the shot.

'He shot himself?... My dad shot himself? Is my dad dead?'

'I'm afraid he is, Jase.'

'You mean my dad is dead?'

'Yes, Jase, he loved you very much but he couldn't go on living without your mum, he was in too much pain,' Susan repeated, unable to find any other words; unable to stop the tears, although she had promised herself not to cry. If only Alan had left something for Jason, a letter, a note, a memento, something, but there was nothing.

Susan put an arm around Jason. Jason was rigid, every muscle tensed against the shooting. He said nothing. He couldn't. His voice was empty. But he could feel himself turning to ice. Susan felt the coldness through his jacket. She brought a blanket and wrapped it around Jason's shoulders. Alan brought a cup of tea.

'Drink this, Jase, it will make you feel better, it'll warm you up.'

Jason sat motionless, wrapped in the blanket, his head lowered, his hands buried in the pockets of the jacket; the cup of tea growing cold beside him. Susan and Alan let him be.

It was several days before Jason was able to return to Orchard Manor to retrieve some of his belongings, his cassettes, his videos, his books, some clothes. By now he had pushed the pain deep inside him, then deeper and deeper, but he could still feel it, especially at night. He asked Michelle to go with him. He didn't want anyone else. Susan had arranged a car to take them and bring them back.

All the doors to the house were locked but he had the keys, they hadn't taken them from him. He wouldn't have given them up even if they had tried. It was still his house. He went straight to his room. But when he opened the door he didn't want to go in. He didn't want Michelle to see it. It wasn't his room. It was empty. Everything was gone except for the built-in shelves. His television was gone. His stereo was gone. Even his bed was gone. The room was all white, his snakeskin wallpaper was gone. The golden snake on the back wall was gone. The white fluffy carpet they loved to lie on and listen to music was gone, replaced by a brown stiff rug.

'Let's get my things and go,' he said to Michelle.

But there was a further shock. His videos and cassettes were smeared with blood and some had bits of flesh wedged between them. His books were the same.

Then he remembered overhearing someone he didn't even know saying, 'Imagine... the kid's father blew his brains out in the kid's room...In his own son's room.'

No one had told him. He hadn't wanted to hear that, but he heard it now. He couldn't stay. He would have to come back another time. He took Michelle's arm and pulled her from the room. The car was waiting for them, the driver surprised they had returned so soon, he had anticipated a nap.

Alan's funeral took place a week after he died. It was held in Sunningdale, in the same church as Diana's. Alan's sister Vilma and her husband Ken made all the arrangements. It was almost as much a media event as Diana's, but with fewer people. Alan's friends were there. His closest friend, the comedian Freddie Starr, flew in that morning from Ireland where he was touring. Charlie Kray was there, again replacing Ronnie and Reggie. Katie was there but she didn't sit with the family; very few people knew who she was. And the press was there in full force.

Jason didn't cry. He remembered that when his dad had cried at his mum's funeral it had set off an explosion of flashing light bulbs and clicking cameras. He wouldn't give the press that satisfaction. He hadn't cried at his mum's funeral and he damn well wouldn't cry at his dad's. Besides, he had no tears. He was all dried up like a desert. With a face like granite, he went through the motions. He stood up, sat down, knelt, he mouthed the words to the prayers, he followed his father's coffin to the grave where he was buried next to his mother, forcing himself to think nothing, to feel nothing, to say nothing.

He only weakened once, when he threw a rose into his father's grave and said, 'God bless you daddy. I love you.' But he said it low so no one would hear. At his mum's funeral at least he still had his dad. They had gone home together. Now he didn't have his father and he didn't have his mother, and he didn't have his home. But he didn't cry.

Although a sympathetic director had told Jason he could take off as much time as he liked, that his understudy was well prepared, Jason insisted on returning to the Barbican a week after the funeral. He felt more at home there. The cast were more like family and he had a special attachment to Juliet Stevenson, who was the only one he confided in. He had learned from his parents that 'The show must go on', and he wouldn't let them down. He wanted no pity. Besides, his role in the play called for him to smash up the entire set each night. He did so enthusiastically, it provided him the one relief he had.

Performances continued until the Christmas break, usually to full houses. The cast were wonderfully supportive. A car had been arranged to pick him up and drive him home. He spent Christmas at his aunt's and uncle's, as had been decided when his father was alive. He didn't want to disturb anything his parents had planned.

Staying with the Blackburns had been a temporary arrangement and he had been with them over two months already. He had to decide on something more permanent. He had two alternatives, either to live with his uncle and aunt in Stoke-On-Trent, an industrial town a long way from London, or live with his half-brother Gary in Los Angeles. Diana and Alan had given Gary power of attorney until Jason was eighteen and had named him as Jason's legal guardian. Jason wasn't especially close to his uncle and aunt and besides they lived too far away. On the other hand he was close to Gary. Gary had lived with them when his parents were alive and he had been happy then. Gary wanted him to come. He wanted to take care of him. He would be more like a dad than a brother.

On December 27th, a little over two months after his father died, and seven months after his mother had died, he said goodbye to Susan and Alan. He really liked them; they had been good to him, he knew that, but they didn't really understand, nobody really understood. How could they, he didn't understand himself. He was sad to be leaving his friends and his home, although Orchard Manor was no longer his home, it would soon belong to someone else. Saddest of all was leaving Michelle, saying goodbye to her. She was the only girl he ever really loved. Now he would be losing her too. And he couldn't bear that. It really broke his heart. They loved each other so much. Michelle cried, and Jason almost cried.

Vilma and Ken drove Jason to the airport. He had told everyone he would probably be back after the Christmas break to finish the run of *Breaking the Silence*. Even though he only took a rucksack with very few of his belongings, he knew in his heart that wouldn't happen. When Vilma and Ken waved goodbye they were both crying, but Jason was not. He had taught himself not to cry.

Albert and Mary Fluck (Diana's parents)

1. *Georgina Dors (Diana's grandmother) and Mary Payne (Diana's mother) Margate 1925*
2. *Albert Fluck holding baby Diana*

Baby Diana 1933

Diana, approximately 13, first glamour shot

1946 on the beach, West Somerset Coast

Early Diana Dors

Diana and Dennis Hamilton

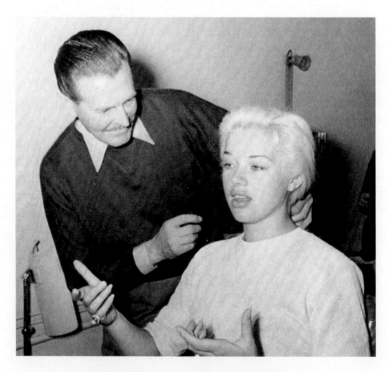

Diana and hairdresser Teasy Weasy

Diana at Cannes, 1956

Diana at Cannes

Diana in her mink bikini in Venice

Doris Day and Diana Dors

Diana and Tommy Yeardye

Luxury Dors

Alan Lake in performance

Alan Lake aged 27

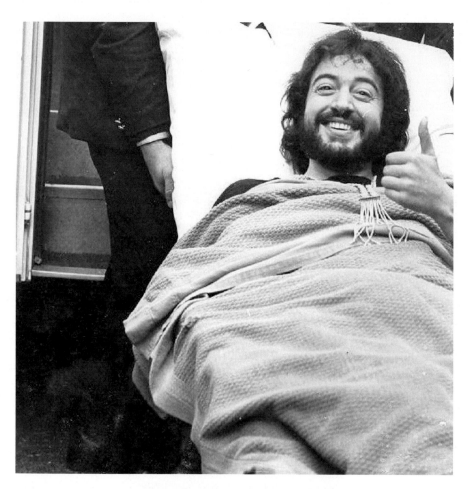

Alan Lake after accident in 1972

Diana and Alan's wedding, 1968
Cyril Lake and Jason's cousins

Alan, Diana and newborn Jason, 1969

Diana and Alan with friends and family at Jason's christening

Jason's christening

Jason's christening with half brothers Mark and Gary

Diana and baby Jason

Diana and 3-year old Jason

Jason, seven years old in 'Just William'

Nine year old Jason

Ten year old Jason

Andrew Ray, Jason and Diana

Left to right: Alan, Captain Flint (parrot), Gary, Jason, Uncle Ken, Auntie Vilma (Alan's sister)

Jason in 'Winslow Boy', 1982

Alan and Jason

Alan and Jason at Diana's funeral, May 1984

Bye my love . . . Alan drops the red rose

Alan Lake drops a rose into Diana's grave

GRIEF: Jason at his dad's funeral

Jason drops a rose into Alan's grave

JASON

Someone once asked Richard Burton why he drank so much. He answered simply,

"Because it dulls the pain."

Chapter 23
How It All Began

'Niema, would you write a book about my life, about my mother, about my father, about me?' Jason blurted out. 'You know my mum was really famous, there would be a lot of interest. It'll be like a tribute to her, my gift to her, October is her birthday, I'd like to do something special, for my father too, there's so much shit flying around from people who didn't even know them…'

'What?' I interrupted, trying to stay the avalanche of words. Jason was always full of surprises but I certainly hadn't seen this one coming.

'A tribute to my parents. A book about my life. It's been such a crazy life. It's a wonder I'm still here.'

'Is that what your urgent phone call was about?'

'Yes. That's it. I've been wanting that to happen for a long time and I've been waiting for the right time to ask you, but I couldn't find the right time so I'm asking you now'. Without taking a breath he persisted as though he had to get it all said before I could interrupt. 'For fuck's sake I'm almost 40… don't know how it happened but it happened and I want to put it all down, set the record straight, while it's still fresh in my mind, that is, whatever is left of my mind after what I've been doing. David thinks it's a great idea.'

Jason and I were sitting in my living room having a cup of coffee. He had phoned earlier insisting it was important that I see him ASAP. That is – I was having a cup of coffee; Jason's cup was untouched. He was too excited, too anxious to talk me into this book idea before I had time to refuse. He was sitting bolt upright, speaking even faster than usual, stumbling over the words, his eyes glistening with mission.

When I could get a word in edgeways I said, 'It's out of the question. Remember, I'm from Canada, I don't know all that much about your mum. In Montreal when I was growing up we weren't even allowed into the cinema until we were 16. It's your story, why don't you write it?'

'Me? I can't write, besides I'm almost dyslexic. You're the writer. But I have a great memory, it's practically photographic. I'll fill you in. I can remember things in detail, even things that happened when I was still in nappies, and I have lots of photographs no one has ever seen. It's perfect with me living right below you... We can sit in the garden and talk... I'm in contact with some of my mother's friends, you can get lots of information from them, most of them have always refused interviews but they wont refuse me. David will help too, he knew my parents well. He thinks the book is a fantastic idea', he repeated, as though playing his trump card.

Jason was so wired he was unable to stay seated. Standing up he continued to enthuse about the book with such burning obsession it was as though his life depended on it, while I sat leaning into the pillows, just looking at him. He was certainly good to look at, especially in that state of animated intensity. He looked more in his late twenties than late thirties with endearing boyish energy and passion. Not surprising. Both his parents were beauties judging from the photos he had showed me. His mother was a virtual beauty queen, and his father drop dead gorgeous and Jason had inherited some of the best bits (and also some of the worst bits) of both. Tall and lean and dangerous like his father, sparkling blue eyes, full sensuous lips and the humour of his mother and the combined charm of both.

* * * * * * *

I had come to know Jason through my friend David Malin (the David of the 'fantastic book idea') and I had come to know David Malin through my friend Dwina Murphy-Gibb, wife of Robin Gibb, of the celebrated Bee Gees. I had met David back in the late Eighties, in the heady days of youth and around-the-clock celebration. Each new year for several years running, Dwina and Robin had hosted a spectacular New Year's party in their magnificent home, a 12th century converted monastery near Oxford, called a Prebendal, where in times past bishops had been educated. The event was in the tradition of a Scottish Hogmanay welcoming the arrival of the new year.

The ritual began at the stroke of midnight with a mysterious stranger, tall, dark, handsome, young and virile, crossing the hearth bearing a lump of coal, a gift of warmth to set the luck for the rest of the year. David was that mysterious stranger. Cloaked in black he fit the bill to perfection, exuding a dark, enigmatic quality I was compelled to explore. Although he later told me that Barry Gibb's wife Linda said he was more like a demon than a good omen; and there was a touch of truth in that, which was perhaps part of the attraction. In any case we became instant friends. We both lived in

London and maintained contact during the intervals between the Hogmanays, indulging in some king-sized happenings, blissed out on the fading embers of hippydom. Then, as suddenly as I had found him, I lost him. He disappeared from London and from my life. I often wondered what had happened to him, but the few people we knew in common had no answers.

* * * * * * *

Almost two decades went by and in the interval I had acquired a holiday flat in Broadstairs, a kind of left over seaside town from the 50's, on the east coast of England. The flat was in a converted historical 18th century customs house right on the beach, called Eagle House. One day walking along the beach my eyes almost spun in their sockets. Coming toward me was the infamous, elusive David, as deliciously gorgeous as he had been almost 20 years earlier with just the right touch of jadedness to verify a life of adventure tinged with dissipation. I did a double-take, but it was really him. He had returned to the place of his birth and to the family home, which was now his, in Ramsgate, a town a walk along the beach from Broadstairs. We were delighted to see each other and, as sometimes happens, our friendship continued as though there had been no interruption, with outrageous parties, outrageous people, sunrises on the beach, feasts by the sea and a slightly dampened-down craziness – but only slightly.

David was a high-profile musician and composer who had worked with the Stones, Pink Floyd, the Beatles and just about everyone else in the music business. In the years he had lived in London, through his musical connections, he had met and become friends with Diana, and especially close to Alan. David had a wonderfully original and zany sense of humour which endeared him to Diana and an off-the-wall madness which endeared him to Alan. Dubbed 'The Candy Man' for the special gifts he procured, he became a regular visitor at Orchard Manor.

Diana adored him. Anyone who made her laugh had an automatic five-star rating. Although she would mumble disapproval at the antics David and Alan indulged in, secretly she found them amusing, often hilarious. Like the time she discovered them fencing in the garden, stark naked, during a thunderstorm.

'Will they ever grow up?' she sighed.

Often, after an exhausting night of theatre or cabaret performance she would hurry to David's flat in central London where he lived with his partner Susie, flop onto the sofa, still dressed in one of her glamorous skin-tight sequined gowns, unzip the gown with a sigh of relief, moaning, 'David, roll me a joint for god's sake.' It was David who had rolled her very first joint. And it was David who had found her collapsed with laughter, lying on his kitchen floor, her head in the refrigerator.

David was 12 years older than 10 year old Jason and had adopted the role of surrogate older brother. Jason found him a laugh, had fun playing with him, and loved his company. The surrogate brother relationship continued until the 15 year old Jason left for California after the suicide of his father. When Jason returned to England at the age of 18, after a disastrous three years in California, David was one of the few people he managed to contact.

Arriving from Los Angeles Jason had headed for London but left almost as soon as he got there, fed up with journalists following him, aiming questions at him like stinging darts, reminding him of everything he wanted to forget. Instead he decided on Brighton, a town he was familiar with through his many visits with his mother, and where he knew several of his parents' close friends. One of the closest was the actor, child star Andrew Ray, he of the amyl-nitrate-white-jelly-bean escapade. Andrew still lived in the same place and the first thing Jason did was visit him.

As it happened, Andrew and David were inseparable friends, as a matter of fact it was Andrew who had first introduced David to Diana, taking David to see her perform in cabaret, promising 'You'll love her'. David more than loved her, he thought she was sensational; her choice of material, delivered with wit and humour, brilliant; her singing voice beautiful and her dancing, world class. He found her charisma so overwhelming, he said, 'When Diana walks into a club it's like the parting of the Red Sea... People have to shield their eyes from the glare of Diana.'

When Jason discovered Andrew was in touch with David he whooped for joy and urged Andrew to surprise David with a visit. Andrew didn't need much urging. Jason had secured a special welcome-home treat almost as soon as the plane touched English soil, a delicacy called 'Purple Om', definitely not for beginners. The surprise visit was not made empty handed. Jason and Andrew arrived on David's doorstep bearing gifts. David, a connoisseur in these matters, protested with a loud 'No' when presented with the offering and immediately swallowed some.

The surprise visit went on for three days with crazy, ecstatic, out-of-their- heads, beautiful debauchery, compliments of the 'Purple Om', making spaced-out, sexed-up music together, tripping in the heavens with a ravenous desire to caress the stars, to taste the moon; Jason convulsed with laughter as David and Andrew relived the wild, abandoned times. Like the time, high on one thing and another, David, catching sight of eggs in Andrew's shopping bag, had a sudden impulse to throw them at Andrew, both screaming with laughter at the resulting egg-etched masterpiece.

David's impulse grew into an art requiring skilful practice, throwing eggs into open bus windows, car windows, even at parts of the anatomy of unsuspecting friends. Eggs were bought and thrown by the dozens. The culmination of this obsession was a massive egg-throwing party hosted by David, where inadvertently someone threw an egg through the window of a stopped police car, splattering both the car and the police officer inside. An irate policeman marched into the flat, so outraged he failed to notice the forbidden substances being hastily concealed. David managed to appease the officer, grovelling unashamedly, apologising profusely and finally charming him into submission. The episode ended with David cleaning the police car while Andrew scoffed, 'David's got a job at last.'

That three day orgy initiated a new relationship between Jason and David, crossing the time barrier, closing the gap between child and man. Jason was now an adult and the older-brother relationship became one of equals. They were not only good friends but close brothers. And that friendship survived, even flourished, in the bizarre twists and turns they were swept up in during the years following Jason's return: falling in love with the same woman, Jason becoming a father at age 20, David becoming a father and separating from Susie, the mother of his daughter, becoming caught up in webs of intrigue often fuelled by drugs and alcohol, hating each other, loving each other, but always befriending each other.

Once, in a philosophical mood, David and Jason were contemplating the celebration of the 20th anniversary of the Beatles' *Sergeant Pepper* album, first released in 1967 – 'It was 20 years ago today...'

David said to Jason, 'Lakey, before we know it another 20 years will have rolled by and we'll be 20 years older but one thing I know, wherever we end up we'll still be brothers.'

David's prediction had come true, almost 20 years had rolled by and Jason and David were still close brothers although, by now, living in different places. David had moved to Ramsgate hoping to leave a destructive London lifestyle behind him. Jason, however, had remained in London indulging in that same destructive lifestyle, the only positive aspect of which had been acquiring a partner called Marcella, who was as grounded and reliable as Jason was undependable and unhinged. The first time Jason visited David in Ramsgate he fell in love with the area. That visit occurred at precisely the right time as by now the inroads of abuse had worn so deep there were few bets placed on Jason's survival. Not only David and Marcella, but Jason himself knew he had to get out of London to preserve his sanity, if not his life.

As it happened, during David's many visits to Eagle House we had discussed the vacant flat on the floor below mine and how great it would be to have it let to like-minded friends.

And so it came to be that when Jason visited David in Ramsgate, knowing how much Jason loved the sea, David said, 'There's a flat going in Broadstairs, it's right up your street. It has your name written on it.'

And that's how it all began.

Chapter 24
A Book is Born

The combined powers of persuasion of David and Jason were more compelling than the gravitational pull of the moon on the sea. How could I, a mere mortal, resist? Besides, I got drawn into Jason's story and especially into Diana's story. The more research I did, the more I read, the more people I talked to, the more interested I became. I was intrigued by Diana's enduring popularity. Almost everyone I spoke to over a certain age had had some form of contact with her. Some had seen her in films, seen her on television, seen her live in cabaret, read about her in magazines, seen photographs of her, read her columns or followed her story in newspapers. Many had met Diana and had some story to tell. I even met people who had pin-ups of her, both men and women.

Even those too young to have had personal contact with Diana were enthralled by her. After all she was on the cover of a Beatles album, in the front row, as one of their heroes. And in a recent episode of *Eastenders*, arguably the most popular British television soap, featuring a fancy-dress party, the hostess, addressing one of the younger guests said, 'Oh, you've come as Marilyn Monroe.'

'No', was the reply. 'I've come as Diana Dors.'

A recent incident was indicative of the profound affection the British public held for Diana, even more than 25 years after her death. After years of planning, a magnificent art gallery named for Turner, one of the most famous English artists was recently opened in Margate, the seaside town where Turner did much of his painting. Jason had been invited to the opening because the gallery planned on exhibiting photographs of Diana in a future exhibition.

The honour of opening the gallery, a very prestigious accolade was bestowed upon the eminent English artist Tracy Emin. Of course the mother of the artist proudly accompanied her daughter, thrilled to partake in such a prestigious occasion especially as her daughter was at its forefront. After the ceremony she was introduced to Jason. She shook his hand enthusiastically and typical of Jason he kissed her warmly.

She beamed with delight and said, 'I adored your mum. One of my most cherished memories is seeing your mum in person. I remember her driving down the road in a pink Cadillac. I waved to her and I could hardly believe it, she looked right at me, smiled and waved back. I was so chuffed. It made my day.'

Later she confessed that despite her pride and delight at the great tribute paid to her daughter, the highlight of her evening was meeting Diana Dors' son.

I was impressed. Diana's persona was indelibly engraved on the UK psyche, her image was not only alive but thriving. And not only on the UK psyche. She was popular as far afield as Japan. She was not only a famous actress she was a phenomenon. I couldn't help but be captivated.

Besides, I have always been fascinated by people who have wild dreams and manage to achieve them against the odds. And Diana Dors was a prime example. At the age of eight, when the teacher posed the usual question to her class, 'What would you like to be when you grow up?' Diana stood up and without hesitation or embarrassment announced, 'I am going to be a film star and have a big house, a swimming pool and a cream telephone.'

How did an ordinary-looking girl with mousey brown hair, who wore glasses, had a patch over one eye, who came from an ordinary family, attended an ordinary school, lived in an ordinary town, dare to have such a huge passionate dream, a dream that challenged the seemingly impossible; and even more astonishing, how did she make that dream come true? I was impelled to find out. And so the endless hours of research began.

I was lucky in that, because of their past relationship with the young Jason, many of Diana's and Alan's close friends, like Freddie Starr, who had played important roles in their lives, and who had never before agreed to be interviewed, were willing to talk to me. Not only willing, but delighted to relive the joys and sorrows of the heady days they all shared. And, of course, there were Jason's close friends: David, who got me started on this project; Maya, the mother of Jason's daughter; Ruby, the daughter herself; Jason's half-sister, Katie; and a string of lovers. Some of what they told me has been integrated into the first part of the book, more will be told and integrated in this, the second part.

* * * * * * *

The first thing I had to do was fill a huge gap in the story. I knew Jason was 15 when he was sent off to California to live with his half-brother, Gary, who was only seven years older and had returned to England at eighteen. But what I didn't know was what had happened to him in the intervening three years. I knew he had not only been suddenly orphaned at 15 but homeless, penniless and, most important, that he knew little of the real world. Everything had been handed to him, love, care, money, every sort of luxury and privilege. From all appearances he was the quintessential silver-spoon baby. But had the opulence of that silver spoon sheltered him from dealing with the real world? Had it fed him the sustenance which would make him able to deal with the overwhelming tragedies which had suddenly befallen him?

From what I had learned, his infant and toddler experiences had come from one nanny after another. His adolescence experiences had been largely forged by filling the bong, dealing with a drunken father and a superstar mother. Had his cosseted existence prepared him for the rough and tumble of life in the raw, life stripped of privilege and entitlement?

Diana's story, and Alan's story, was embedded in Jason; he was part of that story, a continuation of that story. I needed to know how their stories were played out in Jason's life, how they had impacted on him. I needed to know how he had survived the years in which he had been suddenly severed from their lives, cast out on his own, orphaned.

Chapter 25
Los Angeles – Reality Check

Fifteen year old Jason sat pressed between two people on the economy flight to Los Angeles. If he had boarded the plane bewildered, confused or sad, these emotions were overwhelmed by the energy of the flight – the announcements, the loading of overhead compartments, the bustle of the cabin crew. Although the plane was crowded and the seats not what he was accustomed to, having always flown first class, as an UM, unaccompanied minor, he received special attention from the stewardesses – an extra pillow, a coke before take-off - which made up for any discomfort. And he received extra-special attention because the cabin crew had been informed who he was and what had befallen him. When one of the stewardesses approached him saying he had been invited by the captain to visit the cockpit, he was thrilled. And when an announcement came over the loudspeaker, 'Jason Lake to the cockpit please, the captain is waiting,' he hurried up the aisle, flushed and animated like a Hollywood star about to receive an Oscar.

The captain and co-pilot allowed him to press buttons and turn knobs that made needles fly and lights flash; to listen to airport control and to sit in the captain's seat as though he was flying the plane. And Jason rose to the occasion. He was comfortable with adults, and because he had taken flying lessons the knowledge and expertise he exhibited impressed the flying crew. When he talked about latitude and longitude they even allowed him to turn the dial to make a course change. His charm, good manners, and no doubt his heart-breaking circumstances, elicited an invitation from the captain to join him for lunch. Jason was thrilled.

With all the privileges and concern Jason hardly had time to reflect upon the past or the future; about leaving England, about his mother, his father, or even Michelle; no time to think about Hollywood, where he was headed, to remember the wonderful times he had had there with his parents and half-brothers or to wonder what would happen to him or even where he would live. He had no concerns on that score. His experience with Hollywood accommodation left little to be desired, even the hotel he had once stayed in with his mother was super-luxurious. Then there was Rod Stewart's mansion where they had all stayed, and the mansion his mother had bought where his brothers had lived with their father, and the beautiful estates with Olympic-sized swimming pools, tennis courts, guest quarters and lavish gardens where they had visited his parents' friends, Liberace, Pamela Mason (married to James Mason), Bob Hope, Terry Thomas and many others. He was kept so occupied during the flight and was so exhausted from the exhilaration and excitement, that when he finally returned to his seat, oblivious of discomfort, he fell into a deep sleep, and slept soundly for the rest of the journey. This total involvement in the "now", this blocking out the unbearable sorrow of the recent past, was the beginning of a process which was to have dire consequences for the rest of his life.

The cabin crew said goodbye with such warmth and affection, wishing him luck, giving him mementoes: specially wrapped chocolates, a small replica of the plane, a pilots' cap; it was as though he was a well-loved son. He was delivered into the hands of Gary with cheeks smudged with lipstick and ribs crushed from embraces. He was happy to see Gary. Gary was family and he welcomed Jason with a bear hug, and led him to the waiting car.

Jason was so high on the adventure of the plane ride that he chatted incessantly, telling Gary about the cockpit, the captain, the stewardesses even detailing the lunch menu, but making no mention of their mother's death or his father's suicide, not even asking Gary the question which had deeply troubled him, 'why hadn't Gary come to his mother's funeral?' It was as though he wanted that plane ride, that distance, that ocean to shut the door on what had gone on before, to separate him from a grief he didn't want to feel – he'd had enough of grief. He was going to Hollywood now and Hollywood was the good times, the fun, the time of family, of privilege of luxury, of all the things that were his life. He was so engrossed in re-living the plane ride he was hardly aware of where they were going. But where they were going was not to Hollywood.

Gary had a small, two-bedroom, non-descript apartment which would have fitted nicely into the lounge at Orchard Manor, in an even more non-descript suburb of Los Angeles, in what was known as 'The Valley'. It was the essence of congested suburbia, thick with cheek-to-cheek houses lined with bumper-to-bumper cars, the air chocked with smog and the streets so crowded with people

Jason thought a parade was in progress. For someone accustomed to acres of green, acres of privacy, he found himself encased in a concrete jungle.

This was certainly not the Los Angeles Jason had anticipated. He wasn't exactly disappointed, he was too overwhelmed, too astounded. Besides, he couldn't take the setting seriously, it was too much like being in a movie where the set was sure to change after the next take and move to a new location. But he soon discovered there was no next take, no new location.

However, it was Christmas, school was out, the air was buzzing with excitement and Jason's natural curiosity about almost everything kept him interested, if somewhat perplexed. One of the first things he did was search for, and find, a quiet, deserted little piece of country tucked into a canyon a short climb from The Valley, complete with a tree house, and he was somewhat comforted, somewhat reassured. He had found somewhere he could relate to, his own private hideaway where he could be by himself, something he was used to, where he could smell the country.

All went relatively well at first. Gary, who was on holiday, kept Jason busy, taking him to see the Christmas decorations in Beverly Hills, to visit friends, to a special Christmas dinner with his dad and brother in a famous restaurant where Dickie was recognised and fawned upon being the host of *Family Feud*, a popular television show. And Jason was accustomed to celebrity treatment. At least there was something familiar, something he understood.

There was no shortage of money. Gary had received £20,000 which had been hidden in the albatross and each of them had received £50,000 from the estate – Gary being given Jason's share, as Jason was too young to manage money. Gary bought Jason first a scooter and shortly afterwards a car, albeit from Jason's share of the money; they went to expensive restaurants, bought new wardrobes, a state-of-the-art entertainment centre, and Gary employed a maid – half of everything charged to Jason.

But once school resumed after a prolonged Christmas holiday there was a radical change of scene and things began to go pear-shaped. Gary returned to work organising media events in connection with his dad's television show, and had little time for Jason. Worst of all, he enrolled Jason in the local school, an impersonal institution, with thousands of students and a maze of passageways and corridors.

Jason was used to having his own tutor and didn't take kindly to the rigours of discipline, accustomed to setting his own agenda. He hated almost everything about going to school, the regimentation, the anonymity, the schoolwork which he found boring, having already covered many of the subjects and the teachers who were dismissive of him. And not only did he hate school, he began to hate Gary for sending him there.

Gary was attempting to take his role as surrogate parent seriously but his parenting skills were extremely limited. He didn't have a clue how to deal with the wilful, indulged, 15 year old Jason, who had so recently suffered an appalling tragedy. How could a 22 year old, parent a severely traumatized 15 year old who had already buried the trauma so deep it was invisible to the naked eye? He couldn't. Gary's parenting consisted of imposing rules, forcing Jason to obey them and grounding him if he did not. The technique was an abysmal failure. Jason had little experience with obeying rules. The more Gary insisted, the more Jason rebelled, devising ingenious methods of thwarting Gary and his rules, like inventing a way of clocking into classes without attending, so that Gary was unaware of his truancy.

Jason's needs or how to deal with them were not high on anyone's list of priorities. In effect there were only two adults in Jason's life who had any interest in him, his half-brothers Mark and Gary. Because of a falling out, Gary had forbidden Jason to see Mark. Although Jason ignored the ban sneaking off to visit Mark, by now Mark was married and busy with his own career. And Gary was too inexperienced, too occupied with his own fast-lane lifestyle. He had his own obsessions, his own expensive habits to contend with. Jason became a latchkey kid without any real adult care, supervision, guidance or example.

The one thing Jason found appealing about school was the girls. Their admiration, their attention, their praise was the only feel-good approval on offer and he made the most of it. In England, he had been a 'somebody', he had not only been doted upon and admired by his parents and their friends, but he had been envied, applauded by the wider world as being the child of a famous celebrity. It had simply been enough to be the son of Diana Dors, it was its own vocation, its own reward. But in L.A. he was a 'nobody', unknown and pretty much unwanted and had to make use of whatever pluses he had to obtain some credibility, some standing, to shore up his ego. Being tall, agile and good-looking, he was popular with the girls, and his English accent had them in fits of adoration. 'Say banana!' they would beg, and when he obliged, lingering over the soft 'ah' sound, emphasising the English melodious pronunciation in contrast to the hard American whine, they screeched and fluttered, 'Oh my god, it's so radical!' as if he was a pop star.

Jason was precocious when it came to dealing with females. Whereas most adolescent boys were tentatively inching their way through the labyrinth of femininity, he had already found the way. After watching his dad's porn movies at the age of 10 and listening to his parents and their friends discussing sexual adventures, sex was not some unfathomable hidden mystery. There was no beating around the bush with 'birds and bees' stories. After all, his mother was a sex symbol and his father a porn star. He got the story straight, complete with photographs, films and live models. Just as Diana had adored men from a very early age, Jason adored women when he was still in kindergarten, as was confirmed by Jozy Pollock.

* * * * * * *

Many years later, when I was in the process of writing this book, I was in California visiting my daughter when I got an excited phone call from Jason. Through Facebook he had made contact with Jozy, who had been a close friend of his mother's, probably the closest, and whom he had known since childhood. Jozy was now living in Los Angeles. Jason told her about the book, and about me writing it, and that I was in California at that very moment, not far from Los Angeles. She was not only willing, but eager to meet me. She invited me to visit and stay the night. I was delighted.

Diana and Jozy had met in the late Fifties and became instant soulmates. Their close friendship continued until Diana's death in 1984. Initially Jozy accompanied Diana on tours, acting as dresser, girl Friday, confidante and dear dear friend. They loved being together, bleaching each other's hair, polishing each other's nails, relating intimate experiences, revealing secrets, confessing hopes and desires. Most importantly, both loved to laugh, and found any excuse to burst into fits of laughter. Both had stunning figures and long blonde hair. They looked so much alike that on several occasions Jozy substituted for Diana, signing autographs while Diana was backstage. Often Diana would come to the theatre with rollers in her hair and wearing no make-up, and together they would create 'Diana Dors – glamorous sex icon'. They both had the same exuberant, fun-loving attitude to life. In a card Diana sent to Jozy, Diana addressed her as, 'High-stepping Jozy.' They were so intimate, knew each other so well that when Diana published 'Dors By Diana' in 1981, she wrote in the copy she gave Jozy 'To Jozy – who – (with the exception of a few chapters) could have written this for me! Love D.D. Christmas 1982'.

Jozy married the handsome American superstar magician Channing Pollock, moved to America, and became his stage assistant. Their act became so famous they even performed for the queen; they were on the prestigious 'Ed Sullivan Show' several times, and they toured with Liberace, who played piano for their act. When Jozy eventually divorced Channing and became engaged to Nigel Olsson, Elton John's drummer, she entered the elite celebrity world of rock and roll musicians, enjoying a champagne life style. Elton John became a close friend and she got to know celebrities like John Lennon and Errol Flynn. But throughout her jet-set, super-groupie lifestyle, she was in constant contact with Diana. They exchanged long, intimate letters, pouring out their hearts to each other. When Jozy showed me some of them I marvelled at Diana taking the time to write such long, detailed letters when exhausted from back-to-back performances. They met frequently, their paths crossing in various parts of the world and later when Jozy spent long periods in England.

Jozy was a frequent visitor to Orchard Manor and knew Jason since he was a toddler. She was a beauty then, as testified by the many photographs she had in her apartment, among them photographs with John Lennon, Errol Flynn, and Elton John. She was still beautiful when I met her some thirty years later, now glowing with serenity rather than burning with explosive energy.

Jozy remembered Jason as 'rambunctious, but sweet and charming,' as a lovely, intelligent, but mischievous child, 'bright as a button', Diana and Alan's prize, but 'oh so naughty'.

'He was always trying to peek at me when I was taking a shower. And one day when I was visiting Orchard Manor he actually tried to kidnap me. He said "Jozy, I want to show you something in my room." So I went up to his room and he immediately locked the door and took the key out and I said, "Jason give me the key," and he said, "If you try to get it I'll either swallow it or throw it out the window." So we sat there for a while and he was showing me some of his things, his scrap book, drawings and eventually I said, "Jason, I have to go downstairs, they'll be missing me," and he said, "They don't want you downstairs. But I want you here. You're staying up here with me." So finally after about half an hour I managed to get out of there and Alan says to Jason, "So you really like your auntie Jozy." And Jason says, "I don't only like her, I love her." The little devil, he was only six years old and he was already hitting on females.'

* * * * * * *

With that background and with his need for appreciation and affection – after all he had been the apple of his parents' eyes, with admiration and love overflowing - it wasn't long before Jason had an L.A. girlfriend, and it wasn't long before he lost his virginity to her. And it wasn't long after that that he crashed his car and wanted Gary to buy him another one. Gary eventually did buy him another car but only after extracting concessions and promises which Jason proceeded to ignore. It didn't take long before school became an irrelevance. The teen-age drug scene was thriving in Los Angeles and drugs were a speciality Jason excelled in. Hanging out, listening to music, volume turned to deafening, scoring drugs, death defying car racing and sexual adventures replaced maths and English.

Jason had crash-landed into the real world without a safety belt and without preparation. He had been raised on a diet of indulgences, without rules or structure, protected from the real world by the cushioning of wealth and fame. In his early, formative years he had had more contact with nannies, governesses and tutors, who catered to his every whim, than with parents who set boundaries – something which is often true of children of celebrities, especially when the mother is the celebrity, and the father is an alcoholic. His indulged upbringing had never equipped him to deal with real-world situations, with the mundane, the tedious, the dull, the demanding. He had lived in a world of excitement, of fun, a world in which he was loved, cherished, adored.

As he once said to me, 'What did I know about the real world? I never lived there.'

In his quest for excitement, in his quest to live in the "now", to obliterate the pain of the past, Jason began hanging out with, as he put it, 'Friends in low places', risking his life in show-off challenges and dares, scoring drugs from shady dealers, stealing bits and pieces when Gary refused him money, and inviting trouble. And trouble didn't need much inviting. He was shot at twice. The first time he and a friend scraped enough money together to buy a $10 bag of marijuana. Jason drove down a dark alleyway to make the exchange. However, the dealer snatched the $10 without producing the marijuana. The friend arm-wrestled the dealer through the open window and managed to retrieve the money. Jason sped down the alleyway at 80 miles an hour in an effort to get away when suddenly a male figure appeared from nowhere and there was a flash accompanied by a loud bang. To his utter astonishment Jason realised they were being shot at. Luckily they weren't hit. But the second time he wasn't so lucky.

Having no experience with gang culture, Jason befriended a member of an L.A. gang and took to hanging out with him on a corner of Hollywood Boulevard. He had been warned against frequenting corners on Hollywood Boulevard but it was not yet dark and there were many people about so Jason ignored the advice as, in any case he was apt to do. He was admiring a metallic blue pick-up truck with tinted windows and silver rims.

'Nice truck,' he said to his friend, when suddenly the truck window was lowered and an Uzi machine gun appeared and began firing. Shop windows shattered, people screamed, panic ensued. But before anyone knew what had happened, the van sped away. In a state of shock Jason had dived to the ground and it took him a while to realise he was bleeding. A bullet had gone through the back of his calf. The friend, who was a member of a rival gang and the target of the shooting was not hurt. Bleeding profusely, Jason managed to get home and dress the wound, having learned first aid from his father. He told Gary the bandaged wound was the result of a football injury, but a bullet hole remained as a permanent reminder. The friend was shot dead two weeks later.

* * * * * * *

Jason had been 14 when his mother died, and for five months he had struggled with coping not only with her death, but with a father who was so distraught he was practically a mental patient. The role of father and son became reversed. It was the son who attempted to comfort and console, to provide distractions, to administer solace. It was Jason who took his father to a Greek island for a much-needed rest. Although he was unaccustomed to responsibility, he was suddenly overwhelmed by it.

Then, barely 15, he had to cope with the terrible tragedy of his father's suicide; with the abandonment, the shock, the horror. His sorrow, his bewilderment, his anger were so profound they had been unable to find expression. He had not even allowed himself to cry because, as he said, 'I was beyond grief, beyond tears, and if I had started crying, I wouldn't be able to stop. So I didn't start.' His questions, 'Why did you leave me?' 'Didn't you love me enough?' 'Why in my room?' had remained unasked, let alone unanswered.

And now, in Los Angeles, suddenly transposed to a place, to a life, so alien to him that at times he hardly knew where he was. And although he was playing 'bit shot', hero, master of the fearless, of the audacious, he yearned to be a child again, to be back home, to be held, comforted, to be cared for. So desperate was his need that at one especially empty moment, he phoned Michelle in England begging her to come and live with him. But Michelle did not come. Even she had abandoned him. There was no one to care, no one to be concerned for him. And if there was no one to care about him, he began not to care about himself. It is little wonder that in the three years he spent in Los Angeles he was virtually out of control. Wanting only escape from a festering wound he had no way of addressing, he plunged into a defiant rebellion, a wild recklessness that was a primal scream.

Drugs were his comfort, his answer to neglect. If he couldn't count on people at least he could count on drugs. When he was high he didn't have to feel, to understand, to be lonely. Drugs were living in the now; they 'dulled the pain'. No stranger to the world of drugs, he had long ago been exposed to their benefits. Now sorely in need of those benefits, he spent more time being stoned than straight, listening to ear-splitting, mind-numbing music – heavy metal, thumping rock, hardly eating or sleeping, living on hyped-up energy fed by drugs and sugar, until he collapsed with fatigue, slept for 24 hours, then resumed the cycle. His eyes became sunk in their sockets and so bloodshot that when he went to classes, that is if he went to classes, he wore dark glasses.

He began to lose weight. His diet was so atrocious it was a wonder it could sustain life. From childhood Jason had been a poor eater. He would spit up any bit of nourishment Diana tried to coax him into eating. Try as she might he refused to eat anything but sweets. Diana would sneak cod liver oil into his chocolate drink, multi vitamin liquid into his Coca Cola, but Jason always detected the fraud. Despite persuasion and bribery the no-eating pattern continued unless sweets were the main course. Jason even had his own account at the sweet shop. When I met Kim Waterfield he told me Jason had always carried a little sac with him. Curious, he had asked Diana what it contained.

'His sweets,' she replied with an air of resignation. 'He won't go anywhere without them and only if I allow him sweets will he eat anything nourishing.'

Now in Los Angeles, with no one to be concerned about his diet or to make deals with him, he could eat all the sweets he wanted. Sweets were only punctuated by crisps and the occasional microwaved Lean Cuisine. Existing on drugs, alcohol, sweets and Lean Cuisine, it's a miracle Jason had the strength to become out of control.

The worse Jason's behaviour became the more rows he had with Gary, the more threats and rules Gary would make. But the more rules Gary made, the less Jason obeyed them, and the more determined Gary became to wield authority over him. One day Jozy Pollock was in town, she of the juvenile kidnapping attempt. Eager to see Jason, she invited him to a concert to meet Elton John and Sting. Jason could hardly contain his excitement. Jozy was the good times; she was home, family, affection; she was all he had of his mother. And meeting Elton John and Sting was the icing on the cake. He began counting the days. He even started attending classes.

But by now Gary had accumulated a long list of pending punishments, unsettled scores, and he chose that occasion to settle them. Knowing how much Jason was looking forward to that very special event, how much it meant to him to spend time with Jozy, and perhaps jealous because he hadn't been invited, he grounded Jason, locking him in his room. No amount of pleading, of imploring, of beseeching, of promising, would change his mind. Jason was devastated. His longing to see Jozy was something akin to despair. But Gary was adamant. He had finally found an effective punishment.

He had turned a potentially nurturing experience into a sentence. He had triumphed at last.

But the triumph was short-lived. Jason could not forgive him, could not forgive the injustice, the hurt, the malice. It wasn't long after that incident that he disappeared. Jason, his current girlfriend Deborah, and another friend drove to San Francisco to attend a three day 'Grateful Dead' music festival, living in a tent, high on acid and any other drug they could get their hands on, not sleeping, stoned up to their eyeballs both day and night, hardly aware of the difference. Jason once again sought comfort the only way he knew how.

That escapade was the final straw for Gary. He was beyond fed-up, beyond exasperation. He had tried his best. He had even sent Jason to a $10,000 summer school in Arizona but Jason with his supply of drugs, had ended up corrupting anyone who came within range. Now all Gary wanted was to get rid of Jason, to get him out of his house, out of his life. Without further ado he packed Jason's belongings and moved him into a motel just far enough away so he could forget about him.

The motel was a sleazy place in a dodgy area where hookers brought their clients, renting rooms by the hour. Jason hated it, but he had no choice and no one to complain to. He remained there for several months until Gary finally upgraded him to a small one-bedroom flat that needed as much love and attention as Jason did. Gary gave him no money, knowing he would only have spent it on drugs. Jason lived on his own in this rundown apartment in semi-squalor for almost six months, stealing food from supermarkets, sneaking out of restaurants without paying, his apartment a 24-hour alcohol and drug abuse centre.

Finally Jason turned 18. He was officially an adult. Gary's birthday present was a ticket to London. He gave Jason $300 – telling him it was all he was going to get until he could prove he had a job – put him on a plane, and with a final 'Bye Jase' and a limp wave, he turned his back and walked away.

If, three years earlier Jason had arrived in Los Angeles an innocent without experience of the real world, three years later he was leaving Los Angeles; a connoisseur of Lean Cuisine, female virtues and mind-altering substances; an authority in the art of lying and stealing. And with these new-found skills and with $300, he returned to the country of his birth to begin a new life.

Chapter 26
Back in the UK

Sitting on the plane en route to London Jason was even more uncomfortable than he had been on the flight to L.A. over three years earlier. He had grown several inches, most of them settling in his legs, and economy flights were not known for their legroom. There was no invitation to the cockpit or lunch with the captain. He was an unknown, stripped of his pseudo-celebrity status. But if Jason had gained nothing else in the three years he was in Gary's care he could have written a book on the art of survival, and Chapter One would have been titled 'Finding a Place to Live'. With this in mind, as soon as the plane touched English soil he phoned Rob Barker. Rob had worked as an all-around house help at Orchard Manor while Jason was growing up. It was Rob who had cared for Jason when his dad had been at his mother's hospital bedside day and night, and it was Rob who had informed him of his mother's death in his father's absence. Rob was pleased to hear from him and said he was welcome to stay until he sorted himself out. With accommodation arranged Jason was free to celebrate his homecoming.

After the Purple Om high of the welcome home blast with Andrew and David, and the subsequent low of the aftermath, Jason was faced with real-life challenges. Although he had temporarily solved the accommodation problem, the financial problem loomed large. The $300 he had arrived with evaporated quickly. Fortunately the comedian Freddie Starr, his dad's closest friend, came to the rescue.

As far back as he could remember Jason had adored Freddie Starr. He was like a favourite uncle, and throughout Jason's young life he had often phoned 'Uncle Freddie' for a chat and a laugh. One of the first things Jason did after the Purple Om recovery was phone Uncle Freddie. Freddie, delighted to hear from him, invited Jason for dinner. When Freddie realised Jason had returned to England virtually penniless, he produced a wad of money and, despite Jason's protests, insisted he accept £1,000 to begin his new life.

'Hey Jase, that's the least I can do. But don't spend it all in one place,' he joked.

That £1,000 sorted Jason out for the short term, but the long term required serious consideration. Jason reviewed his options. He could get a copy of *Spotlight*, the guide book for actors and audition for acting work. He had had more than a little success as a child actor and later as a teenage performer, receiving good reviews both for his role in *Breaking the Silence* and earlier in *The Winslow Boy*. His acting talent had even been acknowledged by Diana who had initially discouraged him from going anywhere near the acting profession.

'It's filled with disappointments,' she had warned.

In a letter Diana wrote to Jozy expressing her hurt regarding her estrangement from Mark and Gary, and her difficulties with Dickie, she also wrote about Jason's acting success.

'Jozy, you were a wise girl never to have a family, they are a continual worry, disappointment and sadness, although I must say Jason is shaping up well. He just finished starring in *The Winslow Boy* at the Lyric Theatre for a season. He got the part on his own merit, having auditioned several times and was even, though I say so myself, extremely good on stage. You can imagine how nervous Alan and I were on opening night.'

However, Jason dismissed the idea of tackling the stage. He had returned from his Los Angeles sojourn in a state of mental disarray. He didn't have the stillness required for organising auditions, the patience for learning lines, the focus for committing to a career or the discipline for living on actors' wages. He needed money and he needed it now.

Although his relationship with journalists had been less than cordial, even hostile and although he had shunned the reporters who were waiting for him when he arrived in England, he had learned from his parents, especially from his mother, how the media could be used to advantage. He decided to bite the bullet. Contacting the *News of the World*, he offered them an exclusive interview for £5,000. They agreed. The press was eager for anything containing even a whiff of Diana Dors. The article appeared with the headline 'Jason Returns Home After Rows With Brother.' Although he disliked the article it was instant money, he didn't have to wait for a pay cheque.

In an uncharacteristic responsible gesture, although by now he was leaning more and more towards the responsible, instead of spending the money on indulgences, Jason used it to buy a one-bedroom flat in Brighton. He was able to get a mortgage because he had invented a job and with proceeds from the article could produce the down payment. This was the flat he invited Maya to visit.

Maya, a stunningly beautiful woman, was a little more than a friend of David's. David was living with Susie at the time and his little-more-than-a-friend relationship with Maya was becoming increasingly complicated. So when David introduced Jason to Maya it was almost with a sense of relief, knowing he could predict the outcome. If Jason was partial to 'pretty' he was a slave to 'stunning'. The attraction was mutually instant.

Before the auspicious introduction, David had set the stage, 'Maya, You're going to love Jason.'

Maya more than loved him. She found him 'shiny, bubbly and ebullient,' as she told me. Being warm and compassionate, older than Jason and also the mother of a seven year old boy, fathered by the actor Peter Firth, she couldn't help being affected by Jason's story, it played profoundly on her mothering instincts. And Jason was at his best, handsome, charming, and loveably orphaned. And if he was a winner with the groupie-minded teenagers, he was a killer with a mature, nurturing woman.

Maya took Jason to her heart. Without ever having met Diana or Alan she took against them for what she considered inappropriate parenting. She took against Diana for her absences and neglect during Jason's childhood, and for what she considered Diana's selfishness in not giving Jason adequate attention. She took against Alan for his drunken behaviour, as setting a bad example for Jason, and especially for his suicide which left the 15 year old Jason orphaned, without so much as arrangements for his future, and she took against them both for introducing Jason to drugs and pornographic films at such an early age.

Maya took it upon herself to compensate for what she perceived as Jason's lack of attention, affection and love, although Jason had never felt such a lack, on the contrary he had never doubted his parents' love and had been surrounded by both attention and affection. Although, in retrospect he did admit that participating in the adult world, especially in the drugs and pornography sessions at so young an age was not to be recommended and had, as Diana herself had feared, deprived him of much of his childhood. Maya admired Jason for emerging from the hell he had been through 'lovely, energetic, warm and affectionate,' instead of emotionally crippled.

Most of all, Maya felt a spiritual connection with Jason, a special attachment as though their relationship had karmic significance, as though she had been ordained to make Jason whole. Jason, for his part, lapped up the spiritual significance especially as it was accompanied by genuine affection and love. Their relationship blossomed to the point where they were unable to be apart. Either Maya would visit Jason in his Brighton flat or Jason would visit Maya in her London flat. Maya loved the fact that, as she said, 'Jason wanted to be by my side all the time.' It satisfied her mothering desires, and her mothering desires satisfied Jason's need of mothering. For a while it was perfect, a union made in heaven.

Then in 1989, less than two years after Jason had returned to England and over a year since he had been with Maya, there was a property crash. Jason's flat, which had increased in value by £10,000, suddenly decreased in value by the same amount. Jason stopped making mortgage payments, and lived rent-free for six months, until the bank repossessed the flat. Maya had a maisonette flat in Little Venice, a lovely London neighbourhood, and had already asked Jason to move in with her. In the summer of 1989 Jason left Brighton and went to live with Maya.

Shortly after the move Jason was pleasantly surprised to discover, with Maya's help and perseverance, that Lynne Brooke, the lawyer who dealt with Diana's estate, had £50,000 in a trust fund for Jason from the sale of Orchard Manor. By now Jason was determined to sort out his life, concentrate on developing a career, and even, god willing, earn some money.

Music was Jason's passion. He lived and breathed music. He not only listened to music both night and day, but played music every chance he had, strumming on a guitar, beating on a drum, or improvising on the piano. From the time he had discovered when he was seven years old that he was able to remember any tune he heard and play it on the piano, whenever he had access to a piano he could play for hours, oblivious of everything else. Working in some aspect of the music field, perhaps as a musician, composer or producer, or possibly a combination of all three, was his obvious calling. So aside from paying for rent and living expenses and buying a car, he bought the latest state-of-the-art equipment to set up a music studio.

Jason's only grumble concerned Rory, Maya's active, alert, ten year old son whom she adored. Although Jason was fond of Rory, he resented not having Maya's exclusive attention. That resentment was magnified on a two-month holiday in Thailand. For the first three weeks of the holiday, Maya and Jason were on their own enjoying a blissful time together. In fact the time was so blissful that Maya became pregnant. Both Maya and Jason wanted a child to consummate their love, as the ultimate fulfilment of that love.

Their daughter Ruby was conceived on a remote Thai island in exquisitely romantic circumstances. In the Cave Of The Goddess on one of the most beautiful beaches in the world, Ruby came into being. And later, to celebrate the conception they both instinctively acknowledged and confirmed by a shooting star lighting up the heavens, Jason and Maya swam together in a sea lit by moonlight, the stars rippling in the water and shining in the sky. If they were living in fantasy land, it was a fantasy they both shared.

Jason was 20 and smitten with romance. The only thing standing between him and nirvana was the arrival of Rory. Jason, riding high on the wonder of love, wanted to prolong that wonder, to revel in that love, he wanted to be amorous, tender, adoring. But he needed Maya's exclusive attention to express the ardour he felt. Maya could no longer satisfy that need.

For Jason, Rory became a thorn in the side of love. If Maya, too, was riding high on romance, the arrival of Rory necessitated a modification of that romance. Maya had practicalities to consider: making sure Rory ate properly, that he applied suntan lotion, that he was kept occupied and amused, that he was assured of dedication rather than rejection. And that took time and a shift in focus. She could no longer devote herself exclusively to the love between Jason and herself. The responsibilities of motherhood conflicted with the luxury of romance.

Jason had no such responsibilities. He was young, he was in love and he was loathe to share that love. He became resentful, he sulked, he grew petulant, angry, spiteful. Maya became irritable, explosive. Like Diana, who had complained to Jozy that she had two children to contend with – Alan and Jason, Maya also had two children to contend with – Rory and Jason. Although there were occasional flare-ups, the magic of that night in the Cave Of The Goddess could not be reignited. Jason returned to London smouldering with disappointment. Maya returned to London pregnant with his child.

Ruby was born in October, 1991 after a horrendous home birth. Maya almost died after losing five pints of blood. Jason, helpless and panicky, cradled baby Ruby in one arm, mopped up blood with the other and prayed for Maya's life, while the midwife, even more panicky, phoned for an ambulance. Although Maya survived the ordeal, the birth placed a great strain on their relationship. So when Ruby was four months old Jason and Maya decided on a long holiday, a two-month trip to the U.S, Mexico and Central America.

Maya needed healing after a difficult confinement. The trip was also an attempt to cement their relationship and hopefully to revive the romance of their holiday in Thailand. With money from the £50,000 Jason had received from the sale of the estate, they travelled first to Florida and then to Mexico and Guatemala. They wanted to visit special spiritual places like the Pyramids Of The Lost World in Guatemala, perhaps in an attempt to resurrect the spiritual connection that had been such a powerful component of their relationship.

Trekking through the rain forest, Jason happily carrying baby Ruby on his back in a knapsack; Maya, so awed by the spectacular scenery, especially by the pyramids, that she forgot the trauma of the birth; Rory playing jungle hero and asking endless questions; everyone was in high spirits. Although their method of travel was unorthodox, it was exciting. Each day was filled with new wonders, new discoveries. They couldn't wait to turn the next corner, to be entranced by the next miracle.

However, despite the amazing adventures and the unforgettable surroundings, travelling with a four month old baby and a lively ten year old boy eventually took its toll. In the best of circumstances, travelling often heightens difficulties between people. The strain of being unable to escape each other's company, of language difficulties, of the countless details to arrange – plane tickets, train tickets, bus tickets, accommodation, to say nothing of buying nappies in places where they did not exist – led first to bickering, then to full blown arguments. The resentments became exaggerated, then all-consuming, and finally harrowing. Although Jason adored baby Ruby, was pleased to look after her and enjoyed being with Rory in normal circumstances, the circumstances were not normal and the tensions mounted.

By the time they returned from Central America things had changed radically. Jason had become increasingly restless. Throughout his life he had been shielded from responsibility; he didn't have to contend with hardship, obligations, commitments. Even he admitted he'd been 'spoiled rotten'. Now, not quite 21, he found himself saddled with a partner, two children and a mountain of responsibilities.

The relationship with Maya became increasingly turbulent as Jason baulked at the restraints and demands of family life. He envied friends who were free of parental duties. He wanted to spend time in his studio spacing out on music. He wanted to hang out with friends, smoking dope, coming home whenever he liked, without being berated by an irate Maya, without accusations and threats.

Maya's passionate intensity, which Jason had initially found exciting, was less exciting when it was turned on him. He was tired of their rows, of Maya's temper, of his jealousies. He was fed up with family, he found family hard work, tedious, repetitive. Like his mother he was bored by the confines of normal life. Like her, he wanted a taste of the wild, the bizarre. Mostly he wanted to be young again. He began to disappear for hours, then for days. Maya became angry, resentful, the arguments became stormy, then physical. It was time for a change.

When Ruby was not yet two, Jason took the plunge. He had received £20,000, money remaining from the funds Gary had been given on his behalf. Jason saw this money as his ticket to ride. After being together for four years, he left Maya, Rory and his own little Ruby, breaking all family ties. In truth, he had been about as ready to have a baby as the Pope. Although he relished reports on Ruby's development which he organized through a network of mutual friends, he was not to see her again until she was six years old.

Chapter 27
Ticket to Ride

When Jason left Maya he had almost £20,000 remaining from the money he had received from the estate. As Jason had no concept of how to deal with money, Maya had taken care of most financial issues, and with a sudden yearning for the luxury he had once taken for granted, he rented an expensive flat in Notting Hill Gate, a high-priced London area. And to complement the expensive flat he engaged in an expensive lifestyle – taxis, gourmet restaurants, fine wines, lavish tequila parties and zero-zero, the best quality hashish. Then suddenly the high rolling times were shattered by a startling discovery. Half his money had disappeared in just a few months. Alarmed, he had a moment of panic. At the rate he was spending money he would soon find himself in a seedy flat like the one he had been banished to in Los Angeles. And what about the Indian trip? His heart was set on an extended trip to India but at the speed he was spending money he wouldn't be able to afford a weekend in Blackpool.

Jason's friends had been returning from India with mouth-watering tales of cheap accommodation on beautiful beaches, delicious Indian food and most important, cheap ganja. They painted euphoric pictures of lying on beaches in the sunshine sipping ice cold ganja milkshakes called 'bang lassies' during the day, and partying all night, dancing until the sun rose and it was too hot to dance. And, of course, there was the fascinating spiritual dimension, communing with gurus who believed in attaining enlightenment, a mystical quest which had intrigued his father.

The ultimate inducement came from his close friend, Martin Glover, the bass player for the band Killing Joke, who was known as 'Youth' on the music circuit. Youth had returned from India with rave reviews about the music.

'It's really far out, man. You gotta check it out.'

India embraced all Jason's loves: sunshine, beautiful beaches, beautiful women, Indian food, far out music and, especially, cheap ganja, and if spiritual enlightenment was in the mix, all the better. He was desperate to find a way to replenish the coffers both to finance the Indian trip and to secure his financial future, the latter a consideration which had only recently surfaced. Through an imaginative leap into the bizarre he hit upon an idea.

When Jason was in Central America with Maya he had been impressed by a lucrative tourist attraction. An entrepreneurial Frenchman was selling ten-minute plane rides, flying over spectacular waterfalls in the rainforest, charging $20 a trip. He could easily do the same. He was not far off from qualifying for his pilot's licence. He still had enough money for a small plane and he could set up a sightseeing business in India, where there was an affluent tourist population. Although he couldn't count on spectacular waterfalls, he could rely on nature to provide equally spectacular Indian phenomena. He could see himself as a business tycoon, raking in the rupees while, at the same time, enjoying the alternative Indian scene, expanding his consciousness, while drinking bang lassies and dancing to killer music.

His plan was to first visit India on a reconnoitring mission and set up the Indian side of the project, and then move to India longer term to manage it. The idea was just outrageous enough to appeal to him. In a burst of unusual practicality he set about materialising his Indian vision and securing his financial future all in one fell swoop.

It didn't take Jason long to receive his pilot's licence and even less time to spend £4,000 on a microlite, a small light aircraft, and then arrange to store it until he could ship it to India. He was on a roll. There was only one small piece missing to perfect the plan – a female companion. But even that fell into place.

Shortly after finalising all the negotiations for the Indian adventure he ran into Carmen, the daughter of Chris Squire, the bass player from 'Yes', one of Jason's favourite bands. The musical connection was reinforced by a childhood connection. He and Carmen had been in kindergarten together. However, he hadn't seen her since the days when he had expressed his attraction by snipping off the ends of her pigtails, causing her to retaliate by sticking bubble-gum in his hair. In the intervening years, his technique for expressing attraction had become far more sophisticated, and it didn't take him long to test its effectiveness. The results were instant. The bubble-gum era was consigned to history. Jason found not only the missing piece to complete his plans, but an important contribution to those plans.

As it happened Jason's rent was seriously overdue. Since he needed every penny for the Indian trip he had decided not to waste money paying rent. The only difficulty had been eluding the rent collector. Now with Carmen on the scene the rent collector was no longer a problem. In accordance with his new found frugality, albeit a very selective frugality, instead of paying rent he did a moonlight flit and moved in with Carmen, a move which provided not only a romantic interlude but a safe haven until they left for India. It was reminiscent of Diana and Dennis who, in their lean years became experts at absconding from flats, from country homes, even from hotel rooms, owing rent.

Before Jason and Carmen departed England, Carmen phoned her mother to say goodbye.

'We're off to India mum,' she said cheerfully, and when her mother exhibited dire concern, Carmen said, 'It's alright mum, Jason has a drawer full of cash', which did little to reassure her mother who feared for her daughter's life.

Also, before leaving for India Jason plucked up the courage to visit Orchard Manor. If he didn't have a mother to say goodbye to, at least he had their home which had been so much a part of his mother; her colours, her textures, her style and her prized swimming pool. Orchard Manor was her creation, her work of art, and her presence was embedded in its very being. It was the first time Jason had visited the house since his return from California. He hadn't bid it goodbye when he left for Los Angeles, being too distressed. But now, with Carmen by his side he was able to make the goodbye pilgrimage.

The couple who now owned Orchard Manor were pleased to meet Jason and allowed him free reign. Jason was astonished to find everything exactly where it had been left. The shells and coral he had collected on a family holiday were still in the poolside changing room in the exact same place. His robe was hanging on the same hook. Captain Flint's feathers were in a glass vase on the bar, exactly as he remembered them. Even the Siamese cats were still there to greet him.

The house had been kept as a shrine to Diana Dors, which was both immensely gratifying and immensely heart-rending. But for Jason, visiting the house was like entering the twilight zone, confusing and unreal. He was torn between the desire to linger and the desire to flee, between the desire to remember and the desire to forget. And, by the end of the visit, Orchard Manor, his home, his mother's home, his father's home, was added to the list of terrible losses he was unable to cry for.

* * * * * * *

From a business point of view, the Indian venture was a disaster. It never even got off the ground, falling victim to a major oversight. There was nowhere to land the plane. The beaches were full not only of people, but of cows and the paddy fields were partitioned into small holdings by mud walls. Undaunted, Jason and Carmen simply turned the business trip into a holiday trip and added Thailand and Burma to the Indian itinerary.

During their first Burmese visit Jason hit upon an alternative business scheme to replace the failed one – buying exquisite Burmese antiques, which were ridiculously cheap, and shipping them to the UK for sale at a hefty profit. And to his credit, the project almost succeeded. Although, at the time, visitors to Burma could only get a two-week visa at most, Jason managed, through perseverance laced with charm, to obtain a three-month business visa. However, ultimately the project failed due to financial restrictions imposed by the repressive Burmese regime.

But, despite the abortive business deals, Jason and Carmen had an exciting six-month adventure, travelling through India, Burma and Thailand, riding elephants, river rafting, trekking, conversing with shamans, gurus, holy men, and Jason enhanced the good times by smoking opium with Thai hill tribespeople. If the business deals were a dismal failure, the personal enrichment was a glowing success. If people made pilgrimages to India to 'find themselves', Jason not only found himself, he found his future.

On a beach in Goa he discovered a new genre of music - psychedelic electronic dance music. It was like discovering a new part of himself. It was music that resonated with the inner core of his being, which tied together the disparate musical strands he had been experimenting with into one adventurous whole. It was music that pioneered new dimensions, not only of music but of consciousness. It was music that had its roots in the Sixties' 'summer of love', but which added a Nineties techno twist, using synthesizers in a new and different way, stretching the boundaries of electronic dance music and adding a new psychedelic dimension, a sense of light, of colour, of liberation. It inspired dancing, it reached out to people inspiring communion, inspiring love, it was music that reverberated with the magic of the Nineties – 'Let's get together and love one another.'

When Jason returned to London, in the summer of 1992, although the friendship remained, the intensity of his relationship with Carmen had just about fizzled out. He had only £100 left, having been robbed in India of £1,000. He had nowhere to live. His dream of becoming a business tycoon was in tatters. But he had gained what was most important. He was inspired. He had been introduced to a genre of music that was exactly what he had been looking for, and which was to become a major part of his life.

Jason adopted the new sound and made it his own, he added his interpretation, his energy, his passion. He had found his thing to be, his thing to do, and he set about doing it, devoting himself to the doing with an intensity that did not spare himself or anyone else. If he had been after a taste of the wild he was about to receive an entire mouthful.

Chapter 28
A Taste of the Wild

Jason returned to London from India to a period of sofa surfing before he acquired a two-bedroom flat with two terraces in Holland Park, an upmarket London area, shared with a friend, and paid for by housing benefits. He could hardly wait to dive into psychedelic dance music. With the money he received from selling his plane, he bought electronic equipment and together with two musician friends, Iain Rive and Dan Woda, formed the band US, short for Universal Sound. Although the band had a measure of success, recording several singles and playing numerous gigs, the major happening for Jason was meeting Fraser Clark. Again, it was a match made in heaven.

Fraser Clark was a Timothy Leary convert, deeply committed to the counter-culture philosophy: 'Turn On, Tune In, Drop Out', and to the 'rave' ethos. Although rave was about creating feelings of community and having fun, it specialised in promoting love and dance and more specifically, love through dance.

The rave culture was the 'antidote to urban anonymity'. Dance was its spirit and the beat was its heart. It was based on the idea that a higher vibration could be reached through people dancing together; that dance made it possible for the dancers to open their hearts to each other and allow love to enter. Dance allowed one to be completely abandoned, to embrace the moment, free of obsessions, free of the past.

Psychedelic electronic music was the music of rave, the vehicle making it possible. The music had no lyrics, nothing to distract from the rhythm, the hypnotic beat, the energy, the abandon. It was all about movement, there were no negative connotations that words can incite, no poetry that words can evoke, nothing to separate the mind from the body. Rave was only love, love, love and dance, dance, dance. Together, the music and the dance created the ultimate 'be here now', the ultimate 'carpe diem' experience. The motto being: 'To rave is to affirm'.

Fraser ran an underground nightclub in the heart of London, called Megatripolis, and edited a magazine called *Encyclopedia Psychedelica*, which proclaimed the wonder of psychedelic drugs, marijuana, and hashish, which he believed encouraged feelings of peace and love and created communion. He was a veteran raver, a believer in the ecstatic, an exponent of expanding consciousness.

The club was a lively, exciting place with a wide variety of activities and possibilities. Aside from live theatre and live music, and the indispensable throbbing dance floor, there were not only live speakers like Alan Ginsburg but online internet presentations, initiated by Fraser. These were given by such notables as Arthur C. Clarke, speaking from Sri Lanka, Timothy Leary, and even the Dalai Lama. Although the club had chill out rooms, where people could get to know each other in a relaxed, loving atmosphere, the staple of rave was the dance floor. The club was also the centre for the 'Zippy' movement, a word Fraser coined, a combination of new age ideology and rave culture, and it was these ideas and values he wanted to spread to the U.S by organising a tour which would cover the entire country.

To discuss such a tour, Fraser was holding a meeting at Megatripolis, and by sheer coincidence Jason was at that meeting. Intending to visit a friend but taking the wrong bus he met, by chance, a different friend who was going to the meeting and unwilling to restart his journey, he decided to tag along.

The tour was to be called 'The Zippy Pronoia Tour', 'pronoia' being the antidote to paranoia, the positive counterpart of paranoia. It could be recognised by 'a sudden attack of optimism' an 'outbreak of good will' or an outburst of generosity to someone one hardly knew. Instead of people being suspicious of each other, they conspired, behind one's back, to help one another, to love one another.

Fraser began the meeting by outlining the aims of the tour, which were most impressive. Whereas most tours were just about playing music, this one would be a tour to change the world for the better, to spread happiness, joy, to release the mind from the conventional, the expected, to encourage the freedom to be oneself, liberated, free. Fraser's ideas meshed so perfectly with Jason's, that if Jason had had Fraser's eloquence and erudition he could easily have replaced him.

After his glowing introduction, Fraser passed the microphone around the circle of inspired participants and asked each one what he or she could contribute to the tour.

One girl said, in a tiny wispy voice, 'My name is Marigold and I can offer lavender, incense, and essential oils.'

Someone else said, in a deep hefty voice, 'My name is John and I can carry heavy loads and I make the best chilli known to man.'

The offers were all about carrying, photographing, decorating, designing, but when Jason's turn came he said, 'My name is Jason. I have a band called Universal Sound, US for short. We play psychedelic trance music. I can offer my band.' And that was it.

Since The Zippy Pronoia Tour was conceived with an abundance of philosophy but a shortage of cash, each tour member had to provide their own ticket to New York, where the tour was to begin. The problem for Jason was convincing a very reluctant Iain and Dan to part with money they didn't have and to step into the unknown – both had never even been out of England. They didn't have Jason's background of universal travel, daredevil risks, and were not as experienced with the world of psychedelics, having only put a hesitant toe into the river of ecstasy.

However, through exaggeration, hype and declarations like, 'Hey guys, we're going on an amazing tour! We're going to rock the States. We're going to have the time of our lives and we're going to be massive, humongous, big like the Beatles, only better and richer!' Jason was finally able to instil a modicum of enthusiasm in the other two.

The next problem was acquiring ticket money and the necessary electronic equipment essential for making the music. Money remaining from the sale of the plane was not sufficient and Jason had to approach his friend, Jimmy Cauty, the brains behind the high-profile band, KLF, asking to borrow £1,000. Jimmy agreed the loan on the basis that Jason would give him his vintage keyboards as security and after warning Jason that if he didn't repay the money within six months he would burn them.

When six months later Jason still hadn't fully repaid the £1,000, Jimmy relented, realising if he burned Jason's keyboards he would never get the money back. But being in the burning mood, in the name of art, he burned a million pounds. He began by nailing one million pounds in £50 notes to a piece of wood and then attempted to interest the National Art Gallery in exhibiting the result as a piece of art worth a million pounds. Despite the incentive of donating the exhibit to the Art Foundation for the millennium celebration in 2000, the offer was refused. He then tried to convince various art gallery owners. But no one would touch Jimmy's masterpiece, it was far too ahead of its time.

Taking himself, his art instillation and a team of media people to a remote island in Scotland, he advertised a sensational event – 'Watch KLF burn a million pounds.' The result was a video film extraordinaire. Not content with this astounding piece of theatre, he compressed the ashes into a brick, also worth a million pounds, and invited film critics and art dealers to the showing of a second film called 'The Brick'. For half an hour the invited guests sat looking at a massive screen with nothing on it but an image of a brick – Jimmy's finger to the art world.

* * * * * * *

The Zippy Pronoia Tour had been plotted on the first flush of the internet. Beginning in New York it would cross the North American continent to San Francisco. It consisted of a core of fourteen people – decorators, media people, photographers, roadies, home-grown groupies, a 'vibe instigator', even an on-board philosopher, called Des O'Leary, who when Fraser said, in a moment of ego, 'I may be an ordinary guy, but so was Jesus', countered with, 'This tour may not have much money but it sure has created a few false prophets'.

Aside from the fourteen tour members the numbers swelled and shrank as various people were picked up and put down along the road – the numbers seriously escalating as native groupies and people looking for a home joined the tour. The tour bus had all the necessary trappings, a kitchen, sleeping quarters, a washroom, and, most important, a drug dispensary, open both day and night. The atmosphere was easy, all-inclusive and the structure so loose it was almost non-existent.

To set the mood for the psychedelic good times there was wild attire, outfits to complement the psychedelic music: buckles and bows, glitter, dazzling colours, some glowing in the dark, weird and wonderful hats and footwear raging from guilty military boots to innocent barefootedness. And the tour members, clothed in psychedelia combined with the venue decor to set the psychedelic mood. The venues were bedecked with holographic effects, illusions of flowers, birds, butterflies, angels, drifting through thin floating veils, creating a virtual psychedelic garden to dance in.

And then there was Pincus, a human robot, acquired in New York during the first part of the tour, a major asset and a living indication of the madness, the wonder, the implausible, that lay ahead. Pincus had the appearance of a mutant space warrior from one of the moons of Jupiter, with a face that looked like it was carved from stone. He was a massive seven feet tall, and dressed entirely in black, except for a gleaming metal space helmet. Each of his colossal shoulders was pierced with a protruding metal skewer, and he had a Samurai sword belted to each hip, poised for action. All his movements were robot-like, sharp and staccato and he never uttered a single word. Fraser took one look at him and it was love at first sight – Pincus was perfect.

With his appearance and stance Pincus was the obvious head of security plus money-handler, titles he took seriously. He stood at the entrance to each venue, silent and still, extending his open palm, robot-like to receive the entrance fee, that is when there was an entrance fee, most times there were donations, and depositing the money in a special pocket made for the purpose. He looked so strange, so alien, that no one dared mess with him.

The tour weaved its way across the U.S performing in large venues: 10,000 people in New York's Manhattan Trade Center, 15,000 in Boulder, 30,000 at the Rainbow Wyoming Festival, but also performing in small towns with audiences of 50 people or fewer. When the motley crew exited the bus, in all their finery, Pincus bringing up the rear, the reaction of ordinary folk ranged from celebration to shock. In small Midwest bible towns it was as though there had been an alien invasion and it was best for the good citizens to rush home and lock their doors and their daughters against contamination.

For Jason it was a tour made in heaven. There were no rules, no boundaries. The antics of the tour members were outrageous, the more outrageous the better. Magic mushrooms, ecstasy, acid, marijuana and hashish were available at all times and being stoned was the preferred mode of existence. The gigs were one glorious party, everyone happy, everyone dancing, and everyone in love.

Jason was in his element, he loved partying, he loved women and he loved being stoned. In Boulder, Colorado there were the rainbow gypsy girls to play with and he ended up drinking tequila out of their belly buttons. In Santa Cruz he washed the magic mushrooms down with vodka. In Salt Lake City he ate so much marijuana he spent the night howling at the moon and in San Francisco he was so stoned he was hardly able to perform.

And in between times there were the groupies, pretty, willing, available, fun. There was no one in charge, no one to say 'yeah' or 'nay'; it was all wild, it was all beautiful, it was all sex, drugs and rock and roll. And, of course, it was all totally indulgent, something Jason was good at. The music, which he had been so engrossed in, which had given him so much satisfaction, took second place to the multiple pleasures.

In some ways the tour experience was reminiscent of Jason's childhood where restrictions were few and far between, where discipline was almost non-existent, where he was surrounded by love, by fun times, by wild times, where he was 'spoiled rotten'. It was a throwback to his days of growing up, but just as those days had not prepared him for the realities of life, The Zippy Pronoia Tour served ultimately to reinforce and extend the immaturity, the juvenile behaviour, the instant gratification of those growing-up days, which was perhaps tolerable in childhood but unacceptable in adulthood. It kept Jason unable to 'put away childish things', unable to 'become a man'.

Chapter 29
Even More Wild

From the time Susan Blackburn tried to explain to the fifteen year old Jason why his father had committed suicide, saying, 'Your dad loved your mum so much and he wanted to be with her so much that he did what he did so he could be with her always,' a thought had been buried in Jason's psyche.

Although he didn't think the thought out loud, and although he was not always conscious of it, it had a profound influence on his behaviour, and helped explain that behaviour, even at its most inexplicable – 'If my father took his life to be with my mother, then if I take my life I can be with them both.'

This thought formed the background to Jason's bouts of seriously reckless behaviour, like his death-defying car races in Los Angeles and which was to become particularly evident in the years to come.

When Jason returned to London after The Zippy Pronoia Tour, the high of the tour was in direct proportion to the low of its aftermath. His band had broken up, Iain and Dan being in need of intense recovery therapy; he was broke and living in a run-down squat on the pittance he received from the dole. After the powerful stimulation of the tour, the overload of sensation, everything seemed insipid, tame, washed out. He had overdosed on sex-on-tap, on highs, on the rush of zany, mind-boggling antics. He was drained, limp, without even enough energy to roll a joint.

Then one night he managed to rouse himself sufficiently to attend a friend's party. That party changed his life. Jason met Esther Wyrsch, a Swiss fashion designer who had all the necessary credentials: blonde, beautiful, intelligent, fun-loving, and with the big plus of being into electronic psychedelic dance music.

While dancing together Esther said, 'I really like this tune.'

Jason replied, 'That's funny, cause it's one of mine.'

The die was cast. She moved in with Jason that night.

Things changed rapidly for Jason after that. For one thing he decided he was going to make money, lots of money, he didn't want to live with Esther in squat conditions. It was at this point Jason turned his addiction to being high and to living in the now, into a thriving, money-making business and put his five-star drug education to practical use. With his experience, knowledge, and connections he was able to source the finest quality drugs: Grateful Dead acid from San Francisco, mother-of-pearl Peruvian flake cocaine, top quality hashish from the Himalayas, zero-zero from Morocco, mushrooms from Mexico, and ecstasy from the man who made it – everything except heroin which he resolutely avoided as being damaging to health.

The money poured in and it took no time at all before he and Esther were able to move into a penthouse flat overlooking Portobello Road, the centre of wheeling and dealing both legal and illegal. And it didn't take long after that for him and Esther to disappear for long periods to India, Thailand, Central America, Europe, and the U.S, partly for business, but mostly for pleasure.

Things went beautifully for a while. Jason functioned best with a partner, and especially with a partner who loved travelling and who loved his music. Then suddenly their relationship hit a snag. He discovered Esther was having an affair. Although Esther apologised, making promises, giving assurances, Jason, unable to deal with what he considered disloyalty and especially abandonment, was unforgiving. Without informing Esther, he took himself off to the USA to be with Deborah, his L.A. girlfriend who he was still in contact with, and who was still in love with him.

Deborah had a surprise waiting. Knowing how fond Jason was of partying, almost as soon as he arrived she took him off to her university fraternity party. Being in a 'I don't really care what happens to me' mood, coupled with a desire to show off to the fraternity boys, he engaged in one of those death-defying activities.

The highlight of the party was a competitive drinking game. It involved a contraption called a beer bong, which was used to funnel beer into the participant's mouth to speed up the alcohol intake, while everyone cheered the players on, clapping their hands and shouting encouragement. The winner was the person who consumed the most beer. The record, until that point, was four pints.

Jason in a patriotic mood, determined to outdo the Yanks, to impress Deborah, to prove himself invincible, and especially to restore a shaken ego, asked, 'What's the most beer the bong can hold?'

'12 pints,' came the reply.

'Fill her up,' he said.

'That's impossible dude, it'll kill you, you're not Superman,' someone said.

'Just watch me.'

After five pints, one of the boys brought a dustbin for Jason to throw up in, but Jason turned away disdainfully and went on to the sixth pint amid stunned comments like, 'You're inhuman dude!' As beer was funnelled down his throat his belly became so swollen he looked nine months pregnant. After the eighth pint he thought his belly would explode and after the tenth he felt as though he was drowning. The room was silent now, there were no cheers to spur him on, no comments to challenge him, actually there was little appetite for him to continue. But continue he did.

After the twelfth pint, he bowed, smiled, and calmly sauntered from the room, although he thought he was dying. But instead of dying, he burped a massive burp and a streak of pure white foam, like a mystery projectile, shot into the night, releasing the pressure in his gut. He returned to the room amid cheers and congratulations. 'Hey dude, you really are Superman.'

As though this wasn't enough of an encounter with death, Jason consumed an entire bottle of Jack Daniels. After that, hardly knowing where he was or how he got there, he staggered onto the balcony where another inebriated fraternity man was so drunk he greeted Jason with a slurred, 'Hi, I'm Batman, who are you?' while waving his arms to simulate flying.

'Hey, Batman, I'm Superman. Batman and Superman...' Jason exclaimed, slapping Batman on the back in a gesture of brotherhood. 'I can fly too!'

'Yeah, we can both fly, that's a good one'.

It didn't take much effort for Superman to convince Batman to put their flying skill to the test, by jumping off the balcony.

'I'll race you,' Jason said, 'One, two three, jump!'

And they both jumped off the third floor balcony on to the roof of a car parked on the street below, squashing the car into an accordion. Miraculously, aside from bruises they were both too inebriated to suffer any serious damage.

Jason returned to the party and collapsed on the sofa, his secret intact. He was vaguely aware and completely disinterested in the conversation floating around the room, mostly about football games and football scores. Then suddenly he heard an urgent voice addressing the man seated beside him.

'Hey dude, someone just totalled your car.'

For some time Deborah had been trying to take Jason home but he had resisted. However, at that point he thought, with whatever thinking apparatus he had left, that it was a good idea to leave with Deborah while he was ahead.

But there was still one more twist in the bong drama to be played out. With difficulty, Deborah managed to take the semi-conscious Jason home and put him to bed, certain he would be out for at least 24 hours. However, he woke in the middle of the night with an urgent need to urinate. Still drunk and unable to find the light switch, he staggered into what he thought was the bathroom. He was in the process of relieving himself when suddenly the light went on. He found himself not only urinating all over Deborah's dad's desk, but facing the dad himself. All he could do was mumble apologies and stagger back to the bedroom, leaving the dad confounded and perplexed. Was this the exquisitely mannered young Englishman his daughter had been raving about, whom she talked about marrying?

The next morning, mortified and disgraced, Jason wrote a note of apology to the dad, kissed Deborah goodbye, and beat a hasty retreat to London and Esther. After his outrageous behaviour, Esther's unfaithfulness seemed a minor blip. Jason forgave her. In any case he had already convinced himself they should have an 'open relationship'.

The open relationship resulted in a trip to Ibiza, without Esther. Jason was restless, and after the difficulties he had endured in the U.S, felt he needed a vacation. After a brief period attending to business and securing a bundle of cash he headed for Ibiza.

* * * * * * *

Jason loved the sea. He loved sitting by the sea, walking by the sea, but most of all he loved being in the sea. His dream was to live by the sea, but until that moment came, he spent as much time as he could being in places close to the sea. The finca he had rented in Ibiza, was a beautiful house with thick stone walls, mosaic tiles and an enormous fireplace for cool nights. It was in the hills overlooking a glorious, secluded beach.

Early one morning when Jason had been in Ibiza for some time, he emerged from the sea after a long swim. When he looked up, there sitting on the sand he recognised Jade Jagger, Mick Jagger's daughter, although he had never met her. He smiled warmly and waved. But Jade was not impressed. Probably tired of being recognised by people she didn't know she turned her head away, disdainfully. She had come to this beach specifically because it was hardly visited, and to make sure of privacy she had come especially early, when most of the Ibizan revellers would still be asleep but despite her precautions here was some creep pestering her.

Jason was unaccustomed to women turning away from him and resented the aloof gesture with its obvious dismissal.

He walked up to Jade and with an air of supreme confidence, lightly tinged with arrogance, said, 'You know what darling, you're not the only one with famous parents around here.'

Jade's interest was piqued, 'So who are you then?'

When all was revealed they both laughed and the friendship was instant. It helped that Jason was long and lean and golden brown and 28.

Some time after meeting Jade, word circulated among the Ibizan in-crowd that there was to be a rave at Atlantis beach, a special secluded place which was said to have mystical powers, perfect for a rave. The party was to be set up with all the rave accoutrements: special lighting, psychedelic decor, a powerful sound system and most importantly, drugs. It was Jason's idea of heaven.

Before setting off to Atlantis, Jason and a few friends, among them the infamous Howard Marks, got a head start, smoking marijuana, drinking tequila, snorting cocaine and taking ecstasy – a little party to warm up for the big party. But instead of approaching Atlantis by boat, the normal way, Jason had a great idea.

'Let's go the mountain way, it'll be more fun.'

Unknown to him, the mountain way involved a treacherous climb along a cliff edge with a sheer 400-foot drop.

Even through the drug haze, Jason soon realised his idea was not really a great one. John, Jason's friend and dealer was in the lead, laughing and joking and being a little too happy.

'Be careful', Jason cautioned, 'It's dodgy up here,' when suddenly John tripped and vanished over the cliff. Gone, just like that.

Everyone sobered up instantly and with dread in his heart Jason looked over the cliff, certain John had fallen to his death. He was amazed to see that by some miracle John had been caught on the only bush growing out of the cliff, about 12 feet down with a huge drop below that. Jason called to him, 'It's alright mate, don't move and whatever you do don't look down. I'm coming to get you.' And in one of those death-defying feats he climbed down the cliff, and equally miraculously got hold of John's hand and, with the help of the others, pulled him to safety.

John, trembling and twitching managed to say, 'Jason, you saved my life' and handed him a massive bag of MDMA powder, pure Ecstasy.

It was at the Atlantis beach rave that Jason met Kate Moss. Jade, a close friend of Kate's, introduced them. Kate was already a world-famous model, but Jason, who had spent much time travelling in far off places, was not up-to-date on the celebrity scene.

Curious about a pretty girl, hopefully without a boyfriend, he asked, 'And what do you do, Kate?'

'I'm a model.' Then aware of Jason's blank response, and wanting to correct the impression that she was some no-account model, she added, 'I just split up with Johnny Depp.'

The name meant nothing to Jason, but he recognised the dejection, the abandon.

'Never mind love,' he said. 'I've just found out my girlfriend's been unfaithful to me, so I'm a bit on the rebound too.'

Kate took to Jason immediately. His lack of awareness of her celebrity status signified for her a genuine appreciation, a genuine liking. They danced, they raved, they got stoned together. Jade joined them for a walk along the beach and all three watched the sun come up. Perhaps it was the element of compassion, or the fact that Kate was extremely pretty, or perhaps it was the reward packet Jason had acquired on the way to the party; but a spark had been lit.

When the sun was high in the sky they continued partying at Kate's – drinking, dancing, getting high, laughing, listening to music and then getting high again. Soon it was getting dark again and Jason felt a change of scene was in order.

'I've got this lovely house,' he said. 'Do you fancy coming back?'

Kate fancied, so a taxi was summoned to drive them to Jason's finca. Kate loved the house, old, solid, with beautiful Spanish furniture and with both a pool and roof terrace. She especially loved the garden with its wide variety of fruit trees, fig, orange, persimmon, almond, plum, its own Garden of Eden. They spent the night together, and the next morning Jason woke to Kate making tea and toast. They spent the day together, chilling out, recovering from the partying, talking, enjoying each other's company.

Jason had already booked his ticket back to London but he had two remaining weeks to spend with Kate and they were spent alternating mostly between his finca, Jade's finca, and Kate's finca, sometimes just the two of them, sometimes all three. When he was with Kate at his place he would make her morning smoothies with fruit from the garden, laced with vodka, tequila or both. The afternoon would be spent swimming in the pool, lying in the sun, talking, laughing, before it was time for the first vodka, followed by the first joint. In the evening Kate would get onto Jason's scooter and they would go to one of their favourite seafood restaurants. They both loved seafood, washed down by cold beer and the fish was fresh and delicious. Then they would call Jade and the three of them would cavort on the beach or go to the Rock Bar and drink tequila, champagne and vodka, becoming increasing outrageous as the night wore on.

There was lots of partying, lots of booze, lots of drugs, lots of sex, lots of fun. It was a time of pure hedonism, a time of escaping the sorrows, the grief, the regrets. There were times when Jason and Kate were wild, but there were also quiet times, times when they confided feelings of anguish, fear, desperation. Jason told Kate about his daughter Ruby, about his mother's death, his father's suicide.

'I can still here their voices,' he said. 'They never leave me.'

Kate spoke about Johnny Depp, how deeply she felt about him, how deeply hurt she was. Theirs was not a raging love affair but it was a friendship with affection and compassion.

When the time came, Kate and Jade drove Jason to the airport. After all the fun and good times, there was sadness at parting. It had all been wonderful, it had all been fun, but beneath it all there was an undertow of unhappiness, of unfulfilment. Jason kissed Jade goodbye, then he kissed Kate, a kiss that lingered for a long moment. He left Ibiza with memories of sunshine, friendship and fun, but the sunshine memories were unable to sustain the darkness that was to follow.

Chapter 30
It's Tough Being Us

Jason returned to London and to the Portobello flat which seemed depressingly ordinary after the finca in Ibiza. He was exhausted, disheartened, and broke, and his relationship with Esther had pretty much run its course. Like his return from The Zippy Pronoia Tour, he was apathetic, unmotivated, unwilling to deal with the dreary business of organising his life. Like his mother, he was not good at coping with the mundane, the unexciting, the predictable. Like his mother, he thrived on the highs of life, the adrenaline rushes, and there were no adrenaline rushes waiting to welcome him home.

Then, early in 1999, the possibility of a mini adrenaline rush fell into his lap. Since Esther was Swiss, she was classified as a visitor, not a UK resident, and her visitor visa was almost up. She was on the verge of overstaying her visa and being expelled from the country. However, if she married an Englishman she would have an automatic right to live in England. Without a second's thought, as a gesture of goodwill, Jason offered to marry her.

About the same time *OK!* magazine contacted Jason offering him £5,000 to collaborate on a story about his mum. Jason happened to mention he was planning on getting married that summer and the offer jumped to £10,000 if he would give *OK!* exclusive rights to cover the wedding. Although Jason and Esther were not planning on a wedding, a divorce being more in order, they quickly changed their plans. For Jason, the wedding was an opportunity to indulge in a bit of theatre and for both of them it was an opportunity to get some much-needed money, to say nothing of wedding presents.

At the time Jeff Ihenacho, an old friend of Diana Dors, ran an exclusive shop called 'One Of A Kind', which specialised in vintage clothing. Jeff was delighted to outfit the couple so they could play bride and groom in style. Jason cut a dashing figure in a gold lamé jacket, a white satin shirt frilled at the neck, a wide cummerbund around his waist, and artificial snakeskin shoes. Esther was exquisite in a white antique wedding gown with layers of silk and lace. The show was perfect, with expert casting and wardrobe.

The guests included old family friends, among them Jess Conrad; Ted Smith, Jason's Uncle Horrible; Andrew Ray, of the white jelly bean and Purple Om episodes; David Malin, Jason's closest friend; and of course Freddie Starr, who probably had to cancel an engagement to attend. It was a great party. Champagne flowed, the groom kissed the bride, the happy newlyweds danced as the guests raised their glasses to toast them, and the cameras clicked. After all, a party was a party, and Jason was an expert at partying. Five months later Esther and Jason were divorced.

With Esther gone, there was no need to preserve an air of domesticity. The flat could be turned into a full-time party palace. Jason had developed his drug connections into a profitable business and the business would be even more profitable if it had a central location, a place where there would always be fun, always be drugs, always be girls. Jason knew exactly how to create such a place. His time with the Pronoia Tour had not been totally without practical advantage. He had learned about lighting, about decor, about creating moods and atmosphere to make a high even higher. Essential both to the decor and to Jason himself were pretty women. They provided erotic interludes and visual excitement, and were good at making hash brownies. Jason, with his combination of charm and first-class produce had enticed a bevy of some of the loveliest ladies in town to his den of iniquity.

One of the loveliest was Fi Fi Dennison. She was not only lovely but intelligent and caring, and she adored Jason. She found him not only attractive but amusing, fun and 'gung-ho for anything', and she loved his child-like quality, which, like with Maya, evoked in her feelings of care and compassion. She told me she was 'consistently enamoured of him,' but realised early on that, at this stage of his life he was 'too on the run, too part-time, too on his own path' for more than a friendship. Besides which the lothario aspect of his personality, the need to seduce women, the need for a constant string of affairs, was not something she would consider submitting to. But they developed a strong bond. Fi Fi was one of the few people he could count on, trust, and confide in.

Jason often spoke to Fi Fi about his mother and father, something he did with few other people. He told her how much he missed them, how his father killing himself in Jason's room was somehow a message for him, how the question of why his dad left him on his own gnawed away at him, haunted him, ripped a hole in his heart. Somehow he felt guilty, responsible. He loved talking about his dad, telling stories about him, quoting him, and Fi Fi was a good at listening. He told Fi Fi how much he admired his dad's way with words, with perceptions, how he could encapsulate the essence of an experience in a few words. Like the comment he made after watching a film of himself being drunk.

'I know where he's coming from but I wouldn't like to be him.'

He could also use words to aim for the jugular, like his comment to someone he wanted to devastate, after being insulted during a drinking brawl.

'Your breath would knock a buzzard off a shit wagon.'

Besides, he was incredibly funny and delightfully witty.

One of the stories Fi Fi loved because it gave her a picture of the mad events in Jason's boyhood was about P. J. Proby, the English Elvis Presley. Proby, a heavy drinker, was a good friend of his parents. When they discovered he was on the verge of killing himself through alcohol abuse, they took him into Orchard Manor to dry him out and, in effect, save his life. They looked after him for about a month, until he was well and ready to face the world. One night, during that month, coming home late he accidentally got locked out of the main house, and ended up sleeping in a log cabin on the estate.

After he had left Orchard Manor, his stay there underwent a radical revision in an article he wrote for the *News Of The World*. Needing money and knowing how eager the press was for any story about Diana Dors, he concocted a real winner. He told the journalist how he had been dragged to Orchard Manor against his will and kept in conditions that made Colditz look like a luxury resort; how he was forced to sleep outside on a bed of pine needles (the log cabin mutating to a bed of pine needles). The story enraged his parents.

'That bastard cunt', his dad said. 'That's how he repays us for saving his fucking life. When I get my hands on him, he'll really know what Colditz was like.'

Although Proby realised he had forgotten his favourite guitar at Orchard Manor, it took him three months to work up the courage to phone Alan and ask for it.

As though nothing had happened, he said, 'Hi, it's P. J., I'd like to pick up my guitar.'

'Proby, you cunt, if you set one foot on my property, I'm going to fuckin' kill you', Alan shouted and slammed the phone down.

Another month went by. Then one morning, when Jason was about eleven, Diana was bustling around in the kitchen giving him breakfast, Alan was still fast asleep upstairs, when the gates to Orchard Manor opened and a mini Cooper Estate pulled up to the house. Proby and a big black muscleman got out of the car and walked into the kitchen.

In a loud Texan accent Proby said, 'Where's my guitar?'

'Is that you, Proby?' Alan shouted, being woken from a deep sleep. A few minutes later Alan stomped down the stairs, holding a shotgun.

The black man took one look at the furious Alan and the gun and said, 'I'se leaving boss.'

'What's eating you dude?' Proby stuttered.

'I'm going to fuckin' kill you, Proby,' Alan said, raising the shotgun.

Jason sat open-mouthed, his spoon of cornflakes immobilised in mid-air. Proby bolted from the kitchen and jumped into the car. Alan, standing by the kitchen door pointed the gun at the petrol tank.

'Alan, remember your dignity!' Diana exclaimed.

Alan froze and Proby made his get-away. It took several years before Proby got his guitar back and they could all laugh about the incident.

One night after a disturbing talk with Fi Fi about his dad's suicide, Jason was so agitated that before going to sleep he took a massive dose from his escape arsenal. That night he dreamed he was his father, immersed in the torment of his wife's death. The despair was excruciating, he could feel it in every cell of his body. The pain was unbearable. His head was splitting open, his skin was on fire. Knowing only that he must stop the pain, crazed with despair, he rushed into Jason's room, took the gun from the drawer where it was hidden in case of a police search and without thinking, without knowing, without considering, he ended his torment. Jason woke up shaking, covered in sweat, but with a powerful realisation. His father had not left him a message by committing suicide in Jason's room. He had been too desperate, too insane to make plans, to consider consequences. He had shot himself there because that's where the gun was. Jason himself knew that mindless desperation, had experienced it in his own life. The relief was overwhelming, the forgiveness total.

* * * * * * *

By now, Jason's flat had become legendary – it was *the* place to hang out, listen to music, dance and get high. The party was twenty-four-seven. It was reminiscent of Diana's flat in the early days when she lived with Kim, where there was always a party happening, loud music, dancing, people coming and going, a centre for good times, but with alcohol replacing drugs.

One day, in the midst of the usual festivities there was a buzz on the intercom. Jason answered.

'It's the police. We're coming up.'

'Ha! Ha!' Jason scoffed. 'Stop fucking about, mate. Who is it really?'

The voice was hard and official. 'We have a warrant for the arrest of Mr Jason Lake.'

Jason turned to ice, his worst fears were happening. It would be a major bust. The flat was a veritable drug emporium with every drug known to man and then some. Lines of cocaine were laid out on the coffee table, a sheet of acid containing 1,000 trips was being used as a place mat, a jar containing 300 tablets of ecstasy decorated the mantelpiece, and the air was so thick with marijuana that, as Jason said, 'You could have cut a lump out of the air and skinned up.' And there were girls in various states of consciousness and attire, dripping off the walls. The flat reeked of debauchery. The press would have a field day, 'The son of Diana Dors was found...' He would end up in jail for a minimum of fifteen years. He couldn't deal with jail. He'd rather die. He didn't mind dying. Dying was easy, it was living that was hard.

'We're coming up,' the officer shouted, this time more aggressively.

Jason could feel the life draining from his body, he was melting into the landing. Soon he would be a little puddle of butter like in one of the stories his dad used to read to him. Stoned, wobbly, agitated, he descended the stairs. If he could head off the police, stall them, at least he would gain time for his friends to hide the evidence. He met the officers halfway up the staircase.

'You look a bit nervous, Mr Lake,' one of the officers said.

'Well you just told me I'm being arrested, that would get on anyone's nerves,' Jason replied, as he ascended the steps backwards, pausing on each one, desperately trying to gain time, as the two officers, one big and burly, the other tall and thin, edged him up the stairwell.

In a tone of mild outrage, in a suddenly acquired posh accent Jason said, 'What's all this about, Officer?'

'Are you Mr Lake?'

'Yes Officer, I am indeed Mr Lake.'

'It's about failing to appear for a traffic offence.'

Failing to appear for a traffic offence. Is that all? How wonderful! Perhaps he wouldn't melt after all. But he wasn't off the hook yet.

The officers had backed him right up to the door of the flat and were intent on entering. Jason managed an extra moment of stall.

'But Officer, I spoke to one of your colleagues the other day and I thought we had settled the matter.' Then realising they were going to enter the flat no matter what, he took the initiative, 'I have his number inside, come in and we'll sort this out.'

Although he was inwardly trembling, he swung the door open with panache.

'Come in officers, welcome,' he said, hoping he had given the occupants enough time to dispose of the gear. The officers entered. Everyone was sitting around the room smiling benignly, as though they were part of a knitting circle, cups of tea replacing the cocaine which had been snorted off the table.

'Smells a bit exotic in here, doesn't it sir?' the burly officer said.

'Okay officers, I must confess,' Jason said. 'My friends and I were having a little puff in the privacy of my home,' and then in an attempt to make light of the situation, he added, 'I ate the rest when I knew you were coming up the stairs. Sorry, but there's nothing left to offer you.'

'You know we can search this place.'

'Please, be my guest,' Jason said graciously. But before they could take him up on the offer, he said, 'I'd like to go to the station Officer, I'm keen to clear this matter up.'

He had to get them away from the flat. They went out into the Portobello Road. The market was in full swing, stalls laden with fruit, vegetables, flowers, stallholders hocking their wares offering irresistible bargains. Jason donned his dark glasses, he had to turn down the stimulation, to exit the kaleidoscope. A police van with five policemen was waiting. He was ushered into the back by the thin policeman. The burly one got in front with the driver. The procedure was so routine that hardly an eyebrow was raised either by the shoppers, the stallholders, or the people crowding the street.

As soon as the van set off the burly policeman turned around and began interrogating Jason.

'Where were you born Mr Lake?'

'London,' Jason replied.

'Which hospital?'

Jason was becoming edgy. *Which hospital? What did 'which hospital' have to do with anything? What were they up to? Some diabolical scheme they had concocted in order to press charges. I must be careful not to give them too much information.*

'I can't remember the hospital. I was only a little baby at the time.'

'Well, I know exactly where you were born,' said the burly policeman.

Bloody hell, they must have a file on me the size of a telephone book.

'You were born September 11, 1969, in Princess Charlotte Hospital', the officer said, with the satisfaction of someone who had just answered the million dollar question.

'Have you been checking my records?' Jason said.

'No, it's much more mystical than that.'

Fucking hell. Now I've got a cosmic copper on my hands.

'Do you know how I know that?'

Jason shook his head.

'It's because I was born right next door to you, in the same hospital.'

This is definitely a set-up.

'Your mum was Diana Dors, wasn't she? You're Diana Dors' son. You and me were born in the same hospital on exactly the same day.'

Jason could hardly believe his ears. *So that's why they hadn't searched the flat. The coppers had known who he was from the start.*

Thank you Mum, thank you coppers, thank you guardian angels, thank you, thank you, thank you.

When they got to the police station, the burly policemen shuffled through some papers, and then said, 'Sorry Mr Lake, our mistake. You did sort it out with my colleague. Sorry to have bothered you. I wouldn't have liked to arrest Diana Dors' son.'

Jason almost kissed the officer, then taking advantage of acquiring the moral high ground, he cheekily said, 'Can you give me a lift home officer?'

'By all means.'

By the time they returned, the flat had been evacuated except for Nicky, a faithful friend who had stayed behind to look after things, certain Jason would not be coming back. When she saw the squad car pull up in front of the house, she panicked, convinced the police were returning to search the flat. But instead, Jason got out of the car and casually waved goodbye to the police officer, and the police officer casually waved back.

That encounter with a fate worse than death put the fear of God into Jason. Reality had scored big time. Jason had to admit he was not invincible and vowed he would never put himself that close to incarceration again. He decided to close up shop, that is, after selling all the drugs he had stock-piled, so he'd have enough money to sustain a lifestyle which, although still extravagant and generous to a fault, would have some built-in restraints, some self-imposed restrictions. The drug mecca would cease to exist. He would turn away customers with a 'Sorry mate, no more anything, shop's closed'.

To embark on this new agenda, he dismantled the den of iniquity. He dismissed his harem. He tore down the Indian spreads with their tent-like chill-out sanctuaries, disposed of the low Moroccan benches, the lanterns, candle-holders, the exotic decor and returned the flat to a proper conventional dwelling. Perhaps it wasn't the romantic retreat it had once been, but it was a hell of a lot better than a concrete cell with a bucket to pee in.

Everything went well to begin with, he settled down to playing music, visiting friends, eating proper meals instead of sweets, avoiding spirits, even taking out a gym membership, although he didn't get much further than the membership card. He was down to one girlfriend, Fi Fi Dennison who, because she was beautiful, sexy and a good listener, had survived the drug mecca closure.

All this time Jason had remained close friends with David Malin, the bond between them going back to his childhood. David had been a regular at Orchard Manor and had also been a regular at the Portobello flat. They had shared many wild times and sometimes had even shared girlfriends. David, too, had been a product of a celebrity past and often in discussing that past, reflecting upon its rewards and its pitfalls, trying to make sense of how it impeded upon the present, the alcohol, the drugs, the lust for that dangerous edge, David would sigh, 'Jase, mate, it's tough being us', and there was an element of truth in that declaration.

David was important to Jason. He was one of the few connections Jason had with his parents, with his childhood. Jason and David could sit for hours, stoned and mellow reminiscing about 'the good old days', about the antics that went on in Orchard Manor. One of their favourite recollections, one which always evoked laughter concerned Ted Smith.

Teddy had been one of Diana's best friends. He would make her laugh to the point of becoming hysterical and begging him to stop. Diana, with her taste for naughty bad boys had always been drawn to criminal types. Teddy fit all the categories. He had graduated from being a stuntman for Tom Jones to being a criminal, although, as a criminal, he was a self-confessed total failure. He had been involved in one of the first credit card scams, robbing the Bank of America of sixteen million dollars, and then being caught and jailed in Singapore. He had failed in his attempt to smuggle gold and he had failed in every other crime he had attempted. He had made an art form out of failure. He described himself as 'the most unsuccessful villain of all time'.

Although Alan and Ted were good friends there was always an undercurrent of competition in the friendship, each trying to outdo the other. Ted was a handsome man with the look and swagger of an eighteenth century pirate. Although he was big and powerful, when he was sober he was physically gentle, but verbally violent. He and Alan were always squaring up to each other, most of the time it resulted in amusing banter, but after one drink too many Ted could turn nasty and pick a fight. Alan, often equally drunk, would have no objection to a fight especially as he always won. A few punches would be thrown, a bit of posturing and that would be it.

But on this particular night, a night both Jason and David will never forget, things were different. Ted had reached his drinking limit and then some, and had become especially obnoxious, baiting Alan, intent on provoking a fight.

In his gangster twang he taunted, 'You think you're so fucking tough, Mr Lake. I can take you on anytime, you and two more like you.'

Alan who had given up drinking by now, was determined not to rise to the bait. With an air of boredom he said, 'Not again Teddy, you know where this is going.'

'Yeah, I know where this is going, it's going right up your ass.'

'Give it a rest, Teddy,' Alan said, in a tone of complete disinterest. Diana had seen it all before and was reading a magazine.

Teddy, sparing for a fight and resenting Alan's indifference, and Diana's apathy, slinked off to the kitchen. There was a rattling in the cutlery drawer and Alan prepared himself to be accosted by Teddy brandishing a knife. Teddy entered the room reeking of menace. He confronted Alan, his right hand behind his back, concealing the knife. In a sudden gesture of defiance, and with great panache, he drew his weapon. However, in his drunken confusion he was pointing a spoon instead of a knife.

In a voice reverberating with derision, Alan said, 'What are you going to do with that Teddy, eat me to death?'

Everyone collapsed with laughter including Teddy himself.

* * * * * * *

Jason was doing fine, leading as clean a life as it was possible for him to lead, taking pride in resisting temptation, even in the closure of his drug mecca, enjoying having the flat to himself, enjoying spending time with a friend or two, with David, with Fi Fi. Then one day calamity struck. An old friend came to visit who had just arrived from Peru with half a kilo of uncut cocaine. That visit tipped the scale. No armour could have saved Jason from that assault. 'Just a few lines for old time's sake.' Then – 'One final last-bastion splurge.' That last-bastion splurge turned into a first degree nightmare.

Jason graduated from a splurge to a full-blown addiction, freebasing crack cocaine. He not only graduated, he married crack cocaine. He had found his ultimate bride, his goddess. He wanted no one else, nothing else. Everything else became irrelevant. He would retire to his private attic space where no one was allowed, not even Fi Fi, and worship his goddess.

As he said, 'All I wanted, all I needed was another hit, and after that hit I wanted another hit, and after that I wanted more.'

His flat, from a hippy style haven with beads, flowers and Moroccan kalim, became a crack house with bare walls and soiled linoleum, and queues waiting outside the door. He was his own best customer. He didn't eat, he didn't sleep, all he did, all he wanted to do, was smoke crack. He had retired from life with mistress cocaine his only companion. In one of his death-defying moods, he smoked crack until he was green around the eyes, until his six-and-a-half-foot frame became a 90 pound skeleton, until he hit rock bottom.

Then, by one of those chance events that intercede to rescue life, to defy death, his friend Alex Cesari, who claimed to be a descendent of Julius Caesar, and his lovely partner Mia, paid Jason a surprise visit. They were appalled at what they encountered. Alex and Mia had a house on Pantelleria, a tiny volcanic island off the coast of Sicily, with natural hot springs and caves which emitted steam, known for their health giving properties. Without asking permission or seeking consent, kicking and screaming they dragged an unwilling Jason off to their home in Italy. Jason was so cunning that, unknown to them, he devised a way of smoking crack on the plane which outwitted the smoke alarm. After three weeks in Italy detoxing, being escorted from hot springs to steam caves and back again, sweating, cursing, screaming, suffering an excruciating withdrawal, he was cured. Alex and Mia had saved his life.

It was not long after returning from Pantelleria clean as a whistle that Jason met Sally Boyden, an Australian child star, talented, beautiful and sexy. They met at a London nightclub. Late in the evening three burly bouncers were attempting to evict a young woman who had become boisterous. As they dragged her past Jason's table, the woman obviously distressed, Jason, stood up and in a gallant gesture, with a bow, handed her a flower. Sally, sitting at a nearby table witnessed the incident and was impressed. They moved in together shortly afterwards. Things went well for a long while.

They were good together, productive. They played music together, performed together, Sally singing and Jason playing keyboards. They were even part of the Golden Jubilee celebration, performing for the Queen. Their main project was writing a children's book called *Punctuition*, a learning vehicle which was both fun and educational, helping children learn punctuation marks. It involved comic characters who represented different aspects of punctuation, getting into various amusing situations. One of the leading men was Full Stop, a big fat character who plodded along a sentence until he finally stopped, ending the sentence; and Prima-Donna-Comma, his leading lady and best friend because she helped him pause and catch his breath as he plodded along the way of a sentence. The book almost became a children's television show, along the lines of Sesame Street.

Then one day Sally and Jason had a confrontation which escalated into a full blown row. For whatever the reasons, real or imagined, Jason felt Sally was losing interest in him and was about to leave him. As with Esther he was consumed with feelings of abandonment. There were accusations, counter accusations, cursing, swearing and Jason became so enraged, so violent, that instead of hitting Sally, and in one of those 'I-don't-give-a-fuck-if-I-die-tomorrow' moods, he shouted, 'Fuck you Sally', and dived off the three storey balcony head first, onto the pavement below. He broke not only his skull, his neck, his arm, hip and foot, but also the concrete paving stone, cracking it with his head.

He woke up in an ambulance screaming for painkillers, which were refused until the injury could be assessed, and then slipped into a coma. Four days later he woke up in the hospital, covered in bandages, his arm and leg in traction, with a 24-hour psychiatric nurse to guard against another suicide attempt.

When three months later he was allowed to leave the hospital, he was able to function, but only with strong painkillers. He wanted nothing more to do with Sally. Rosemary Warcup, a dear and compassionate long-standing friend, insisted he stay with her and her husband Adam. Rosemary was a healer, known as 'Healer to the Stars', among them Geri Halliwell and Kylie Minogue. She gave Jason daily healing sessions, mainly through Reiki, a Japanese healing technique. It took Jason a full year to recover. He stayed with Rosemary and Adam all that time, rent free. Jason called Rosemary, 'my angel' and said, 'I'd take bullets for her', so deep was his gratitude.

Then, at a Halloween party, he met Marcella. It was love at first sight. He was intrigued by her hazel-green eyes, long dark hair and her innocent yet naughty smile. They became inseparable. The only problem being that Marcella managed a bar. Jason thought it was a perfect arrangement. Each night he would go to the bar to be with her, and, of course, there were drinks on tap. Alcohol was plentiful and it was legal. It didn't take him long to get into the old abuse pattern. And it didn't take long after that for him to start drinking excessively. After a year his drinking was out of control. That's when he visited David in Ramsgate and that's when he ended up living in Broadstairs, or as Fi Fi put it, that's when 'Jason took early retirement in Broadstairs.' And that's when I became part of the picture.

Jozy Pollack

Alan and Diana, Orchard Manor Swimming Pool

Stained glass mural, Orchard Manor Swimming Pool

Deborah and Jason on the road to Grateful Dead concert

Jason at 18, back from LA

Jason and baby Ruby

Maya and baby Ruby

Pinkus

David Malin

Jason and Esther at a rave

Sally and Jason

Jason with Duran Duran

Viking Bay, Jason's home view

Jason with Gregory Peck and Ruby

Marcella

Ruby and jason, 2008

Jason with half-sister Katie

Jason on the beach with piano

Jason and Lucky

Jason, September 2011

Jason at his parents' graves

Chapter 31
Freddie Starr

Jason's upbringing had been studded with celebrities, actors, musicians, comedians, even celebrity gangsters; they were the stars shining in his boyhood heaven. One of his favourites was Britain's much loved comedian, the irreverent diamond-in-the rough Freddie Starr, he of the £1,000 gift for Jason to begin his new life after returning from California. Freddie had not only been Alan's closest friend but also Diana's personal jester. Jason adored him. Although Uncle Freddie visited frequently, his visits could never be often enough for Jason.

Freddie was completely tuned into Jason's sense of humour, knew exactly what Jason found funny and would make him laugh until his sides ached and he was rolling on the floor in painful delight. Jason considered Freddie more his friend and playmate than his parents' friend. They spoke to each other in different accents, mimicked how different people walked and talked, even how they looked – Freddie being a brilliant impressionist, with a face that could create a hundred moods: Jason called it his 'bendy face' – and with a repertoire of physical skills that could, in a flash, transform him from a haughty Flamenco dancer to the limping Hunchback of Notre Dame, to say nothing of his versatile singing voice.

Best of all, the young Jason loved Freddie's pranks, the more tasteless the better, especially when Freddie let him in on some prank or other, swearing him to secrecy. Jason would proudly guard their secret although hardly able to contain his excitement, waiting for that magic moment when the hilarity would explode. Like the time Freddie played a trick on guests he had invited to a party. Freddie took his guests on a tour of his estate on a hydraulic cart mounted on the back of a tractor. Then passing through a muddy patch he slowly tilted the cart. The startled guests, unable to believe what was happening shouted for help, but none was forthcoming. Jason, spared the indignity, sitting up front with Freddie, howled with laughter as the guests, attempting to maintain their balance, scrambled up the cart, clinging to each other with shrieks of dismay as the cart gradually discharged them into the mud, party clothes and all. Jason and Freddie were naughty kids together revelling in the mischief concocted by Uncle Freddie and applauded by Jason.

Jason loved visiting Freddie's massive estate which featured racehorses, flashy cars and even Freddie's own helicopter. Speed was Freddie's middle name.

'A helicopter is cheaper than paying all those fucking speeding tickets,' he said.

Freddie always took Jason to the stables to see the horses and let him feed them lumps of sugar, carrots and apples. Jason liked the feel of a horse eating a lump of sugar off his hand, it made tingles go up his spine and he loved stroking their coats, smooth as silk.

Much later, when he was fifteen and his father had died and he no longer had parents Jason found comfort in Freddie's presence. In the short period before Jason went to Los Angeles Freddie was there for him, making sure he was okay, and when Jason was taken in by family friends, Freddie made it a point to visit Jason as often as he could. Although he was busy to the point of exhaustion, he always found time for Jason, but by then Jason found it harder to laugh with Freddie and things weren't as much fun.

Then, much later, when Jason was eighteen and he had spent several turbulent years with his half-brother in Los Angeles, returning to London virtually penniless, it was Freddie who had given him £1,000, to help him get started. He saw Freddie only now and again after that, but they telephoned each other, regularly at first, then gradually less often, but they always stayed in touch. Freddie was a workaholic, constantly touring and performing, but he was always delighted to hear from Jason.

When eventually Jason moved to Broadstairs he phoned Freddie to let him know where he was living.

'Broadstairs,' Freddie said. 'That's close to Margate, right?'

'Right,' Jason replied. 'Less than a ten-minute drive. Why?'

'I'm playing in Margate on August 18th at The Winter Gardens. Let's see, we're in May now, that's only a few months away. Why don't you come along? I haven't laid eyes on you for years. I bet you're a big boy now with big strong muscles – know what I mean,' he chuckled, 'and that you're not rolling on the floor on your own any more. Come early so we can have a chat. And you can give your uncle Freddie a big bear hug like you used to. To be honest Jase, I could do with a big bear hug myself.'

'Nice one', Jason said. 'Maybe you can come back to my place afterwards. I want you to see it and I also want you to meet Marcella, my new lady.'

'Sorry mate, I'd love to, but I have to leave right after the show... I have another gig at the other end of the country next day, I'll be driving all night.'

'Maybe next time,' Jason said.

'Maybe next time. But don't forget this time, make it your business to be there.'

'Wouldn't miss it for the world. I'll be there all right,' Jason said, delighted by the possibility of seeing Freddie in the flesh.

'And bring the little lady.'

'Will do.'

Jason invited me along for the big event. I had never been to the Winter Gardens, a magnificent Edwardian seaside building, home to some of England's top entertainers, including the Beatles. We got there so early that the place was deserted, and I had time to be impressed by the grandeur of the venue. Jason announced our presence to the doorman and we were told to get drinks at the bar while Freddie was informed of our presence. As I stood in the beautifully refurbished bar, drink in hand, gazing out to sea, a feeling of uneasiness took hold. Freddie was not expecting me. What if he wanted to see Jason on his own? What if I was intruding?

'Are you sure it's okay for me to be here?' I asked Jason. 'Maybe he won't be up to meeting strangers.'

'Freddie's cool,' Jason said. 'You're my friend, don't worry. I really want you to meet him.'

Before I could express any more doubts an usher arrived to escort us to Freddie's dressing room.

Freddie Starr's eyes lit up when he saw Jason, and his smile radiated concern and affection. It was the smile – a mixture of disbelief and gratitude – of a father greeting a favourite son who had just returned from the trenches unscathed. He embraced Jason with the promised bear hug, then holding him at arm's length he gazed into his face with the tenderness of a mother gazing at her new born, his own face clouding over with misgivings.

'It's been too long mate, much too long. It's all that time spent chasing my tail, trying to catch up with myself.'

It was minutes before he realised that Marcella and I were present. We had hung back, clinging to the door, trying to be unobtrusive. He shook hands warmly as Jason introduced us.

'So that's the little lady,' he said, putting an arm around Marcella and nodding approval. 'Why don't you all sit down, make yourselves comfortable.'

We crossed the room to the sofa, Jason sitting on a chair close to Freddie. As soon as we were seated Freddie's gaze returned to Jason as though he wanted to lock Jason's image into his heart.

'You know Jase, it's as though it happened yesterday. I still live with the guilt every fucking day… I've never told you this before, but if I hadn't attended to those damn horses, Alan could be alive today.'

Jason's presence had broken the time barrier, Freddie was in another world, another time.

'You know he phoned me. After all I was his closest friend. It was the day of the anniversary when he first met your mum. It's over 20 years ago but I remember it like it was yesterday. "Freddie, I just can't go on without her… it's no use," he said. His voice was a whisper, like he could hardly talk… I knew he was crying. I'd never heard him sound so desperate and so miserable, and don't forget I spent a lot of time with him after your mum died. But this was different, I knew it was the real thing… I panicked, "Alan, I'll be right over… I'll just put the horses away and I'll be right there." I raced over… it didn't take me long, maybe half an hour. When I got there he was dead. Police all over the place…'

His eyes had been lowered as he spoke but suddenly he lifted them and looked intently at Jason.

'If only I'd just left those fucking horses alone, I would have got there in time… I'm sorry Jase, I'm so sorry.'

'It's not your fault… it's what he wanted to do, don't blame yourself,' Jason said, close to tears himself, transported into Freddie's hell, his own hell relegated to second place. Somehow their roles had become reversed and he was now trying to console Freddie.

Freddie looked as though life had drained from his veins, his arms hung limp at his sides, his neck seemed too heavy for his head. Remembering had rekindled the anguish. He was trapped in the chilling 'if only' syndrome, with its relentless pursuit, undiminished by time, defeating any rationale used against it.

His confession was so poignant, his features so sunk in grief, that silence was the only response. I too was close to tears. After a few minutes Freddie lit a cigarette, inhaling deeply, his head bowed.

Then suddenly there was a knock on the door.

'Five minute call Mr Starr.'

Freddie rose from his chair as though he was a hundred years old, looking miles away. He embraced Jason distractedly, 'Goodbye Alan,' he said, confusing Jason with his father. Alan was so embedded in his consciousness, that for a split second the distinction between father and son blurred and for a moment Freddie Starr was re-united with his best friend.

'Fuckin' hell…what am I saying… it's you Jase, sorry mate,' he said, shaking his head as though attempting to dislodge the confusion. Jason put his arm around Freddie but said nothing.

We followed Freddie out of the dressing room in silence – he on to the stage, us taking our seats in the audience. Only a true actor, a seasoned performer could have given the superbly funny performance he delivered that night. He had the audience howling with laughter while he was drowning in invisible tears.

Chapter 32
Gregory Peck

Among Diana Dors' many endearing qualities was her love of animals. Her home was never without animals. Her books abound with references to her pets. She even includes photographs of them.

'I have a houseful of pets and I love them all,' she wrote.

Her pets were not only cats and dogs but also a variety of jungle birds, and once, even a pig. One of her legacies to Jason was this love of animals.

Because Alan shared her compassion for animals, Jason grew up in a household where animals and birds were part of the family – some rescued from a life of misery and abuse. One such bird, a macaw Jason named Captain Flint, was rescued by his parents from the clutches of Billy Smart's circus.

When Jason was about ten his parents took him on one of their regular circus outings. Billy Smart was a good friend and they had carte blanche to wander where they pleased. Jason took full advantage of this backstage pass, arriving early to pay his respects to the animals, especially to the birds. He had been intrigued by a large, brightly-coloured macaw he had seen on a previous visit and couldn't wait to see it again. The bird had been caught in the Amazon rainforest, before the practice became illegal, and bought by the circus in the hope of making it a circus feature. However, the wilful Macaw declined celebrity status and, despite expert trainers, stubbornly refused to learn a single trick. Rejected as a failed performer, he was put out to pasture, spending his days chained to a perch, his audience confined to a small group of circus boys who used him as a source of light entertainment.

As Diana, Alan and Jason approached the macaw they saw two of the boys teasing the bird, prodding it with sticks, delighting in its frenzied screams and snapping beak. They enraged the bird until it flew at them, flapping its great expanse of wings, only to be yanked back by its chain. Again and again it attempted to attack its tormenters and again and again the chain tore at its leg. They were so appalled by the bird's distress, so in sympathy with its valiant but futile attempts at self-defence, that, then and there, they decided to rescue it.

The asking price for the macaw was over £1,000, but aware of his customers' eagerness to acquire the bird, the manager added £500 for the perch. Diana and Alan balked at the increased price.

'It's easily worth that,' the manager argued. 'Let me tell you something, that stand has been on television. It's even been on Blue Peter.'

'I don't care if the stand had its own TV show. I'm not paying £500 for a fucking bird stand,' Alan protested.

Fearing they would forfeit the bird, and being unaccustomed to money depriving him of what he wanted, Jason urged his parents not to abandon such a splendid creature to the cruel pranks of heartless boys. A settlement was finally reached and Captain Flint joined the Siamese cats Sara and Dilly, short for Dillinger, and Percilla the pig, rescued as a piglet at Jason's school fete, where its pen had boasted a poster indicating the various butcher cuts it would become. Jason harboured a secret plan. One day, when he grew up, he would take Captain Flint back to the Amazon rainforest and release him into the wild.

And so Captain Flint came to live at Orchard Manor, the magnificent mock Tudor mansion, set in three acres of land, with its indoor swimming pool surrounded by marble columns, its water lit from beneath by multi-coloured lights, and its stained glass mural lit by sunshine. Although being ensconced in a cream-and-pink living room, furnished with gilt chairs, gilt-framed mirrors, deep-pile cream carpets, a cream brocade settee and cream satiny curtains wasn't quite what Captain Flint had in mind, he not only made the best of his surroundings, he took control of them. The cats hated and feared Captain Flint, who terrorised not only them but the entire household with his wild screams and threatening beak. He allowed neither man nor beast to approach him, flapping his wings in anger and biting anyone or anything that came within range.

With his mum's encouragement, Jason undertook to tame the haughty Captain Flint. Each day he came a little closer to the bird, talking to it and throwing it bits of food. His patience was rewarded when, after about a week, he was allowed to stand next to Captain Flint without arousing signs of hostility. Encouraged by his progress he attempted to stroke the bird, gently drawing a pencil across its breast, not daring to expose his fingers to the macaw's powerful beak. But Captain Flint wasn't having it. He snapped the pencil in two. Undaunted, Jason persisted and after repeated pencil snapping, Captain Flint relented, and permitted Jason the occasional pencil caress.

One day Jason arrived in the living room for a morning training session. But Captain Flint had vanished. The celebrity TV perch had been abandoned, its chain hanging limp and useless. Captain Flint had chewed right through it. Jason panicked. He raced around the room looking for hiding places, but Captain Flint was nowhere to be seen. Then he noticed that the sliding gold-plated door which led from the living room to the swimming pool was slightly ajar. One of the many guests who frequented Orchard Manor had gone for an early morning swim, or perhaps a late night one, and had neglected to shut it. Jason crossed the threshold with beating heart. There, on the head of a life-sized statue of a black panther sitting on its haunches, sat Captain Flint, preening himself. Perhaps the panthers – there were two of them – were reminiscent of the jungle and soothed his wild heart. With the skill of an Amazon hunter, Jason retrieved Captain Flint, throwing a Persian hand-loomed rug over the bird and carrying him kicking and screaming back to his perch. Captain Flint was slow to forgive the indignity. It was several days before he favoured Jason with a scarcely audible 'hello', the one word he had acquiesced to utter.

Although Jason wooed Captain Flint with the patience and determination of a Romeo, it took over a week before he was granted a full pardon, and several more weeks before he succeeded in persuading Captain Flint to perch, first on a broom handle and then on his arm. When finally Captain Flint allowed himself to be finger-stroked, a triumphant Jason convinced Diana and Alan, who in any case took pity on the chained macaw, that it was time to remove the chains and allow the bird to fly freely.

Jason's triumph was short-lived. Captain Flint, scorning civilised behaviour, reverted to the wild creature he remembered being. He chewed the elegant furniture, pecking lumps out of antique tables and mirrors. He flew at strangers and staff alike.

'Here comes Flint Airways,' Jason would announce, as the Captain zoomed overhead landing on an original oil painting or on a silver candelabra, or even on the five foot by five foot television screen. He delighted in emitting raucous, piercing screeches both day and night, frightening guests, staff, and even family members out of their wits, disrupting household activities – the cook threatened to resign – and depriving Diana and Alan, whose bedroom was above the living room, of much-needed sleep. Captain Flint's fearlessness, his obstinacy, his wonderful panache, which they had so admired in the circus shed, seemed far less admirable in the pink-and-cream living room. The crunch came for Diana when the wily Captain Flint began using the curtains as a ladder to climb to the rail, where he perched disdainfully, first preening himself and then indulging in matters more personal, splattering not only the fine satin curtains but the very walls.

'Jase, dearest,' Diana said to her son one day. 'We're going to get Flinty his own special house outside, so he can have fresh air and more room to fly. It will be much better for him. He'll be much happier.'

Jason was secretly relieved, Captain Flint was beginning to keep even him awake at nights. Together with his dad, he helped build a glass gazebo for Captain Flint. He fitted it with a radio so that the captain wouldn't be lonely and a heater so he wouldn't be cold. He even bedded down with Captain Flint for the first few nights, to make the transition to the new home less stressful. A bird specialist was engaged to trim the captain's wings to prevent him from heading for the Amazon jungle. Each day Jason would open the Gazebo door and stand guard while Captain Flint waddled across the lawn and sat on a beach tree until Jason guided him back into the Gazebo. Gradually, as his wings grew back, he was able to fly across the garden and back into the gazebo on his own. From perching on Jason's arm, he took to perching on his shoulder, sharing as many of Jason's activities as were deemed to be bird-friendly. Jason and Captain Flint remained buddies for the next five years, up until the time Jason was forced to leave his home, and with it Captain Flint.

* * * * * * *

One summer's day, over 20 years later, while Jason was already living in Broadstairs – I hadn't moved there permanently yet but was often staying in my flat – Jason went to visit a friend in Ramsgate. Walking along a busy street bordering the sea, he spotted a seagull lying on the road. He rushed into the road to rescue it from oncoming traffic. The bird, still a baby and unable to fly, had probably fallen out of its nest. It was barely alive - its foot had been severed and was dangling from a splinter of bone. With the traumatised seagull cradled in his arms, Jason frantically approached shopkeepers, pedestrians, residents, until he got the address of a vet.

The vet cast an indifferent eye over the gull – regarded as a nuisance in this seaside town – and after a cursory examination said matter-of-factly, 'You'll have to put it down.'

Jason was outraged. 'You're not killing my seagull!' he protested, staring at the vet as though he was a serial killer.

'It's badly injured. That's the best thing to do.'

'Give it back, I'll take care of it myself.'

'I can't do that,' the vet said more gently, realising he was dealing with profound determination, let alone genetic imprinting. 'Its foot has to be amputated. I'm not allowed to release an injured bird. That's RSPB regulations.'

'So you're qualified to kill it, are you? If its foot has to be amputated, why can't you amputate it?'

'I can but it will cost you £100.'

'That's ridiculous. I want to speak to the RSBP.'

The vet obligingly phoned the RSBP and a distraught Jason pleaded for the bird's life. After some deliberation, and at Jason's insistence, it was decided the gull could be released to Jason if the vet agreed to amputate its foot and if Jason agreed to care for it, following the vet's instructions.

'I'll do whatever the vet tells me to do,' Jason promised.

Seeing how distressed Jason was, and how determined to save the seagull, the vet, obviously touched, and not wanting to be considered a murderer, agreed to amputate the foot free of charge, and to release the gull into Jason's care.

He was about to conduct the amputation, with what looked like a blunt scalpel, when Jason interrupted the surgery.

'Wait a minute, aren't you going to give it an anaesthetic?'

'No. It won't feel anything,' the vet said, and chopped off the foot.

The bird flapped its wings in panic and shrieked a seagull cry of pain.

Jason winced, 'You said it wouldn't feel anything. The poor bird is in pain. Can't you do something?'

'It's over now,' the vet said applying medication, bandaging the stump and handing the gull to Jason, all in about three minutes.

Jason nested the gull in his arm, gently stroking its head as the vet explained that antibiotic ointment had to be applied to the wound each day, covered by a fresh bandage.

Jason brought the injured gull back to Broadstairs and set about caring for it with the tenderness and devotion of a new mother. This time, however, there was no glass gazebo home with a celebrity perch, the gull had to make do with a cardboard carton, cut with air holes, and lined with hay bought from the local pet shop. But as a small compensation, Jason placed the carton in the small conservatory adjoining the living room of his flat. Jason bought his seagull tinned pilchards, and was delighted when the gull began to eat and drink. As promised, Jason faithfully attended its wound, dressing it every day. However, each time he lifted the gull from its box, he had to hold it at arm's length, keeping it out of reach, for, as it grew stronger, it pecked him whenever it could access any exposed flesh.

'What kind of gratitude is that?' I asked him one day, as I was leaning over the balcony, watching Jason attend the seagull and saw the bird's beak clamp down on his hand.

'It's nothing, it doesn't hurt', Jason said dismissively, 'He doesn't have much of a peck. Actually I've named him Gregory Peck.'

'How apt,' I said.

'More apt than you think,' Jason replied. 'Gregory Peck was a friend of my mother's. She thought he was great. My Gregory has a lot to live up to'

As we spoke, Gregory Peck twisted his neck, and in a flash landed several quick pecks on Jason's arm. He wasn't much into living up to anything. Jason smiled, to show there were no hard feelings.

'It's okay. It doesn't really hurt. His wound must be bothering him,' Jason explained in the gull's defence, not wanting me to think badly of his Gregory or to give him bad press. Holding him as far away as possible, Jason stroked Gregory's head. 'He's upset. I have to calm him down. Anyway, it's time for his dinner. Maybe it's just that he's hungry. He loves fresh fish.'

By this time Jason was going to the fishmongers, who saved cut-offs of fresh fish for Gregory. Gregory was becoming known as the luckiest bird in town.

Each day, aside from getting his wound cleaned and dressed, Gregory underwent an exercise regime.

'I have to get his wings strong so he'll be able to fly,' Jason explained, as he held onto Gregory's chest, while Gregory flapped his wings, in a vain attempt to fly.

We all became fond of Gregory. Each time I came to Broadstairs, the first question I asked Jason was, 'How's Gregory doing?'

'He's doing great,' was the inevitable reply. 'His wound is drying up. I'll be able to take the bandage off soon.'

Children living in the building came to see Gregory. Jason would proudly display him, stroke his head, and allow him to flap his wings. Gregory became quite a celebrity. Word got around. Children would come from the beach to see him, adults would visit him offering advice on seagull care.

Some wagged their heads in disapproval, 'You're spoiling that bird.'

'You'll never get rid of him. Why would he want to leave?'

'How do you expect him to cope in the real world?'

However, mostly everyone approved of Jason's devoted care. Zoe, the mother of three children who doted on Gregory and who were lucky enough to live in the building, visited him regularly, becoming a sort of surrogate mother in residence, checking on Gregory and administering to him when Jason was away.

As part of the exercise regime Gregory was permitted to roam freely in the conservatory for a limited period each day. However, one day he wandered into the living room, and although there was no sumptuous furniture to deface, he did a good job with the carpet. Like Captain Flint, he was banished from the living room.

The time came when Gregory was fit enough to be put on the grass in the communal garden. A select group of well-wishers were invited to see Gregory take his first steps. Someone suggested Jason charge an admission fee. Holding Gregory in cupped hands, Jason carefully lowered him to the ground. Gregory hobbled forward a few feet, flapped his wings pathetically, hobbled another few feet and then remained stark still, refusing to budge. Jason scooped Gregory into the comfort of his arms, stroking his head, to lessen the trauma.

I was reminded of a Balinese 'touching-the-ground' ceremony I had witnessed some years back. In Bali babies are not allowed to touch the ground until they are six months old. Until that time they are held in someone's arms, passed from aunt to brother to grandfather to cousin to a choice of adoring relatives in the large extended families. The infant is never left on its own, sleeping with the parents at night and carried by some family member by day. Then, at six months of age, in a lavish ceremony, attended by family and friends, the baby is placed on the ground for the first time. I was invited to attend one such ceremony. The expression on the parents' faces when the baby left the comfort of their arms and was set down on its own – a mixture of anxiety and pride – was much like the expression on Jason's face when Gregory took his first steps on the grass. The Balinese baby, like Gregory, attempted to drag itself forward a few feet, and then, arms flailing and looking bewildered, it sat bolt upright and remained stark still, refusing to budge a further inch. The parents' reactions were also much like Jason's, as the mother scooped the baby into her arms, kissing and stroking it, to lessen the trauma.

After this first attempt, Gregory was put in the garden each day, fortified by bits of fresh fish. Gradually his hobbling distance increased. Then he began practicing levitation, flapping his wings and raising himself off the ground. Finally the day came when he flew from one end of the garden to the other, a distance of some hundred feet. At this point he was so used to human company that he would practice his flying skills without fear or embarrassment, unperturbed by the children in the garden cheering him on.

After several weeks, Jason became confident enough to leave Gregory in the garden on his own. Zoe would keep an eye on him. One day, Jason left Gregory in the garden while he visited his Ramsgate friends. Zoe was in charge. I had several visitors that day and we were leaning over our garden fence, watching Gregory's antics, a favourite pastime, when, to our astonishment, he limped down the garden, picked up speed, and in a sudden burst of confidence, spread his wings and flew over the beach huts, which lined the garden wall and dropped into the sea. We watched in horror as he tried to lift himself out of the water but was unable to. Zoe ran out to the beach, but before she got to Gregory, the waves had washed him ashore. He sat on the sand, soaking wet, unable to move, looking sad and bedraggled. Meanwhile, I had phoned Jason on his mobile and was giving him a blow by blow description.

'Zoe is on the beach. Don't worry, the kids aren't trying to chase him. Zoe's about ten feet away. She's stooped down on the sand. She's inching closer on her hands and knees, she's getting even closer. Gregory isn't moving. He's not trying to get away... She's got him!'

We all breathed a sigh of relief. Zoe returned with a dripping wet, sandy Gregory. She cleaned and dried him while Jason beat a hasty retreat from Ramsgate to change Gregory's sopping wet, dirty bandage. Everyone had some comment about the event.

'That was scary, he's not ready to be on his own.'

'He probably would have drowned, he was weighed down by water and then by sand.'

'It's a good thing Zoe got to him before the kids did.'

But the worry was over. It was great to have Gregory back – he had become one of the family. Life resumed its normal pace.

Several days later, Gregory was again in the garden, surrounded by bits of fish, when another seagull came to visit him.

'Gregory has a friend,' Jason called up to me.

The visitor hopped closer to Gregory, helping himself to Gregory's fish. Gregory generously shared his meal with his friend. However, when the fish was gone, so was the friend.

'With friends like that, who needs enemies,' I quipped.

'That bloody seagull ate up all Gregory's fish,' Jason said, scooping up the empty dish with one hand, and Gregory with the other.

Suddenly something strange happened. The usually silent Gregory emitted a series of loud squawks. Within seconds, there was a cloud of agitated seagulls circling the garden, flying over Jason's head, screaming and diving. Gulls seemed to be coming from all directions. It was too much like Hitchcock's *The Birds* for comfort. Jason quickly disappeared with the flapping, squawking Gregory. As soon as Gregory had gone, the seagulls flew off, screaming their objections, or warnings, or whatever. Only Gregory knew for sure.

About a week later, I was watching Gregory in the garden. By this time his wound had healed and the bandage was off. He had perfected a sort of hopping limp, and was able to cover the garden territory with ease. I was thinking how well he was doing, when suddenly he hopped down the garden, picking up speed like a plane on a runway, and spreading his wings took off, flying over the beach huts, over the water, and landing on the pier about two hundred yards away. He flew with such grace, it was as though he had been doing it all his life. All at once, the limping ugly duckling had become a beautiful swan. Jason chased after Gregory, running across the beach to the pier. The roof of the pier cafe and the pier itself were gathering places for seagulls. Young seagulls perched on the roof, older, bolder ones waited for handouts by cafe tables and by benches along the pier where people sat eating fish and chips – some raided rubbish bins. Jason returned empty-handed.

'I'll keep looking for him,' he said, 'but he's with his mates. Maybe he's found a family. Maybe it's best for him that way. Did you see how beautiful he looked in the air. I guess it was time for him to go.'

If Jason hadn't released Captain Flint to the Amazon rainforest, at least he had released Gregory to the sea.

That evening Jason invited me for a glass of wine. 'To celebrate Gregory,' he said.

Gregory's escape and the subsequent chase, evoked in Jason reminiscences of another escape, another chase.

'I've got to tell you this story,' he said. 'It's about the pet pig we had when I was a kid. We spoiled her rotten. My mum used to feed her with gold-top milk and cornflakes. Her name was Percilla. She lived in this special pen-house my dad had built for her. But she had this habit of escaping into the neighbour's garden, rooting up his vegetables and rolling in the mud. After doing it one time too many, the neighbour threatened to shoot her. In order to keep the peace, and save Percilla's life, my dad promised to make sure Percilla would never bother him again.'

'This one day the *News of the World* came to our house to photograph my dad. In the middle of the shoot, out of the corner of his eye, my dad saw Percilla heading for the neighbour's garden. He went berserk. He grabbed a stick and began chasing her, trying to catch her before she got herself killed. The photographers weren't sure what it was all about, but they began chasing my dad to find out.

Check this, there's my dad chasing a pig with a stick and there's these photographers chasing my dad with their cameras.'

'Percilla had too much of a head start, she managed to root up the garden and roll in the mud and when she saw all the people rushing toward her, she panicked and jumped in the swimming pool, dropping lumps of mud in the pool and leaving a mud slick on the water. The photographers loved it. The cameras didn't stop clicking. Even the neighbour got into the act. Next day the story was splashed all over the *News of the World* complete with photographs. The readers loved it even more. The journalists saw they were onto a good thing, and Percilla stories became all the rage. They went on for months. "Is Percilla up for the chop?" "Will Percilla allow Pierre, the French pig, to become her lover?" It was wild. Percilla became a big time celebrity.'

'Gregory Peck was somewhat of a celebrity too,' I offered. 'Maybe not big time like Percilla. But he was a little-time celebrity, after all he had to live up to his name.'

'A toast to Gregory, the little-time celebrity,' I said.

'May he fly in peace,' Jason added.

We raised our glasses.

Chapter 33
Entering Bleak House

Sometimes one finds a special place where the balance is perfect and the creative spirit flourishes. For Charles Dickens, Bleak House was that place. It was his favourite residence, the place where he did much of his best writing. More like a castle or fortress with its towers and turrets, it stands on a cliff, aloof and almighty, looking down on Broadstairs, poised to protect it from invaders coming from across the sea. Woven into a tapestry of times gone by, it evokes a haunting wistfulness, a dreamy speculation.

In 2002, when I first came to Broadstairs, I couldn't wait to visit Bleak House, probably in the hope that some of its magic would rub off on me. Dickens was one of my favourite writers and Bleak House was his muse. After paying my entrance fee, I was left to my own devices, with most areas being roped off. At first I was disappointed. Although Bleak House retained a powerful, forbidding exterior, the interior, or that part open to the public as a Dickens museum cum souvenir shop, was shabby with neglect, smelled of mould and dust and was badly in need of love, or at least care. However, as soon as I crossed the threshold to Dickens' writing room, something extraordinary happened. I was overwhelmed by a sense of significance, by the power of place. Although smeared with dust and patched with damp, or perhaps because of it, the room breathed of Dickens, was haunted by his presence. His writing desk, facing the window with its magnificent view of Viking Bay; his chair, its stuffing poking through the worn leather; his scarred bookshelves; his lamp; were all there, silent and waiting.

All my senses became engaged. As I stood by his desk on its raised platform, the better for him to contemplate the choreography of sea and sky, I became aware that I was in the exact location, gazing at the exact scene Dickens saw each time he raised his eyes to consider a word or refine a phrase. As I watched the waves winking in the sunlight, the seagulls streaking against the sky, their cries filling my ears as they dived to earth, I leaned into the chair, the leather soft and yielding, and drifted into a strange communion. It was part meditation, part contemplation; it was a mingling with the creative impulse, the mystery of inspiration, the mystery of the man – the writer, the magnificent story teller, the reformer. My head resounded with the secrets embedded in the ether. The room, the desk, the chair, the sea, the secrets, we were all perfect together. And I was on a great pilgrimage.

When my friend Cedric came from Canada, I took him on my Bleak House pilgrimage. But the experience was very different, much more earth-bound – the essence of pilgrimage being difficult to share. Cedric, always curious about people and places, got into conversation with the person selling postcards. She was a chatty mild-mannered woman, who turned out to be the owner of Bleak House. She lamented the fact that since her husband had died some years previously, the house had fallen into serious disrepair, but she lacked the money to do anything about it. However, she was adamant that, no matter what, she would never sell. Bleak House would always remain in her family.

I was therefore taken aback when I learned, less than two years later, that Bleak House had been sold and that the new owners, Richard and Jackie Hilton, were to use it as a family home. Local people were up in arms when the news broke:

'Bleak House should never have been sold to a private family.'

'Bleak House is a heritage site. It belongs to Broadstairs, to Kent, to England, to the world.'

'The Hiltons will ruin Bleak House.'

As renovations began, rumours proliferated with every hammer stroke:

'The Hiltons have no respect for Bleak house.'

'They are creating a modern monster'

'They are destroying the atmosphere, the significance; they are obliterating history.'

All this without a shred of evidence.

If Broadstairs was Charles Dickens' 'favourite watering hole', Charles Dickens was Broadstairs favourite son. Every year the town hosted a delightful but very serious Dickens Week, where all was authentic Victorian – dress, bathing costumes, cricket matches – all scrutinised by the Dickens police, to assure that no participant broke the authenticity rule. Modern wristwatches, sunglasses, or any non-Victorian item of clothing was strictly forbidden. The week was a

Dickens celebration, with readings from Dickens' books, theatre performances adapted from his novels, talks, games – a Dickensian feast.

I was delighted when someone informed me that in honour of Dickens Week, the Hiltons were opening the garden of Bleak House to the public, where afternoon tea would be available, the proceeds going to charity. My sister-in-law Gitte was visiting from Canada and we seized the opportunity to have tea in the very garden where Dickens had entertained his guests.

The garden looked festive, with tables covered in pretty cloths, fresh flowers on each table, and a canopied stall serving tea and cakes. The stall was almost elegant. China cups and saucers decorated with flower patterns replaced the usual plastic cups and paper plates; a silver samovar instead of an electric kettle; graceful teapots instead of the brown chunky kind, and scrumptious-looking cakes on trays covered with doilies.

As I stood by the stall watching the girl pouring tea, something unpredictable happened, something unusual. Sometimes I meet someone with whom I have an instant rapport, even before speaking to them. A twinkle in me connects with a twinkle in them and there is a mysterious, enigmatic connection. This was such a time. The girl serving tea looked like a radiant Snow White, with long dark hair and an English-rose complexion. There was a sparkle about her, an energy that invited fun; she looked mischievous, ready to laugh, as though she had a private source of merriment. She noticed me admiring the chinaware.

'They're the real thing,' she laughed.

'I know. I really like the real thing.'

'Me too,' she laughed again.

As I ordered tea and we discussed the merits of the different cakes, I indulged my compulsion to know more about her.

'What's your name?' I asked,

'Nina.'

'That's a coincidence. Mine is Niema, almost the same. Where do you live Nina?'

'In Broadstairs.'

I was surprised. For some reason I didn't expect her to be from Broadstairs. I thought the stall, the dishes, the tables and chairs, had been catered and arranged by some specialist company which she probably worked for, in one of the larger towns. I'd never seen such cakes in the local bakeries.

'Where in Broadstairs?' I was not one to let go easily.

'Here.'

'What do you mean "here"? In Bleak House?'

'That's right.'

'Who else lives in Bleak House?' I was puzzled. Had it been converted into a rooming house?

'Just me and my mum and dad.'

Although I was confused, something was almost falling into place. 'Then you must be one of the Hiltons.'

'That's right.'

She didn't seem the least bit put out by my extensive interrogation.

'Are you related to the hotel Hiltons?'

'My uncle owns hotels.'

I was on a roll and it was hard to stop, it was like digging for treasure, but another customer stepped up to the stall and I was prevented from getting carried away and asking to see her birth certificate.

Although she was busy, Nina brought the tea and cakes to our table and sat with us for a few minutes. We chatted easily and laughed a lot.

'Nina, I really like you,' I said. 'I hope I see you again.' She inspired directness.

'Sure. Come visit me whenever you like. I have my own flat in the house.'

When I said goodbye to her, she said, 'Don't forget to visit me. Come any time.'

I didn't visit. Some encounters are better left unrepeated. Besides, I've become more English and can't just drop in on people I hardly know. But fate destined otherwise. Several months later there was a notice in the local paper about a charity event sponsored by Bleak House. The well-known medium Sally Morgan was to give individual readings in the Bleak House gardens: £5 for 5 minutes. Tea would be available and a tour of the house could be booked. I went along with my friend Joyce. If nothing else, we would be donating to charity.

Nina was again serving at the stall, bright and cheerful. This time the garden was filled to capacity with locals, come in the hope of having a peep at the mysterious goings-on at Bleak House, as much as to acquire a fleeting glimpse into their futures. There was a long wait to see Sally Morgan. We ordered tea, and Nina, although busy, immediately brought a pot of tea to our table.

'You never came to visit,' she admonished with a laugh. Fortunately, she couldn't linger and I was spared having to make excuses.

The weather wasn't up to much. It was drizzling slightly and somewhat chilly. It didn't take long for the combination of cups of tea, chill and drizzle to affect my bladder. The Bleak House loos were out of bounds. After all it was now a private residence, and this was a public event. The public loo was in the car park, not that far away, but far enough. I sidled over to the stall, waited for a lull and plucked up my courage.

'Nina, I have to go to the loo rather badly. Do you think I could use the loo in the house?'

After all, she had invited me to visit, and although this wasn't the visit she had in mind, perhaps it would do for a start.

'Sure. Just go around to the front and tell my father or mother – whoever opens the door – you're a friend of mine and you have to use the loo. They won't mind.'

Although this was awkward, if not downright embarrassing, and no way to meet the owners of Bleak House, I had waited too long to have much choice in the matter.

Richard Hilton, Nina's father, answered the door; a big man with a kind face, dressed in a loose-fitting white cotton top and white trousers, looking like a combination of my favourite guru and my favourite uncle. I apologised for the bother and stated my mission.

'No bother, darling. Come right in.'

He led me through the kitchen.

'This is Jackie, my wife.'

Jackie smiled at me, a pretty petite woman, who looked more like Nina's younger sister than her mother, with her long blonde hair and exquisite figure.

When the deed was done, Richard said, 'Would you like me to show you around the house? The tour doesn't cover much. I'll show you the room Queen Victoria slept in, it still has her bed.'

Although I had seen some of the house when it was a museum and had visited the caves under the house, which had been used by smugglers, this was a most unexpected and welcome invitation, indeed.

'I'd love to see the house. Thanks.'

Richard was so easy and unassuming, it felt like I had known him all my life. He took me through the house and I was impressed by how lovingly it had been restored, with careful consideration to authenticity. I was delighted to find the Bleak House rumours totally unfounded and just that: rumours. Exactly the opposite was true. Richard showed me the section of the house destroyed by a recent fire.

'I'm going to restore it to the way it was originally, no matter how much it costs me' he said.

'How did you come to buy Bleak House?' I asked.

'Now that's a story,' he said.

'A long time ago, when I was a young man, I went to see a medium, more for the hell of it than anything else, although no doubt I could have done with some answers. The medium told me lots of things, then she said something that almost made me laugh out loud. "One day you are going to own a castle by the sea." She might as well have told me that one day I'd be Prime Minister. I was a bricklayer at the time, with trouble making ends meet. How could I take that seriously? "I'll tell you what," I said. "If I ever own a castle by the sea, you'll be the first one I invite to visit.'

'The years passed and I had long ago forgotten all about the prediction. Then one day, Nina and I were having a meal at Marquesi's. Although I was living in Ramsgate at the time, I hardly ever went to Broadstairs. You know Marquesi's, the Italian restaurant on the seafront. It's gone now.'

I knew it well. It had been one of the oldest and most elegant restaurants in Broadstairs.

'I was looking through the local paper, waiting for the food, and a notice caught my eye. It said that the Japanese wanted to buy Bleak House. I was curious. Where's Bleak House? I asked Nina. "Just turn your head to the left and look on top of the cliff and you'll see it," she said. I turned around and there, on top of a cliff was this castle overlooking the sea. Suddenly it came back to me, Sally

Morgan's prediction – the castle by the sea. I knew I had to have it.' He shrugged his shoulders, 'That's how it happened.'

'Is that why Sally Morgan is here now?'

'Right. That's why she's here now and sleeping in Queen Victoria's bed.'

'What a story,' I said. 'It's like a fairy tale.'

'That's exactly what it is, my fairy tale'

* * * * * * *

I didn't see the Hiltons for several months after that. By then the summer had arrived and Richard Junior, one of the Hilton's sons who was living abroad, had returned to England to spend the summer with his parents. Jason had met him in a pub and they had gone out drinking together several times.

One lovely summer Sunday a group of us were sunning on the beach when Jason joined us and announced that Richard Junior had invited him to Bleak House.

'I told him I was with some friends,' Jason said. 'And he said, "Bring them along."'

No doubt Jason had neglected to mention that 'some friends' were a few revellers short of a party – there were thirteen of us plus two nine-year-old boys. I was the only one who had been to Bleak House, and the others jumped at the opportunity to see it.

Richard, Jackie, Nina and several of their friends were relaxing in the garden after their Sunday lunch when we trooped in. I don't know if Richard Junior had informed his parents of the invitation. In any case he couldn't have prepared them for an invasion, as he was unaware of it himself. Whether they had been forewarned or not, we were welcomed like honoured guests. Chairs were brought into the garden, glasses were filled with champagne and wine, introductions were made and glasses filled again.

As the afternoon evolved everyone became increasingly mellow and increasingly bold – the garden, the champagne, the sunshine, the hospitality all worked their magic. Gradually the invasion of the garden spilled over to claim the house. Some people settled comfortably in the living room, some listened to CDs in the music room, some even made their way under the house to explore the pirate caves. I was impressed by the Hiltons' generosity – not only was their home opened to people they didn't know, but they made sure their glasses were continuously filled.

I remained in the garden talking to Richard. He was pleased Jason was one of the guests. He seemed to know there was some connection between Jason and me and wanted to talk about him. He told me he had met Jason's mother many times and that his father had been a good friend. But although he had been aware that Diana and Alan had a son, he had never met Jason and had often wondered what had become of him. He had lost all contact after Alan died.

'Do you know what happened to Jason after his father died?' he asked.

I told Richard the whole story, sparing no details. How a distraught, traumatized Jason had been sent to live with his half brother Gary in Los Angeles. I told him how Jason had spent three fraught years there, how he had pretty much slipped through every net, had stopped going to school, had gotten into drugs; I told him about the shooting, about the sleazy accommodation ... the whole story.

When I finished Richard shook his head in a mixture of incredulity and concern. We were both silent. I was almost as affected telling the story as Richard was listening to it. Richard was basically a family man with traditional family values. He had five adult children, several grandchildren, and a wife he had known since they were at school together. The idea of the young Jason being left without parents, without a home, without anyone to care for him, was deeply troubling for Richard.

'I wish I had known... both his parents gone and everyone else letting him down,' he shook his head again in a gesture of non-comprehension. 'I knew nothing about all this, nothing at all... You know love, had I known, I would have done something.'

I imagine it was at this point that Richard was overtaken by a compulsion to make amends for the collective neglect. Perhaps he promised himself to attempt some form of embrace, some form of redress. If he did indeed make such a covenant, such an undertaking, and future events attested to the fact that he did, it was an undertaking the complexity of which he could not have anticipated, even though some of its ramifications were to become evident that very night.

Chapter 34
The Party

The warm afternoon sunshine gradually gave way to early evening chill, and people began to filter into the house. The languid afternoon, the quiet explorations, the sunning in the garden, had spent their appeal giving way to more robust pursuits. The knots of people in twos and threes, as if by some unspoken signal, dissolved into a steady flow towards the house.

The music room was the centre of gravity and like a magnet, the sound of music emanating from its open doorway drew people in until the sofas were full and people were sitting on cushions on the floor. The earlier musical strains, which had been subdued, wistful, bluesy, metamorphosed into more raucous rhythms. Slowly, imperceptibly, without any formal declarations, a party atmosphere began to develop. Someone started dancing; others joined in. The room was large and the polished parquet floor perfect for dancing. As the rhythms became increasingly seductive, the dance floor became increasingly compelling. There was an air of excitement, of expectancy, of things about to happen.

Our group was a loose gathering of friends and acquaintances – a disparate combination of latter-day hippies, present-day free spirits, and committed entrepreneurs; the diversity of lifestyles, of interests and occupations, united by a taste for fun and adventure. We had approached Bleak House with tentative, respectful steps, treading softly, not only because it befitted the entry into such a revered, distinguished monument, but also because we knew our second-hand invitation wasn't exactly above board, or even whether we had been invited at all. However, the Hilton's warm reception complemented by champagne and wine were the signals we needed to relax inhibitions, something we were all good at.

The music room had a karaoke set-up and a sound system to die for. Richard, after making sure everyone's glass was filled, picked up the microphone and began to sing. Richard was in anyone's estimation a handsome man: tall, powerful, elegant, with an expression of good humour and intelligence, but when he stepped up to the microphone, he became a Star. His presence resounded throughout the room.

Like an embrace it gathered a motley collection of individuals and transformed them into an audience. When he sang *My Way*, it was better than listening to Frank Sinatra; he had a rich, mellow voice, tender and passionate, the kind that chills the spine. I later learned he had sung professionally at one time. Richard Junior followed and his voice was almost as impressive as his father's, but minus the chill factor. Everyone cheered and clapped and the party from a hesitant beginning began to gain confidence. The music which followed was irresistible, perfect for dancing. Whoever the appointed disc jockey was, he was obviously well-practised. How could anyone hold out against the Stones' *Brown Sugar* or *Honky Tonk Women*, or the Bee Gees' *Stayin' Alive*? We danced in groups, in couples, on our own. We danced sipping from glasses, pausing only for refills. The good times were definitely rolling and we were rocking and rolling with them.

When Jason approached the piano hardly anyone took any notice. But when he struck the first chord it was as though a bolt of electricity had shot through the room. All dancing ceased. We became riveted, mesmerised by the sounds.

It is difficult to describe the music Jason played. It was an improvisation of moods and feelings juxtaposed against each other, a collage of opposites, both disturbing and pleasing. The feelings were passionate, soulful, tentative, self-assured, harsh, tender. They were composed of fragments of familiar refrains, household melodies, favourite musical phrases rising out of, and embedded in a cacophony of discord. They evoked a kaleidoscope of moods, evolving one from the other, overlapping each other. They were like a rainbow in a dark sky, at times overwhelmed by darkness, at times shining through the darkness. They were glimpses into the heart of agitation, of conflict, into the heart of harmony, of elation. The moods, the feelings were entwined in each other, embracing each other, destroying each other – it was a medley of Jason himself.

I had never heard Jason play the piano. And as I stood there glass in hand, gripped by the music, I recalled a story he had told me.

'My dad had a very close friend called Claude,' he had said. 'He was a massive giant of a man, with hands like dinner plates. They met in a pub and had one hell of a punch-up. After nearly killing each other, smashing tables and throwing the pieces at each other, they realised neither one could finish off the other. They were too well-matched to become enemies, so they became friends instead. They were great friends. They even kept souvenirs of their first meeting – broken bits of tables – which they celebrated from time to time with champagne and bear hugs. They had a lot in common. They both loved racing cars and I remember speeding madly through the countryside, whizzing through narrow lanes both of them singing at the top of their lungs.'

'Early one morning I was messing about as my mum was trying to get me ready for school. That's when I was still going to school – I was about seven or eight at the time. Suddenly something strange happened, something that had never happened before. I began to hear the song *Silent Night* in my head. I could actually see the notes dancing before my eyes. I had never played the piano before. My mum had tried showing me some things on the piano but I wasn't interested, didn't want to know. But for some reason I went to the piano, sat down and picked out the notes to *Silent Night*, note after note, until I got it right. When I got it right, I played it over and over. I had no idea why I was playing *Silent Night*, it wasn't even Christmas. While I was playing the phone rang. It was Claude's wife, Maggie. She told my mum that Claude had just died – he had been suffering from a brain tumour for some time. I heard my mum let out a kind of wail. I didn't know what happened but I knew it was something terrible. Then Maggie asked, "Who's that playing Silent Night?" "It's Jason. Why?" Then the bombshell hit. "It was Claude's favourite hymn." That really spooked my parents. It still spooks me.'

* * * * * * *

Jason rose from the piano to shouts of 'Cheers' and, inspired by his playing, the dancing gained a new momentum, a new fervour. Although I had drunk relatively little having shared a glass with my friend Andrea, the music, the dancing, Jason's playing, remembering his story, had combined with that relatively little to make my head spin. Besides, although it had been quite some time since I had such a good time dancing, I was exhausted and hot. I was seriously in need of fresh air. I left the music room and headed for the garden.

The evening had moved into night and was warmer than the late afternoon. The air was soft, the sky lit with stars. Richard was sitting in the garden sipping from his glass.

'Taking the air,' he said.

I plonked down beside him. 'I needed a break. The dancing and the music were getting to me.'

He had obviously heard Jason's playing, for he said, 'That boy certainly knows how to play the piano.'

'I'm amazed,' I said. 'I've never heard him play before. He taught himself. He told me he only started playing after his dad died. The people he was staying with had a piano and he began playing whatever came out of his head. Then he started to work out tunes he heard on the radio like *Eleanor Rigby*, playing them over and over, driving everyone crazy. I remember him saying, "If I could hear it, I could play it." He doesn't have a piano, so when he gets the chance to play he really goes for it.'

'He's welcome to use our piano any time he likes.'

'That's a great offer. I'm sure he'll be delighted to take you up on it.'

When I returned to the music room the party was not only going strong but had reached a new dimension. The dancing had grown increasingly abandoned – twirls, leaps, stamps, limbs flailing, hips grinding. Everyone was dancing, including the children who were weaving among the adults in darts and skips, playing an innovative game of tag-dance. Whereas before the atmosphere had been mellow, it now had manic overtones inspired by the frantic, heavy-metal type music which had taken over. Although it was growing late, there was not even a whisper about leaving.

Jason was dancing by himself, wrapped in his own dance world. It was a kind of erratic, intense dance, the movements angular, sharp, more an expression of conflict than joy. Whereas earlier in the evening he had made sure to dance with everyone, paying special attention to the females, employing his unique brand of charm to make them feel lovely and wanted – something he had a natural talent for – coaxing those onto the dance floor who seemed a little hesitant; now he was not aware of anyone else. I watched him with a sense of unease. Then suddenly, as though he had received some urgent message, he made a dash for the piano. He rushed right by me without seeing me. His eyes had that certain glassy look they acquired when he had overdone the drinking, especially the vodka, like artificial glass eyes; the blue too bright, too shiny. His body was tense with a wired, barely contained energy.

Indifferent to the dancing and the dancers, he thrust himself at the piano reaching for the keyboard like a drowning man reaching for a lifeboat, and began to play. His playing was explosive, raging, erratic. First it seemed like he was attacking the piano, forcing the keys into submission. Then suddenly he was stroking the keys, caressing them like a lover. It was as though he was communing with the demons haunting him, with the angels protecting him. The piano was his connection, his voice. Although someone had turned the dance music off Jason's playing attracted no audience. On the contrary, there was an air of annoyance at the disruption. Several people left the room, several others continued to dance, mocking his playing, their movements uncoordinated, uncontrolled, like demented robots. It was unnerving.

Then I saw Richard enter the room. The twinkle in his eye had visibly dimmed. He looked tired. I suddenly felt a compulsion to leave. But first I had to get Jason to stop playing, both for his sake and for everyone else's. He was playing himself into a bizarre place and taking everyone with him, including me. I stood beside him and spoke into his ear.

'Jason, it's time to go. It's late. Let's not outstay our welcome. You've got a great deal going here, don't blow it. Don't abuse the privilege.'

Jason continued playing, his back rigid, his eyes blazing. My words hadn't even registered. He was lost in the tumultuous sounds he was creating, in the music he was hearing. He had the look of someone possessed, like a channel for a mad spirit. Then he began to speak, his voice hardly above a whisper. At first I thought he was talking to me and I struggled to hear what he was saying. But he wasn't talking to me or to anyone else. He was locked into some bizarre communication, the music like beads stringing his phrases together.

'This is the most amazing piano I have ever played... it has soul... it's teaching me how to play... it's telling me what to play... I mustn't get in its way... I mustn't get in the way of myself... I have to let go... no thinking... just listening... the piano is speaking to me... I have to listen... It says, "Hear this, hear that... Try this, try that..." I'm playing what it wants me to play... it's telling me what to do.'

He didn't once look at me.

And as though this wasn't enough, suddenly through the blast of notes, through the effort of trying to hear Jason, let alone understand him, I heard the sound of breaking glass. My friend Julia's wine glass had fallen. Broken glass and blood covered the floor. Julia had cut her hand. She looked distraught, perplexed, non-comprehending as the blood ran down her wrist. In a moment Richard was at her side.

'Don't worry darling,' he said, wiping her hand with his handkerchief. 'It'll be alright. We'll get you sorted.'

He led her out of the room, his arm reassuringly around her shoulder in an effort to ease her discomfort, to lessen her embarrassment.

Meanwhile someone had put on some thumping disco music. The belligerent sounds drowned out Jason's playing, causing him to play even more belligerently. First he attempted to play over the disco music, then he attempted to play with the disco music, becoming visibly frustrated by his inability to either override it or accompany it.

Suddenly Jason struck a chilling chord and rose from the piano, his arms extended, his fingers like claws, like an angry ogre rising from a coffin. The disco music had won out and Jason was anything but gracious in defeat. He marched onto the dance floor like a warrior going into battle to defend his honour, and began to dance an angry protest to the curtailment of his playing. His expression was aggressive, incensed, threatening, like his dancing. Someone called Terry seemed to tune into the aggression and joined him. A drunken, hostile duet developed between them, their movements menacing, both real and pretended. The 'real' quickly dominating as they squared up to each other sparring like boxers. Their performance was part dance, part confrontation, and the confrontation was gaining the upper hand. The violence was only a whisper away.

I felt things were going somewhere beyond my reach. I had to leave. It was no longer fun and I wanted to preserve some aspect of the good time. Someone had switched off the lights and the room was in darkness except for intermittent flashing strobe lights. I headed across the room slowly, inching through the dancers. Jason and Terry were enacting their dance-drama not far from the doorway, totally absorbed in their bizarre contest. I attempted to get to the door while giving them a wide berth but that was impossible in a crowded room. As I drew close I saw Terry throw a punch at Jason. Jason caught the punch with an aikido-like block, grabbed Terry's arm and flung him into space. The only problem was: I was in that exact same space. He came at me with a whirlwind twirl knocking me off balance. Terry rushed back into the ring while I staggered sideways a few feet, but unable to regain my balance, fell over backwards, slamming into a bookcase.

The room was dark, the dancers immersed in the dance and in each other, and besides everything had happened so fast, I doubt whether anyone had registered the event through the alcohol fuelled haze of euphoria. Certainly not Jason and not Terry. They were so entrenched in combat, so anesthetised by alcohol they hadn't even noticed my presence. Terry probably hadn't even felt the impact. I managed to crawl a few feet into a corner of the room and lay there unable to move. Jo, the girlfriend of my friend Yan was one of the few people aware of what had happened. She rushed to my side.

'Are you alright?' she asked.

'No.' My head ached and pains shot across my back.

She took me in her arms and held me. We remained like that for some minutes, Jo rocking me gently. The music and dancing continued uninterrupted.

When finally I was able to be dragged to my feet, I could think of nothing but escape. I left unseen by the back door leaning heavily on Yan. It was a short walk from Bleak House to Eagle House but it seemed like walking a marathon to me, every step like a dagger stabbing my back. Maya, who was visiting Jason, helped me to bed with powerful painkillers and a hot water bottle. I lay motionless, head throbbing, back contracted with pain waiting for the painkillers to kick in. When they finally did and blissful relief came, I tried to recall what had happened and why. I thought about Jason and his glazed out-of-reach look. I thought about his dance, that is if the quasi- martial arts contortions could be dignified by classifying them as dance. I was sure he was still in the music room, still performing. He would have to be prised out of Bleak House. In the state he was in he wouldn't know when or even how to leave, wouldn't be capable of rational behaviour. I wasn't furious about what had occurred, although anger certainly came into the equation, I was simply bone-weary, tired of trying to understand, to forgive, to make allowances.

When Jason was that drunk, like his father, he slipped into some darker aspect of himself. Also, like his father, I knew he would recall nothing next day, and would be smitten with remorse for causing hurt to someone he cared about. But, again like his father, this would not deter him from repeating the same steps, walking the same path again and again. He was like some helpless junkie hooked on excitement, on stimulation, on intensity, needing to be constantly high on something or someone. He was unable to tolerate the ordinary, the everyday. He craved living on the edge, on the wild side. He sought out danger, thrills, daredevil feats, exhilaration, even crisis, thirsting for the ultimate high, for the ecstatic, the euphoric, and if he could only reach these states of heightened being through alcohol, then so be it. Whereas most people sought comfort and stability in routine, he abhorred routine. He had been reared on excitement, on drama, on the extraordinary, the spectacular. He had imbibed their intensity, their adrenaline rush, with his mother's milk and yearned to experience them over and over again. Too much was never enough. He knew no limits.

I adored Jason; he was charming, thoughtful, loving, interesting, and he was a loyal friend. I was especially touched by his tenderness with animals. I felt a great deal of compassion for him, and he certainly deserved compassion, but he was a hard pill to swallow. When he was high he was unpredictable, unreachable, impossible. I wondered how long anyone could tolerate or forgive his self-absorbed, irresponsible behaviour; his flirting with self-destruction, his need for violence inflicted both on others and on himself; his abuse of the people closest to him, followed by contrition and regret; his self-indulgence; his lack of control, of discipline. Would he have to take things to the limit, as his father had done, before he learned to appreciate, to cherish, not only others but himself, or was he a victim of his genes, a victim of his celebrated, celebrity-riddled past? I fell asleep wondering.

Chapter 35
Is it Alright to Cry Now?

One day, long after the Bleak House episode, long after my back had more or less healed, long after I had forgiven Jason, had watched him struggling to sort out his life, making promises, breaking promises, confronting his demons, slowly winning, but very slowly, I opened my door to a beaming Jason. In the palm of his hand was the tiniest bird I had ever seen, no more than two inches long. He told me a bird's nest had fallen three floors, from the roof of the building onto his concrete patio. When he lifted the nest he found a baby bird under it. He was certain it was dead but when he picked it up, to his amazement it was alive.

'How could a bird survive smashing onto the concrete? That has to be a miracle. I'm calling her Lucky,' Jason said, looking at the small fluffy ball in his hand, his eyes shining with unadulterated love. 'I'm going to raise her to be my pet love bird.' Of course for Jason, if 'love' was involved the dove had to be a 'her'.

'You know, doves are different from seagulls. Seagulls are wild, you can't really tame them but you can teach doves, you can train them. Remember that ungrateful Gregory Peck? He went back to the wild as soon as he was better, even with part of his leg missing. And he never comes to visit me, he never writes, he never phones,' he added jokingly. 'But Lucky will be different.'

'She's so small,' I said. 'Doesn't she need her parents to feed her?'

'I'll be her parents. I'll feed her with a syringe. I'll take good care of her.'

And he did. He made her special baby bird food. He fed her every hour or two both day and night with a mush of porridge and vitamins. Jason, who hated leaving his bed before noon unless it was to sunbathe or to go his AA meeting, set his alarm to wake him throughout the night. In the evening he would put Lucky in her nest with a hot water bottle, wrapping the bottle in layers of towelling until it was the right temperature and changing it in the morning. He lined her nest with feathers he found on the beach so she would feel at home and at night he covered the box with a blanket, and a pillow on top of the blanket to keep the warmth in.

'It's important to keep her warm,' he explained.

Against the odds, Lucky thrived. At first she had refused food, and Jason had to force her beak open. But soon she began to open her beak on her own, demanding food with loud chirps as soon as Jason was in sight. When he picked her up she fluttered and flapped with excitement, frantic to get fed. And when she was fed, calm and content, she sat in Jason's hand watching television with him while he stroked her.

She grew amazingly quickly and soon Jason was able to feed her every three or even four hours, instead of hourly. Feeding time became a huge event. She was so eager to get her food that she'd hop about skittishly, her beak open, making 'feed me' noises, but not remaining still long enough for Jason to get the syringe into her beak. At first some of the food would miss her beak and smudge her with sticky goo. But after a few days Jason perfected the technique, holding her wings down with one hand and popping the syringe into her beak with the other. He had infinite patience with Lucky and didn't mind how long he spent getting everything right: the syringe washed, the food mixed in proper proportions and at the right temperature, the box and, especially, the nest cleaned.

Jason adored Lucky and was as proud of her as any parent of a precocious child.

'Look how she hops into my hand when it's feeding time… Check out her new feathers. She's growing up, that baby fluff is disappearing… Doesn't she look sweet sitting in her nest…? She knows me now, look how she sits on my finger. I'm taking her for walks and she loves it.'

With Jason's devoted, totally committed care, Lucky was indeed becoming a lovely plump baby with real feathers. Jason had pulled it off. He had done the pretty much impossible. Lucky was the ultimate love bird.

When Lucky was several weeks old and had grown to a mighty four inches, complete with grown-up feathers, Jason felt it was okay for him to have a break from the twenty-four-seven caring. He asked me if I would look after Lucky for one night while he and Marcella went to a prestigious music festival. Adam Adamsky, a friend of his who he played music with, was not only playing at the festival but was instrumental in organising it. Adam would take them there, give them free tickets and backstage passes, which meant free everything.

The idea of looking after Lucky did not appeal to me at all, actually it frightened me. I had held her in my hand several times, stroked her, marvelled at her progress but I had never cared for a bird, and caring for Lucky, who needed feeding with a syringe and who was Jason's precious treasure, was especially scary. It was like looking after the crown jewels.

'I don't really want to do it Jason, and I'm going to a Cherry Festival with Andrea and Joyce on Saturday, we'll be away all afternoon, besides I don't know how to feed her. I've watched you do it and it looks like I'd need a doctorate in zoology.'

'That's no problem, I'll show you how. By now she can go four hours without feeding so the Cherry Festival is no problem. You'll practice feeding her until you get the knack, it's really easy. I'll prepare her food and give you all the instructions you need. It's only for one night. We'll leave Saturday and be back Sunday by noon.'

In the end I agreed, as I usually did. 'But Jason, remember, it's only for Saturday night, You'll be sure to be back early Sunday?'

'Positive.'

After my reluctant agreement I underwent an intensive bird-caring course. I took notes. Hot water bottle at night, a fresh one in the morning, feeding every three hours, with an extra hour's dispensation for the Cherry Festival. And when I had finished the written part of the course, I graduated to the practical part: the feeding lessons. The first time I fed Lucky, I got porridge over her face and on her wings, one eye was stuck shut, glued by the porridge. I felt awful. The poor little bird looked pathetic, her feathers all sticky, and I looked like I had been in a porridge slinging competition.

'You see Jason, I'm no good at it, look what I've done.'

'You just need a few more lessons. It's no problem, now I can give Lucky her first bath,' Jason said cheerfully, anxious to put a positive spin on the situation.

'No, I can't do it,' I protested.

'Of course you can, you'll get the hang of it, you just need practice.'

So I practiced and finally managed to get the porridge down Lucky's beak instead of in her eyes and on my clothes. Jason arrived that festival Saturday with Lucky's paraphernalia: her box, a blanket to cover the box, a pillow to cover the blanket, her nest, a hot water bottle, miscellaneous cloths, a syringe, her porridge, her vitamins, and Lucky herself. And so Lucky took up temporary residence in my living room.

I took my duties seriously. Although Andrea, Joyce and I were having a good time at the Cherry Festival, I made sure to be back in time for Lucky's feeding and I was pleased it went relatively well. I didn't go out that night for fear I would not be back in time for the next feeding. Instead, I washed the cloths ready for the next day, cleaned her box and put Lucky to bed following all Jason's instructions to the letter. I even sang her the little song I used to sing to my daughter at bedtime.

I awoke early Sunday morning after a restless night and, with fear in my heart, I removed the pillow, then the blanket, and peered anxiously into the box. What if I had done something wrong? Lucky was so fragile. I breathed a sigh of relief to find her sitting happily in her nest, her beak wide open, chirping for food. I fed her, put her back in her nest, folded her clean cloths and her blanket, washed her feeding utensils, and waited for Jason and Marcella, hoping they would return before the next feed.

By late afternoon they were still not back. Instead Jason phoned, 'Would you mind if we stayed another night? We're having such a great time.'

'I absolutely mind,' I said with more than a little annoyance. 'I don't want you to stay another minute, let alone another night. I can't cope with the responsibility. You must come back now.' I was adamant, forceful, determined.

'Okay,' Jason reluctantly agreed. 'We'll be back as soon as we can.'

'Not as soon as you can. Now!' I insisted.

'Okay, now.'

I was greatly relieved. Lucky was relatively clean, her box was tidy, her cloths were washed and folded and her feeding apparatus ready and waiting. I had done well. Jason would return to a well looked after Lucky.

But Jason and Marcella did not return, not now and not later. Annoyed and frustrated I went through the ritual of the feeding and the bedding. After another anxious night I woke early unable to sleep, went straight to Lucky's box and removed the covers. Lucky was squeezed into a corner of the box, dead. She looked so small, so fragile, so pitiful. I burst into tears and sat on the sofa crying. At the recollection of that moment my eyes still fill with tears. That poor little bird, so alive and active last night and now dead.

When Jason phoned later that morning, apologising profusely, I interrupted his excuses, bursting into tears.

'Lucky is dead. I found her dead this morning. I don't know why, she just died. I did everything right.'

There was a heavy silence and then Jason said, 'I'm coming right back.'

'Please come back soon. I don't know what to do.'

Several hours later Jason knocked on my door. We fell into each other's arms.

'I'm sorry Jase, I'm so sorry. I know how much Lucky meant to you.'

'I know. It's not your fault,' Jason muttered.

Jason and Marcella buried Lucky in a corner of his garden. What happened after that burial was more than a revelation, it was an epiphany. Jason had what can only be described as a breakdown. We sat in the garden, Marcella, Jason and I and all at once Jason's face contorted with pain and he began to cry. But he didn't just cry, he wept, he sobbed, he wailed, he howled, he cried as though there was no end to the pain, no end to the tears. His body was racked with sobs, his eyes swollen, his face puffy. Marcella cried, I cried, we hugged him, we held him, but he was inconsolable, nothing could stop the weeping, nothing could comfort him, we stroked him, we kissed him, but he was beyond comfort.

At one point, through the sobbing, Jason spluttered and gasped, 'Everything dies on me. Everything leaves me. My mother died, my father died, and now my baby bird died.'

And suddenly I understood. Jason had never been able to cry for his mother, for his father, for all the sadness in his life, for being wrenched from loving parents, from a life filled with promises and sent to a place, to a life where there was no love, no promises.

Jason sobbed, 'It's my fault Lucky is dead. I am to blame. I let her down. I was her parent and I let her down. She missed me so much that she died.'

Was he talking about missing his father, missing his mother, about his father missing his mother, about him missing them both, about his father letting him down, about his mother letting him down?

'This is sent to teach me a lesson. I have to learn from this, I must stop this crying and do something to make things better.'

'Jason, it's alright to cry,' I said. 'You're crying for all the times you didn't cry, for all the things you didn't cry for. It's alright to cry now.'

We sat in the garden, holding each other, crying with each other, crying for Lucky, for Jason, for ourselves. Finally Marcella and I were all cried out, but Jason continued to cry. Maybe he cried a river, maybe he cried a sea, he cried until he was unable to stop crying. Hours went by, maybe days, maybe weeks.

And then, all at once, Jason stood up, looked out to the sea he loved so much, and said quietly, 'It's okay. I've stopped crying now.'

Epilogue

Jason is making a massive effort to turn his life around. He now attends AA meetings regularly. He has acquired all the rights to the Diana Dors estate and is working on a website, www.dianadors.biz whereby people can buy Diana Dors merchandise: posters, photographs, greeting cards, place mats, etc. He has a professional theatre agent, Linda Sears, of 'Sears Management Limited' and is still writing music, currently working with Adamski.

Marcella has remained a close, supportive friend and assists Jason with all his projects.

Jason coincidently met Maya and Ruby in a London park when Ruby was six years old. Maya introduced them. "Ruby, this is Jason." Ruby said, "My daddy's name is Jason. Are you my daddy?" "Yes I am", Jason said. Since then Jason and Ruby see each other regularly.

Maya and Jason are friends and visit each other from time to time.

Jason is also in contact with his half-sister Katie.

David and Jason have remained brothers.

I am still around.

Other Books by the Same Author

Available from: www.niemaash.com

Flight of the Wind Horse, reprinted as **Touching Tibet** (Forward by the Dalai Lama) – Eye Books

"Excellent – Niema Ash really understands the situation facing Tibet and conveys it with remarkable perception." – Tenzig Choegyal (brother of the Dalai Lama)

"Mesmerising" – The Sunday Times

"Almost surreal in its assemblage of improbably colliding facts – a marriage of the bizarre and the beautiful that chills the spine as often as it warms the heart." – The Times

Travels with My Daughter – Eye Books

"Niema Ash is that rare and most admirable character – a born writer. Bravo!" – Irving Layton

"Niema Ash's prose is soaring... I was beguiled." – The Mail On Sunday

"A delightful read... you'll enjoy this one." – The Canada Post

Travels with Loreena Mckennit – (out of print)